CRIMINALIZATION, VOLUME 2

Studies in Critical Social Sciences Book Series

Haymarket Books is proud to be working with Brill Academic Publishers (www.brill.nl) to republish the *Studies in Critical Social Sciences* book series in paperback editions. This peer-reviewed book series offers insights into our current reality by exploring the content and consequences of power relationships under capitalism, and by considering the spaces of opposition and resistance to these changes that have been defining our new age. Our full catalog of *SCSS* volumes can be viewed at https://www.haymarketbooks.org/series_collections/4-studies-in-critical-social-sciences.

Series Editor
David Fasenfest (York University, Canada)

Editorial Board
Eduardo Bonilla-Silva (Duke University)
Chris Chase-Dunn (University of California–Riverside)
William Carroll (University of Victoria)
Raewyn Connell (University of Sydney)
Kimberlé W. Crenshaw (University of California–LA and Columbia University)
Raju Das (York University, Canada)
Heidi Gottfried (Wayne State University)
Alfredo Saad-Filho (Queen's University Belfast)
Chizuko Ueno (University of Tokyo)
Sylvia Walby (Royal Holloway, University of London)

CRIMINALIZATION

VOLUME 2

Where Do We Go from Here?

EDITED BY
GARIMA PAL AND CHIRAG BALYAN

Haymarket Books
Chicago, IL

First published in 2024 by Brill Academic Publishers, The Netherlands
© 2024 Koninklijke Brill NV, Leiden, The Netherlands

Published in paperback in 2025 by
Haymarket Books
P.O. Box 180165
Chicago, IL 60618
773-583-7884
www.haymarketbooks.org

ISBN: 979-8-88890-567-8

Distributed to the trade in the US through Consortium Book Sales and Distribution (www.cbsd.com) and internationally through Ingram Publisher Services International (www.ingramcontent.com).

This book was published with the generous support of Lannan Foundation, Wallace Action Fund, and the Marguerite Casey Foundation.

Special discounts are available for bulk purchases by organizations and institutions. Please call 773-583-7884 or email info@haymarketbooks.org for more information.

Cover design by Jamie Kerry and Ragina Johnson.

Printed in the United States.

Library of Congress Cataloging-in-Publication data is available.

Contents

Preface   VII
Acknowledgments   XV
List of Tables and Figures   XVI
Notes on Contributors   XVIII
Cases   XXIV

1 Bail(ing) Out Adolescent Sexuality from the Legal Quagmire: Decoding Overcriminalization in Pre-trial Incarceration   1
   Upma Gautam and Priya Das

2 The Collateral Consequence of Overcriminalization: Analyzing the Effects of Parental Incarceration on Children   22
   Ira Rana and Anurag Deep

3 Policing Homosexuality post the Transgender Persons (Protection of Rights) Act, 2019: A Critical Legal-Victimological Analysis   35
   Debarati Halder and Rupesh Rizal

4 Criminalization of Addiction – Analyzing the Bihar Liquor Prohibition Law   54
   Dipa Dube and Shekhar Kumar

5 Decolonization of India's Legal System through Transformative Constitutionalism
   Contemporary Legislative and Judicial Developments towards Indianization   69
   Arvind Tiwari and Sonali Kusum

6 Criminalization of Undertrial Prisoners in the Context of Specific Offences: Social Work Responses to Marginalization   102
   Sharli Mudaliyar

7 Rehabilitation and Restorative Justice in Italy: Themes, Methods and Experiences in Adult and Minors Criminal Law Systems   154
   Chiara Scivoletto

8 Criminal Acts of Lynching and Overcriminalization: Empirical Analysis of People's Perspectives regarding Punitive Sanctions   168
   Garima Pal and Tusha Singh

9 Raising the Age of Trying People as Adults Back to 21   183
   Antonio Reza

Index   199

Preface

The title *Criminalization: Where Do We Go from Here?* poses a poignant question that reverberates deeply within the spheres of law, society, and governance. In recent years, there has been a noticeable surge in discussions surrounding the expanding scope of criminalization and its profound impacts on individuals, communities, and the justice system at large.

As we find ourselves amidst a backdrop of shifting norms, rapid technological advancement, and evolving societal landscapes, it becomes increasingly imperative to subject the trajectory of criminalization to critical scrutiny. While the primary objective of criminal law remains the preservation of order and the assurance of public safety, the delicate balance between legitimate enforcement and the risk of excessive punitive actions warrants careful examination.

This volume endeavors to delve into the intricacies surrounding criminalization and its far-reaching ramifications. The authors embark on a journey to dissect various facets of this phenomenon, drawing upon empirical data and scholarly research to illuminate the perpetuation of injustices on the marginalized groups and the efficacy of punitive measures in addressing underlying societal maladies. Moreover, the concept of overcriminalization emerges as a central theme, as the authors interrogate the proliferation of criminal statutes and the resultant erosion of individual liberties. Through meticulous empirical analysis, they illuminate how overcriminalization exacerbates systemic injustices and undermines the foundational principles of justice and fairness by drawing upon the insights of scholars such as Oberman, Cortesi as well as Indian scholars like Upender Baxi, K. Rajagopal, B.B. Pande.

From the phenomenon of pre-trial incarceration to the troubling trend of the criminalization of undertrial prisoners for specific offenses, the authors employ robust empirical evidence to shed light on the complexities and injustices inherent in these practices. Through rigorous analysis, they uncover the disproportionate impact of pre-trial detention and highlight the systemic biases perpetuated by the overreliance on incarceration by law enforcement authorities on the marginalized sections of the society.

Furthermore, the authors confront the grim reality of criminal act of lynching, employing empirical data to unravel the social dynamics and structural inequalities that underpin this heinous act. By contextualizing these incidents within broader patterns of criminalization and social injustice, they seek to provoke critical reflection and spur collective action towards meaningful change.

In addition to empirical analysis, the authors also delve into theoretical interpretation of criminal statutes including the collateral consequences of overcriminalization, policing homosexuality post the transgender persons (Protection of Rights) Act, 2019, and the decolonization of India's legal system through transformative constitutionalism. This volume opens the floodgates for deliberation on the appropriate age for treating individuals as adults in legal proceedings among others. Through rigorous scholarship and unwavering commitment to truth, they pave the way for a future where justice truly prevails.

In essence, *Criminalization: Where Do We Go from Here?* serves as a rallying cry for informed action and introspection. By harnessing the power of empirical data and theoretical insights, the authors invite readers to confront the harsh realities of our criminal justice system and to collectively chart a path forward that is grounded in equity, compassion, and respect for human dignity. Their multifaceted exploration of criminalization offers hope for a future where justice is not just a lofty ideal, but a tangible reality for all, irrespective of geography or background.

With this backdrop, we bring to the readers writings of various academicians and practitioners from across the globe, expressing their viewpoints through the writings contained in this volume and suggesting a way forward. In Chapter 1 of their scholarly exposition titled "Bail(ing) Out Adolescent Sexuality from the Legal Quagmire: Decoding Overcriminalization in Pre-trial Incarceration," *Gautam and Das* meticulously scrutinized the intricate nexus between legal paradigms and adolescent sexual dynamics, anchoring their analysis in both historical jurisprudential evolution and contemporary empirical insights. Through a discerning lens, they unearth the subtle dissonance between statutory rape laws and the fluidity of societal norms surrounding consensual relationships among minors. Drawing from empirical data, such as the prevalence of child marriages at 23.3% in India, Gautam and Das illuminate the incongruity between legal statutes and prevailing socio-cultural realities. They underscore the profound ramifications of over-criminalization, particularly on adolescent girls, who often bear the brunt of punitive legal measures. Legal complexities, including conflicts between mandatory reporting mandates under the Protection of Children from Sexual Offences Act (POCSO) and confidentiality imperatives enshrined in the Medical Termination of Pregnancy Act, are expounded upon, revealing systemic challenges that imperil the reproductive rights and overall well-being of adolescent girls. Moreover, their inquiry delves into the judicial dynamics surrounding bail adjudications, revealing a nuanced interplay between legal precedents and judicial discretion. Empirical analyses of court decisions highlights the divergent approaches taken, ranging from stringent denial of bail to recognition of the commonplace nature of adolescent romantic entanglements. This nuanced understanding is underpinned by the examination of legal provisions, such as the Romeo-Juliet exemption, which seeks to mitigate the unintended consequences of statutory rape laws. Ultimately, Gautam and Das advocate for a recalibration of legal frameworks, emphasizing on education, counseling, and empowerment as more efficacious alternatives to punitive measures. Their erudite elucidation underscores the imperative of aligning legal norms with empirical realities, fostering a more equitable and enlightened trajectory in navigating the complex terrain of adolescent sexuality within the purview of the law.

In Chapter 2 titled "The Collateral Consequence of Overcriminalization: Analyzing the Effects of Parental Incarceration on Children," authors *Deep and Rana* through their research have scrutinized the burgeoning trend of criminalization in India and its collateral impact on children with incarcerated parents. Their study unveils a stark disparity between the staggering number of affected children and the actual prison population, highlighting the urgent need for targeted interventions. Through empirical analysis, they reveal systemic inadequacies in legal provisions such as Article 22(2) of the Constitution, which neglect the mandate of magisterial inquiry into familial circumstances post-arrest. Moreover, the research underscores deficiencies in visitation policies within Indian prisons, elucidating qualitative and quantitative disparities in communication avenues between inmates and their families. Advocating for a paradigm shift in victimology, the study urges the recognition of families of offenders within the criminal justice framework. It calls for policy reforms aimed at addressing the unique needs of children impacted by parental incarceration. Ultimately, Deep and Rana aim to foster a heightened awareness of the collateral consequences of over-criminalization while advocating for robust support systems to safeguard the welfare of these vulnerable demographics.

Rizal and Halder in Chapter 3 "Policing Homosexuality post the Transgender Persons (Protection of Rights) Act, 2019: A Critical Legal-Victimological Analysis," unearth alarming empirical findings regarding the policing of transgender individuals in India post the enactment of the Transgender Persons (Protection of Rights) Act, 2019. Their research reveals a pervasive pattern of police misconduct characterized by false imprisonment, excessive use of force, and custodial abuse directed at transgender persons. Through an in-depth examination of case laws and legal provisions, Rizal and Halder uncover a distressing reality wherein transgender individuals are disproportionately subjected to unwarranted arrests and physical violence by law enforcement agencies. Their empirical findings shed light on the systemic flaws within the criminal justice system, highlighting the urgent need for comprehensive reforms to address police brutality and ensure the protection of transgender rights. This empirical research serves as a clarion call for legislative and institutional interventions aimed at safeguarding the dignity and well-being of transgender individuals in India. By providing concrete evidence of systemic injustices, Rizal and Halder's findings underscore the imperative for policy reforms and enhanced training for law enforcement personnel to uphold constitutional principles and promote social equity.

Dube and Kumar in Chapter 4, titled "Criminalization of Addiction – Analysing the Bihar Liquor Prohibition Law," conduct an analysis of the criminalization of addiction within the framework of the Bihar Liquor Prohibition Law, specifically the Bihar Excise and Prohibition Act, 2016. They examined the foundational principles guiding criminalization, particularly Joel Fienberg's Harm and Offence principles, to assess the law's legitimacy. Their study critiques the law's broad application of penal powers, arguing that it exemplifies overcriminalization and excessive state intervention. Through empirical research, they highlight the detrimental effects of overcriminalization, including the erosion of individual autonomy and dignity. In their analysis, *Dube and Kumar* extensively scrutinize Section 30 of the Bihar Excise and Prohibition Act, 2016, which prescribes stringent penalties for various activities related to intoxicants. This provision imposes imprisonment for offences such as manufacturing, possession, buying, selling, distribution, collection, bottling, importing, exporting, transporting, or removing any intoxicant or liquor. The severity of punishments outlined in this section, ranging from five years to life imprisonment, along with substantial fines, reflects the draconian nature of the legislation and serves as a focal point for critiquing the overcriminalization of addiction. Their findings underscore the need for a more nuanced approach to criminalization, one that balances societal interests with individual rights and avoids undue state intrusion.

In their comprehensive discourse titled "Decolonization of India's Legal System through Transformative Constitutionalism – Contemporary Legislative & Judicial Developments Towards Indianization," authors *Tiwari and Kusum* explore the imperative need to decolonize India's legal system in the context of the country's 75 years of Independence. They begin by defining colonialism and decolonization, emphasizing the process of divesting colonial powers and achieving national liberation. Tracing the evolution of India's legal system from colonial rule to independence, their discourse advocates for 'Indianization' rooted in indigenous legal philosophies, shedding the colonial mindset in contemporary legal practices. By examining contemporary initiatives towards decolonization, including legislative efforts to repeal obsolete colonial laws, their discourse discusses the impact of colonial laws on marginalized communities. It emphasizes the importance of transformative constitutionalism in addressing these issues. In highlighting the persistence of colonial legacy in India's legal framework, their discourse cites examples such as the Constitution of India and the Indian Penal Code. They discuss the challenges posed by colonial inheritance and the need for legal reform to align with modern values. Exploring specific colonial-era laws shaping India's legal landscape, such as Section 377 IPC, Section 124A IPC, and Section 497 IPC, their discourse discusses the implications on individual rights and advocates for their reconsideration. In conclusion, their discourse underscores the importance of decolonizing India's legal system through legislative reforms and transformative constitutionalism. It calles for a reevaluation of colonial-era laws and practices to ensure alignment with India's contemporary socio-political realities and values of justice and equality.

Mudaliyar's Chapter 6 on "Criminalization of Undertrial Prisoners in the Context of Specific Offences: Social Work Responses to Marginalization" examines the criminalization of undertrial prisoners and social work responses, focusing on Prayas, a TISS project in Mumbai. Data from MIS and qualitative insights reveal Prayas's collaborative efforts with lawyers to provide legal aid and bail for underprivileged undertrials across Maharashtra's prisons. Case studies of Rita and Meena illustrate the challenges in meeting bail conditions due to poverty. It elucidates on the social work interventions, including contacting families and providing NGO support, facilitating their release, and furthermore, emphasizes the importance of holistic support in reuniting prisoners with their families. Prayas addresses the issues of overcrowding in Indian prisons, especially with undertrial prisoners. Despite positive efforts, there exist barriers in accessing legal aid resulting in prolonged detention. Prayas's Legal Aid and Bail Project targets undertrial prisoners, providing psycho-social support and facilitating legal processes. Demographics reflect socio-economic vulnerabilities, highlighting the need for wider rehabilitation efforts. In conclusion, they stress on the necessity of criminal justice social work, by placing trained professionals in prisons to aid rehabilitation. Social workers play diverse roles in coordinating with various stakeholders, sensitizing officials, and supporting families, and hence are crucial for successful reintegration and rehabilitation. Continued post-release support, including vocational training, ensures smoother transitions into society, ultimately reducing recidivism and promoting holistic well-being.

Scivoletto's Chapter 7 on "Rehabilitation and Restorative Justice in Italy: Themes, Methods and Experiences in Adult and Minors Criminal Law Systems" delves into the application of probation and restorative justice practices in Italy's criminal justice systems for both adults and minors. The chapter examines how probation serves as a tool for rehabilitation and explores its potential for restorative justice. Scivoletto discusses the legal framework surrounding probation, including international recommendations and Italian legislation, emphasizing its role in reducing recidivism and promoting public safety. In Italy, probation, known as "Messa alla prova" (MAP), is applied both before and after judgment for adults and minors, aiming to prevent imprisonment's negative effects while promoting responsibility and rehabilitation. The chapter highlights the introduction of MAP for adults in 2014, primarily to address prison overcrowding, and its subsequent implementation alongside community service. The MAP for minors, established in 1988, includes educational projects and restorative measures aimed at repairing harm and reconciling minors with victims. Scivoletto explores the outcomes of MAP, noting its positive impact on crime reduction and offender accountability. However, challenges such as unequal application and standardization of projects are identified. The chapter presents results from a research program conducted in the Emilia Romagna Region, offering insights from social workers, defendants, and defense counsels. Despite positive perceptions of MAP, concerns arise regarding its effectiveness in meeting rehabilitation and restorative goals. Collaboration between professionals and judicial institutions, especially judges, emerges as an area needing improvement. Furthermore, Scivoletto discusses the need for the integration of restorative justice practices within MAP, emphasizing the importance of victim involvement and the establishment of restorative justice centers. The chapter concludes by highlighting the ongoing challenges in implementing restorative justice reforms and the imperative for continued research and institutional support in this area.

In Chapter 8 titled "Criminal Acts of Lynching & Overcriminalization: Empirical Analysis of People's Perspectives regarding Punitive Sanctions," the research conducted by *Pal and Singh* delves into the complex issue of lynching in India, a criminal act not specifically defined under the Indian Penal Code. Their study aims to understand public perceptions regarding punitive measures for lynching and the broader issue of overcriminalization. Through empirical analysis, they collect data from 215 respondents across various states and age groups. Findings reveal a predominant belief among respondents in the effectiveness of strict punitive measures for reducing crime, with over 70% endorsing such measures. Concerning lynching, approximately 93% of respondents favored strict punishment, indicating a strong consensus on this matter. Regression analysis indicates a weak positive correlation between general pro-deterrence perspectives and support for strict punitive measures against lynching, reinforcing the hypothesis. Legislative analysis highlights constitutional protections and ongoing efforts by some states to address lynching through new legislation. Challenges included the absence of a specific legal definition for lynching in the IPC and inadequate data tracking mechanisms. In conclusion, the study emphasizes the need for coherent discourse and legislative action to effectively address the issue of lynching in India, by combining empirical research with legal developments i.e. the introduction to the new Bharatiya Nyaya Sanghita to inform policy decisions and societal understanding.

Reza's Chapter 9, titled "Raising the Age of Trying People as Adults Back to 21," delves into the historical trajectory of defining adulthood within the American criminal justice framework, prompting a critical inquiry into the appropriate age for treating individuals as adults in legal proceedings. Initially, the concept of adulthood exhibited multifaceted dimensions influenced by cultural, legal, and biological factors, with age benchmarks evolving over time. Historically, adulthood was recognized at 21 years, a standard later revised to 18 years in 1971 concurrent with the amendment of the voting age via the 26th Amendment. However, the arbitrary nature of this transition to adulthood at 18 lacks biological justification, given ongoing neurological development in areas governing decision-making, impulse control, and judgment until approximately 25 years of age. Empirical research material accentuates the discord between legal adulthood and biological maturation, highlighting the inadequacy of treating individuals as adults at the age of 18. Neuroscientific findings indicate that adolescents often exhibit incomplete cognitive capacity, hindering their comprehension of the ramifications of their actions. Consequently, adolescents may engage in impulsive behaviors without fully grasping the gravity of their offences, challenging the efficacy of punitive measures aimed at deterrence, incapacitation, rehabilitation, restitution, and retribution. Legislative efforts, such as Proposition 57 in California, have aimed to address these concerns by granting judges discretion in adjudicating whether minors should be tried in adult courts. Nonetheless, inconsistencies persist, as illustrated by Proposition 21, which empowers prosecutors to directly charge minors in criminal court for specific offences. These legislative maneuvers underscore a broader societal quandary regarding the appropriate handling of juvenile offenders within the criminal justice system. The historical narrative of trying and punishing children as adults underscores the grave consequences of inflexible age-based thresholds. Tragic cases involving individuals like James Arcene, George Stinney Jr., and Lionel Tate underscore the human toll of subjecting juvenile offenders to adult penalties. Arcene and Stinney, the youngest individuals sentenced to death in the United States, symbolize the systemic failures of a blanket approach to justice. Conversely, Tate's case highlights the potential for rehabilitation and exposes the pitfalls of harsh sentencing policies. In conclusion, the imperative to reevaluate the age criteria for treating individuals as adults in the criminal justice system is unmistakable. Biological, psychological, and societal considerations necessitate a nuanced approach that accounts for individual maturity, culpability, and rehabilitation potential. Aligning legal standards with scientific insights and ethical imperatives can pave the way for a more equitable and just system of justice, fostering accountability, rehabilitation, and public safety.

Garima Pal
Chirag Balyan

Acknowledgments

We extend our deepest gratitude to all the contributors who have generously shared their expertise and insights in this edited volume on overcriminalization. Their dedication to exploring the complexities of this topic has enriched the discourse and expanded our understanding of the challenges and implications of excessive criminalization.

We would like to thank the editorial team at Brill, particularly David Fasenfest and Jason Prevost, for their invaluable support, guidance and expertise throughout the publication process. Their commitment to excellence has been instrumental in bringing this project to fruition.

Special appreciation goes to our Hon'ble Vice-Chancellor, Prof. Dr. Dilip Ukey and Dr. Pratapsinh Salunke for providing the necessary resources and fostering an environment conducive to scholarly inquiry.

We are grateful to our colleague Dr. Anand N Raut and peers for their constructive feedback and encouragement, which have helped shape the direction and scope of this book. A special thanks to student interns Ms. Urja Vashishth, Mr. Samay Jain, Mr. Vedant as well as Mr. Ayushman Tripathi, Research Assistant for designing the book cover.

Our heartfelt thanks go to our families for their unwavering support, patience, and understanding during the long hours spent researching and writing. Their love and encouragement have been a source of strength and inspiration. Lastly, we express our appreciation to all those who have advocated for criminal justice reform and tirelessly worked towards promoting fairness, equity, and justice within our legal systems.

Tables and Figures

Tables

6.1	Occupancy and percentage of undertrial population	105
6.2	Duration of confinement	107
6.3	Occupancy and percentage of undertrial population, Maharashtra Prison	112
6.4	Duration of confinement, Maharashtra Prison 2021	113
6.5	Interventions for release, rehabilitation and livelihood support	145
8.1	Respondent profile for state/union territory	172
8.2	Respondent profile for age group	173
8.3	Strict punishments in general to punishment type for lynching	174
8.4	Awareness of lynching to punishment type for lynching	175
8.5	Regression statistics	178
8.6	ANOVA	179

Figures

1.1	Age of consent by country, 2023	6
1.2	Women aged 19–24 years who got married before age 18 years	9
1.3	Contraceptive use (any method) amongst sexually active unmarried women (age-group wise)	10
1.4	Inter-relationship between IPC, POCSO, PCMA and MTP	11
1.5	Purpose of kidnapping	12
1.6	Impact of criminalization of adolescent sexuality on adolescent girl/boy	13
1.7	Offender relation with victim under POCSO Act, 2012 – friends/online friends/live-in partner on pretext of marriage	14
1.8	Pendency percentage in courts of cases under POCSO	15
1.9	Trial outcomes under POCSO act: 2017–21	16
1.10	POCSO Act: incidence and rate	17
6.1	Occupancy	106
6.2	Share of undertrials	107
6.3	Legal services for the poor-state mandate	108
6.4	Prayas strategy within framework of social work as stated in the proposal submitted	110
6.5	Cyclic representation of arrest to non-release to overcrowding	114
6.6	Total outreach and year wise trend	116
6.7	Services provided	117

6.8	Gender	118
6.9	Age	119
6.10	Education	119
6.11	Occupation	120
6.12	Income	121
6.13	Age, gender, illiteracy	121
6.14	Age, gender, unemployment	122
6.15	Offence-wise case categorization	123
6.16	Gender wise categorization of cases	124
6.17	Punishment	125
6.18	Case categorization bail	126
6.19	Advocate status at case intake	127
6.20	DSLA status at Prayas intervention	128
6.21	Panel advocates	129
6.22	Bail status at intake and Prayas intervention to facilitate bail application through legal aid	130
6.23	Panel advocate, bail and release through legal aid	132–133
6.24	Release	134
6.25	Contact with family	135
6.26	Facilitated bail compliance	136
6.27	Rehabilitation plan	144
6.28	The above stated illustration show Released male prisoners offering support in midst of pandemic	149
8.1	Percentage of people strict laws and punishment for justice	176
8.2	Percentage distribution of punitive perception for lynching	176
8.3	State/UT-wise trend for lenient punishment for lynching	177
8.4	State/UT-wise trend for lynching	178
9.1	In this photograph of Reza's bracelet which consisted of his information and a mugshot	194

Notes on Contributors

Chirag Balyan
is an Assistant Professor of Law at Maharashtra National Law University Mumbai. His area of interest is contours of criminalization, antinomies in liberal theory, and preventive justice. The title of his doctoral thesis is: "Antinomies in the Criminal Justice System: A Normative Critique of the Pre-Trial Detention Laws in India". He has recently published a book with Thomson Reuters titled, Revisiting Reforms in Criminal Justice System in India. He has also published a funded research project titled "Commercial Sexual Exploitation in Maharashtra: a study of public prosecutors" in collaboration with the Government of Maharashtra, India and International Justice Mission. Mr. Balyan regularly publishes in reputed journals.

Priya Das
is a Ph.D. scholar, University School of Law & Legal Studies, Guru Gobind Singh Indraprastha University, Dwarka, Delhi. She obtained her law graduation from GNLU, Gandhinagar and LL.M. from ILI, Delhi and was Assistant Professor at Delhi Metropolitan Education, Noida, and Uttar Pradesh.

Anurag Deep
has been in the teaching profession since 2001. He has served at CPM Degree College, Allahabad and Deen Dayal Upadhyay Gorakhpur University, Gorakhpur as full-time permanent law teacher from 2001 to 2012. He joined the Indian Law Institute, New Delhi as Associate Professor in 2012 and is currently serving as Professor since 2017. He completed his legal education from BHU, Varanasi with merit scholarships. He earned his Ph.D. from Deen Dayal Upadhyay Gorakhpur University, Gorakhpur on the theme "Laws regarding Terrorism and Violation of Human Rights (with special Reference to Cyber Terrorism)." He has reviewed research articles for journals like *Indian Journal of International Law*, *RMLNLUJ*, *JILI*, etc. He has participated in developing courses, syllabus of various Universities. He has discharged the responsibilities in administrative capacity in Gorakhpur University as Warden of hostel, Asst Dean, Student welfare, Asst Proctor, Asst Coordinator – Exams and evaluation, and in the Indian Law Institute as Coordinator LL.M. and Diploma courses, Head-Disciplinary Committee, Procurement committee, Library committee, Tender committee, certificate and Gold Medal committee for convocation etc. He has written a dozen reference letters for students applying for Oxford,

Harvard, Cambridge, and Hague, Rhodes etc. many of these students are selected and suitably placed.

Dipa Dube
is a Professor at Rajiv Gandhi School of Intellectual Property Law, IIT Kharagpur. She held many responsibilities including Dean, Rajiv Gandhi School of Intellectual Property Law; Examination Malpractice Committee Member and Member, Council of Dean, Students Affairs. Her area of interests are gender violence, police & prison, crime against women and victims of crime.

Upma Gautam
is an Associate Professor of Law at School of Law & Legal Studies, Guru Gobind Singh Indraprastha University, Dwarka, Delhi. She has 19 years' experience in teaching and research where she taught many subjects including Criminal Law, Criminal Procedural Law, Criminology, Cyber Offences and its Investigation, Jurisprudence etc., She authored more than 25 research works on diverse topics, and the paper titled Spatial Dimensions of Understanding Nature as a "Person" in Law: Geographical Legal Implications was awarded the best paper in the ICSSR IMPRESS sponsored national conference "Spatial Dimensions of Environmental Problems and Natural Resource Law". organized by the Department of Geography, Shaheed Bhagat Singh College, the University of Delhi at the Conference Centre, North Campus on 3 and 4 September 2019.

Debarati Halder
holds her Ph.D. in Law from NLSIU, Bangalore. She had been a practitioner in law before joining legal academia. She is deeply interested in Cyber Law, Victimology and Therapeutic Jurisprudence. Debarati is also a pro-bono cybercrime victim counselor and she specializes in cybercrimes against women and laws. She was the first in India to propose a law to penalize Revenge Porn. She is a doting mom and a passionate pet parent. She is founder of Centre for Cyber Victim Counseling, co-founder of South Asian Society of Criminology and Victimology, founder & editor-in-chief Gender and Internet, web magazine for cyber law for women, Global Advisory Committee member of International Society of Therapeutic Jurisprudence, Member of World Society of Victimology and Life member at Indian society of victimology. She authored four books with national and international publishers.

Shekhar Kumar
completed his master's degree in the month of June 2018 at IIT Kharagpur and qualified NTA NET in December 2018. Now he is a research scholar at

Rajiv Gandhi School of Intellectual Property Law, IIT Kharagpur. He was also Assistant Professor at IMS Unison University before joining for doctoral studies. He also is actively involved in various research initiatives taken by Prof. Dipa Dube.

Sonali Kusum

has done her graduation in Law with B.A., LL.B. 5yr integrated course and pursued masters in law as LLM with specialization in human rights law. She has qualified UGC NET in Law. She holds a Post Graduate Diploma in Social work and in Human Resource Management. She has submitted a Ph.D. thesis on "Constructing a Legal Framework on Surrogacy in India" at National Law School of India University Bangalore. She has received a Ph.D. in Law degree from the Chief Justice of India, Sharad Arvind Bobde, Supreme Court of India at National Law School of India University, Bangalore. For her research contribution on Surrogacy law in India, she had the opportunity to be invited by Rajya Sabha Committee on Health & Family Welfare to present her views and her suggestions have been included in the Rajya Sabha Report No. 102, August 2017 on the Surrogacy Bill 2016. She is an Assistant Professor at Mumbai Campus, School of Law, Rights and Constitutional Governance, TISS.

Sharli Mudaliyar

is a doctoral scholar at the School of Social Work (SSW), Tata Institute of Social Sciences (TISS), Mumbai, India, holds a post-graduate degree in Law and Social Work and presently researching "Dual Victimization at the Intersection of Drug Use in Sex Trafficking". With a decade of experience, she exhibits profound understanding of marginalized groups particularly victims of human trafficking, incarcerated population and child sexual abuse. Engaged in both grassroots research and field of practice, her trajectory in criminal justice and human trafficking commenced during her Masters in Social Work (Criminology and Justice) at TISS (2012), evolving from a professional social worker to a dedicated researcher, to paving the way for her current pursuit as a doctoral scholar, with a specialized focus on the study of trafficking, which directly stems from her field experience demonstrating her dedication to addressing critical issues emerging from the field. Through co-authored state reports. Her significant contributions in the field of legal aid for incarcerated population with Prayas-TISS include co-authoring influential reports like "Legal Representation for Undertrials in Maharashtra (2018–2021)" which aimed to address criminalization and marginalization of vulnerable undertrial prisoners across six prisons in Maharashtra and advocating for systemic reforms within the criminal justice framework. Moreover, her expertise encompasses crafting policy notes on the Collaborative Model of Social Worker and Lawyer in the Legal Aid System; and forthcoming research report titled "Study on the Role of Social Worker with regards to Women Prisoners and their Children". Drawing from her extensive field experiences, she has actively contributed to the discourse on social work within the criminal justice system in academia as a guest lecturer at TISS and presenting papers at national and international conferences. Additionally, as a Consultant at SSW, TISS, she played an instrumental role in crafting an award-winning submission, leading to SSW, TISS winning the 9th FICCI Higher Education Excellence Award in the category of Excellence in Institutional Social Responsibility, 2023.

Garima Pal
is an Assistant Professor at Maharashtra National Law University Mumbai who continues to make significant contributions to the fields of Criminology, Victimology, and Human Rights. Holding a Ph.D. focused on "Drug Abuse and Alcoholism and the Role of Rehabilitation Centers in Uttarakhand," she has established herself as a versatile and interdisciplinary scholar. Her professional journey is marked by notable positions, including her role as a Research Associate at the Institute of Social Sciences, New Delhi, and a Project Coordinator at NLU Delhi for projects funded by prestigious bodies like the Indian Council of Social Sciences Research, the Ministry of Home Affairs, and the National Commission for Women. Her recent authorial works include "The Palghar Report: Status of Project Affected Families in Palghar," published by Mohan Law House, and "Hate Crime in India," published by Springer Nature. Additionally, on the "Bhartiya Nyaya Sanhita 2023" with Whiteman and Co. "The Palghar Report" has gained significant legal importance, as it has been submitted before the Bombay High Court in relation to an ongoing dispute. This underscores the report's relevance and impact in addressing real-world issues and influencing judicial processes. Apart from her academic and research contributions, she has actively engaged in legal advocacy. She recently filed a Public Interest Litigation (PIL) in the Bombay High Court concerning the appointment of a custodian for the proper execution of living wills. This action highlights her commitment to upholding human rights and contributing to important legal reforms. In addition to these achievements, she is leading two active research projects funded by the ICSSR and the National Commission for Women, focusing on "Social Media Intermediary Guidelines" and "Women Policing in the State of Maharashtra," respectively.

Ira Rana
Assistant Professor, is a dedicated scholar with a focus on research and education. Holding a Ph.D. from the Indian Law Institute, Delhi, her doctoral research delved into the vulnerability of children with incarcerated parents in India, advocating for a necessary legal framework to address their needs. She is also UGC-NET/JRF qualified and has further enhanced her expertise through an online course on Contract Law from Harvard University. With a strong academic background, she is currently serving as an Assistant Professor at Quantum University, Roorkee, and Uttarakhand. Her teaching portfolio spans subjects like Labor Law, Legal English, Law of Contracts, and her research interests lie prominently in Child Rights. In her research endeavors, Dr. Rana has extensively explored the intricacies of the justice and social welfare machinery, particularly concerning the welfare of children. Her hands-on experience includes internships with the Chief Probation Officer in Delhi and interactions with various stakeholders like Child Welfare Committees and Juvenile Justice Boards. Dr. Rana has contributed significantly to academia through publications in esteemed journals and chapters in books addressing socio-legal issues in India. Moreover, she has presented her research findings at national and international conferences, demonstrating her commitment to advancing discourse on critical topics such as human rights, surrogacy, and the rights of vulnerable groups.

Antonio Reza
was named by University of San Francisco as one of 2021's "30 under 30", USF graduates who are changing the world. At USF, he graduated magna cum laude with a BA in communication studies and with minors in sociology and in legal studies. He was also the Northern California student representative for the California System Involved Bar Association, the student president for the National Justice Impact Bar Association, a clinical law student for the Northern California Innocence Project, and a judicial intern for Santa Clara County Judge Vanessa Zecher.

Rupesh Rizal
is an LL.M. student of Parul Institute of Law, Parul University, and Vadodara. He is also a practicing advocate registered with Sikkim Bar Association. He is actively involved in various research initiatives taken by Dr. Halder and has also assisted her for the same.

Chiara Scivoletto
is a full Professor of Sociology of Law, Deviance and Social Change at the Department of Law of the University of Parma, where she teaches "Sociology of deviance", "Sociology of law" and "Criminology". She is also the director of the Course for 'Juridical expert in family and minors' rights in supporting the local social services', held by University of Parma and the Emilia-Romagna Region. In 2018 she was appointed the Chair of the Interdepartmental Research Center (CIRS,) of the University of Parma. At the same University, she was the chair of the Social Work programmes.

Tusha Singh
did her graduation (B.A., LL.B.) at University School of Law & Legal Studies in 2017 and Postgraduate (Criminal Law) at National Law University, Delhi, in 2018. She is currently a teaching associate in Amity Law School, Noida.

Arvind Tiwari
is a well known Criminologist and a scholar in Criminal Justice & Forensic Science, Human Rights, Police Studies & Public Security, Criminal law & Access to Justice, Victimology, Youth Justice and Crime & Development. He completed his Bachelor of Arts, M.A. (Gold Medalist) and Ph.D. in Criminology & Forensic Science at Dr. H.S. Gaur Central University, Sagar, and Madhya Pradesh. He has published several articles in peer reviewed journals and chapters in edited books. He has been engaged in many public policy research projects in the area of Access to Justice Fellowship Project (Tata Trust & TISS), Non-Registration of Crimes: Problems and Solutions (Bureau of Police Research and Development, Ministry of Home Affairs, Government of India), Bail and Its Extent of Abuse Including Recidivism (SVP National Police Academy, Ministry of Home Affairs, Government of India), Community policing and its Impact on Public Order (TISS), Role of Fast Track Courts in Dispenzation of Speedy Justice (TISS), Open Prisons in India (TISS), Status Report on Human Rights in India (TISS), Medical Facilities in Indian Prisons: Role of Doctors and Para-Medical Staff to uphold Right to Health of Prisoners (TISS). He has given over 100 conference presentations such as Presidential address, Keynote address, Special address and Chaired sessions. He has also supervised several successful Ph.D., M.Phil. and Master's students and published several research papers in peer reviewed journals in a span of more than 25 years of career.

Cases

Aaditya v. State of Maharashtra, SCC Online Bom 2540 (2020).
Aarti v. State of U.P, Misc. Bench No. 5503 (2018).
AK v. State Govt. NCT of Delhi, Bail Application 2729 (2022).
Amit Rasao Patil v. State of Maharashtra, SCC Online Bom 917 (2020).
Anhant Janardan Sunatkari v. State of Maharashtra, SCC Online Bom 136 (2021).
Arnesh Kumar v. State of Bihar, 8 SCC 273 (2014).
Atul Mishra v. State of UP, Criminal Appeal No. 4907 (2022).
Atul Mishra v. State of UP, Criminal Misc. Bail Application No. 53947 (2021).
Abul Hassan And National Legal v. Delhi Vidyut Board &Ors., AIR 1999 Delhi 88.
Amalgamated Coalfields Limited and Ors. v. Janapada Sabha Chhindwara AIR 1961 SC 964.
Anil JS v. State of Kerala & Ors., 2010, WP(C) NO. 32519 OF 2010.
Anil Kumar Bhatt v. State of Uttarakhand, 2022 Criminal Jail Appeal No. 47 of 2013.
Ashim @ Asim Kumar Haranath v. National Investigation Agency, SLP(Criminal) No(s). 6858 of 2021 (India).
Bade Rama v. State of Karnataka, Criminal petition No. 6214 (2022).
Bhim Singh v. State of Jammu and Kashmir, AIR 1986 SC 494.
Chander Vir Kaundal v. State of H.P, SCC Online HP 95 (2017).
Dharmander Singh v. State Bail Application 1559 (2020).
D. K. Basu v. State of West Bengal, AIR 1997 SC 610.
Gopika Jayan & Anr. v. Faisal M.A, LiveLaw (Ker) 308 (2022).
Hukum Chand v. State of U.P., 2012, MISC. SINGLE No. – 1019 of 2001.
Hussainara Khatoon v. Home Secretary, State of Bihar (1980) 1 S.C.C. 98 (India).
Independent Thought v. Union of India, 10 SCC 800 (2017).
Indian Alcoholic Beverage companies v. State of Bihar 2016 SCC online Pat 4806.
Jagjeet Singh v. Ashish Mishra, Criminal Appeal No. 632 (2022).
Jayantibhai Babulbhai Alani v. State of Gujarat, SCC Online Guj 1223 (2018).
Joginder Kumar v. State of Uttar Pradesh, 1994 4 SCC 260.
Joseph Shine v. Union of India, SCC Online SC 1676 (2018).
Jayaswal Shipping Company v. The Owners and Parties, AIR 1954 Cal 415, 58 CWN 468.
Kajal v State of Uttar Pradesh, SCC Online All 3909 (2019).
Kuldeep v. State of Himachal Pradesh, SCC Online HP 2659 (2019).

Mohd. Azad Ahmed Ali Khan v. State of Maharashtra, SCC Online Bom 1093 (2018).
Moti Ram v. State of M.P, AIR SC 1594 (1978).
Muhammed Rafi v. Satheesh Kumar M.V, LiveLaw (Ker) 386 (2022).
Mohd. Akhtar v. The State of Jammu And Kashmir 2018 (8) SCJ 265.
Mukesh v. State (NCT of Delhi) (2017) 6 SCC 1.
M.V. Elisabeth And Ors. v. Harwan Investment and Trading, 1993 AIR 1014.
M/s Aamoda Broadcasting Company Pvt. Ltd. &Anr. v. The State of Andhra Pradesh &Ors.,(W.P. (Cr.) No. 217/2021).
Mcleod v. St. Aubyn, (1899) AC 549 (PC).
Nilbati Behra v. the State of Orissa, 1993 SCR (2) 581.
N.V. Sankaran alias Gnani v. The State of Tamil Nadu, [2013 (-) CTC 686].
NALSA v. Union of India, 2015, WRIT PETITION (CIVIL) NO.400 OF 2012.
Navtej Singh Johar v. Union of India, AIR 2018 SC 4321.
Nimeshbhai Bharatbhai Desai v. State of Gujarat, 2018 R/CRIMINAL MISC.APPLICATION NO. 24342 of 2017.
Nimeshbhai Bharatbhai Desai v. State of Gujarat, 2018 SCC Online Guj 732.
Praduman v. State (NCT) of Delhi, Bail Application No. 2380 (2021).
Pratap v. State of Himachal Pradesh, LiveLaw (HP) 23 (2022).
Prakash Singh v. Union of India, (2006) 8 SCC 1.
Rakesh Kumar v. Vijayanta Arya (DCP) &Ors., LiveLaw (Del) - (2022).
R. v. Almon, (1965) Wilm 243.
R. v. Blackburn, (1968) 1 ALL ER 763.
Rajesh Upadhyay v. The State of Bihar, 2023, Miscellaneous Appeal No.354 of 2016.
Rojer Mathew v. South Indian Bank Ltd and Ors Chief, Civil Appeal No. 8588 of 2019.
Roopesh v. State of Kerala, 2022, Crl. R. P Nos.732, 733, 734 of 2019.
R.D. Upadhyay v. State of A.P. & Ors Writ Petition (civil) 559 of 1994 on 13 April, 2006 (India).
Rajnish v. State, Criminal Misc. Bail Application No. 20805 of 2022 (India).
Re: Inhuman Conditions in 1382 Prisons AIR 2016 SC 993 (India).
Sabarinathan v. The Inspector of Police, (3) MLJ (Crl) 110 (2019).
Sanjeev Dhruv Varma v. State of Maharashtra, SCC Online Bom 3813 (2020).
Shembhalang Rynghang v. State of Meghalaya, Crl. Petn. No. 64 (2021).
Shri Wasim v. State of Karnataka, Criminal Appeal No. 2632 (2008).
Skhemborlang Suting v. State of Meghalaya, Criminal Petition No. 63 (2021).
Smti. Ephina Khonglah v. State of Meghalaya, B.A No. 14 (2021).
Sunil Kumar Antil v. CBI, LiveLaw (SC) 577 (2022).
Sunil Mahadev Patil v. State of Maharashtra, Bail Application No. 1036 (2015).

Sunilkumar Dilipbhai Patel v. State of Gujarat, R/CR.MA/19567 (2020).
Suraj v. State of Maharashtra, SCC Online Bom 325 (2021).
S.G. Vombatkere v. Union of India, 2022, WRIT PETITION(C) No.682 OF 2021.
Shri Ishwar Singh v. Land and Building Department and Anr, 2018, W.P.(C) 8178/2018.
Shri Salek Chand Jain v. Ministry Of Social Justice, 2022, W.P.(C) 1542/2020.
Shrimati Sarala v. State Of Chhattisgarh, 2021 WPCR No. 508 of 2021.
Sunil Kisanrao Bagul, Nashik, v. Assistant Commissioner Of Income Tax, ITA No.704/PUN/2022.
Suresh Kumar Koushal &Anr. v. Naz Foundation &Ors., CIVIL APPEAL NO.10972 OF 2013,(Arising out of SLP (C) No.15436 of 2009).
Tara Singh Gopi Chand v. The State, (1951 CriLJ 449).
Tehseen S Poonawalla v. Union of India, (2018) 9 SCC 501.
Vishnu Sitaram Sarode v. State of Maharashtra, SCC Online Bom 2389 (2021).
Vijayalakshmi v. State Rep, The Inspector of Police, Crl.O.P.No.232 (2021).
Vishnu Sitaram Sarode v. State of Maharashtra, SCC OnLine Bom 2389 (2021).

CHAPTER 1

Bail(ing) Out Adolescent Sexuality from the Legal Quagmire: Decoding Overcriminalization in Pre-trial Incarceration

Upma Gautam and Priya Das

1   Introduction

Vinod[1] (aged 19 years) and Gita[2] (aged 17.5 years) were schoolmates, who fell in love, eloped and got married, as a result, Gita got pregnant. Gita's parents filed a case against Vinod for aggravated penetrative sexual assault/rape (POCSO Act) and kidnapping (IPC). On account of the ongoing case, Vinod has been incarcerated resulting in discontinuance of his education, his bail has been rejected by the lower court. Meanwhile, Gita has given birth to a child and is residing with Vinod's parents. The application for bail comes up before the High Court, which grants the bail to Vinod as Gita offers to stand as a surety for him. Vinod is temporarily set free after staying in jail for more than a year.

X v. GNCTD, 2023)

∴

Dharmander Singh (aged 24 years) and prosecutrix (17 years) became friends via Facebook in 2016. Their friendship culminated into physical intimacy and later into marriage. An FIR was registered against Dharmander on 14/10/2018 for the offence of kidnapping, rape, hurt, criminal intimidation, he was arrested on 17/11/2018 and has been in judicial custody since then. He was finally granted bail after spending two years in jail.

Dharmander Singh v. State Bail Application, 2020

∴

---

1   Fictional name.
2   Fictional name.

The number of *Vinod* and *Dharmander* languishing in jail for want of bail are endless in our country. These cases where romantic love with an underaged girl is criminalized, constitute 25% of the total cases under the POCSO Act (clogging the already overburdened criminal justice machinery) (Ramakrishnan & Raha, 2022). Criminalization of romantic relations has serious ramifications on the health and well-being of the youth, their liberty and freedom (of healthy expression of sexuality) (Das & Gautam, 2022). Lengthy trials and denial of bail results in innocent young Romeos languishing in prisons. The growing concern on the criminalization of adolescents engaging in consensual sexual activity (statutory rape) has also been expressed by the erstwhile CJI of India (J. D.Y Chandrachud), legal luminaries as well as the research organizations. However, the Supreme Court's appeal to Parliament to lower the age of consent under the POCSO Act and the Indian Penal Code, 1860 has been declined by the Government recently. Therefore, the gap between the socio-cultural reality of adolescent sexuality and the existing legal framework is going to persist thus necessitating the evaluation of criminalization of romantic/consensual relations.

States in order to maintain and preserve the social order, exercises social control by imposing civil law prohibitions(injunctions/penalization) or criminal sanctions(criminalization) against a deviant act. Criminal sanctions are contended to be a stronger and more efficient mechanism to curtail "real" crime (Cornford, 2015). This monopolized exercise of power by the *leviathan* State labeling a wrongful(harmful) conduct as criminal is what is known as "criminalization". Criminalization is considered a social process as it is heavily backed by the ethos, values and conscience of the society (Cornford, 2015). For instance, pre-pubertal sexual relations has been considered distasteful across the civilizations spatiotemporally (Graupner, 2000). Therefore, the apposite time for entering into sexual relations was after attaining puberty, particularly more so in cases of girls. This forms the basis of the pegging age of consent between 12–14 years traditionally (Greco-Roman period) so as to coincide with the age of puberty (Bullough, 2005). However, with the growing health concerns and other considerations (discussed in Part II), the age of consent has been continually increased world over as well as in India.

The Age of Consent contained in the Indian Penal Code, 1860 (§ 375) coincides with the age of marriage and the age of majority i.e. 18 years. It does not merely perform the prescriptive function of prescribing the age of consent but acts as a baseline to criminalize sexual relations with a girl below the age of consent in blanket fashion. Therefore, any sexual activity consensual or non-consensual with a girl who is below the age of consent is deemed as statutory rape *(thereby criminalized)*. The rationale for criminalizing statutory rape is ensconced between the biological considerations (health concerns of girl) and the social and developmental issues such as lack of maturity, lack of awareness of the nature of the act and its repercussions.

The sexual aggression against or sexual expression of a minor girl is comprehensively and specifically dealt with under the Protection of Children from Sexual Offences Act, 2012, which being a special legislation commands stringent measures and punishments. It is laden with additional safeguards to protect the best interest of the child thus entails harsher punishment and diminishes the chances of obtaining bail thereby further prolonging the duration of pre-trial incarceration.

Stringency of measures and punishment is not problematic in cases of sexual abuse, but the problem lies in treating romantic relations with the same stringency (of measures and punishments). Sexual offenders involved in a non-consensual intercourse and those in consensual intimacy (with underaged girls) are kept at the same pedestal under the POCSO Act. This amounts to gross abuse of expressive function of the criminal law thus amounting to unfair and unjustified criminalization (of teen romantic relations).

This Chapter in its *first section,* attempts to trace the role of legal sanctions in regulating the sexual behaviors of adolescents wherein the concept of "age of consent", its origin and evolution leading to statutory rape law and the underlying deciding factors are contextualized in the backdrop of Global context. It is followed by comprehensive and critical analysis of the intersections in the Indian legal framework pertaining to adolescent sexual intimacy and the attached collaterals. This complex medley of laws aimed at restricting adolescent sexuality ends up jeopardizing their health and life, which is further exacerbated by the uncertain durations of pre-trial incarceration. The last part of this chapter primarily focuses on the incoherent judicial approach in matters of bail which consequently amounts to overcriminalization.

2 Origin and Evolution of Statutory Rape Law (Age of Consent)

Historical analysis of scarce and fragmented information reveals that age of consent and marriage was a private matter left for the families to decide (Lacy, 1968). The fanatic emphasis on female chastity at marriage resulted in age of consent being subsumed by the age of marriage. However, it is pertinent to note that marriage was usually not consummated until the girl had her first menses (Friedlander, 1913). Thus, it can be inferred that age of consent existed only in cases of married girls and roughly coincided with the attainment of puberty.

The intervention of the State in matters of age of consent, marriage and family began in the 1st century during the reign of Augustus, however it was not until the 13th century that the sexual relations with a girl below the age of consent (statutory rape) were criminalized. The 13th century legal code of England mentioned in Eidson (1980) pegged the age of consent at 10 years criminalizing all sexual relations – consensual or non-consensual, with a girl below this age (Oberman, 2000). These initial laws protected the sexuality of only the females in order to ultimately "protect a father's interest in his daughter's chastity" mentioned in Oberman (2000). These laws were least concerned about the physical or mental harm endured by the girl due to underaged sexual union but were primarily aimed at restricting any interference with father's guardianship over her his daughter. Promiscuity as a defense against statutory rape implies that the protection was extended only to the girls believed to be chaste. Thus, it can be inferred that historically statutory rape law was maneuvered to "preserve the common morality rather than to penalize men for violating the law" as suggested by Oberman (2004).

Statutory rape law in England was the pioneer, which was subsequently adopted in the Unites States, India and the rest of the world except for some countries like Pakistan, Iran, Sudan, Afghanistan, Saudi Arabia, Yemen, UAE, Libya, Oman, Kuwait, Qatar and Maldives- where there is no age of consent and marriage irrespective of the age of the girl, acts as the only means to legitimize sexual relation (marked in grey, Figure 1.1).

2.1   Age of Consent: A Global Context

The Age of consent has varied with time and jurisdiction. The survey of age of consent carried out by Magnus Hirschfield in some 50 countries in the early 20th century reveals that it was 12 years in 15 countries, 13 years in 7, 14 years in 5 and 16 in the remaining 5 counties (Hirschfield, 2000). Similarly, in the United States the age of consent was maintained at 10 years till the late 19th century (Cohen, 2008) and the average age of consent was increased to 16 years only by the beginning of the 20th century (Oberman, 2001).

The Age of consent in almost every jurisdiction has seen an increase (Figure 1.1). The reason for this shift is attributed to the need for greater protection to young women from sexual aggression and the simultaneous increase in the age of marriage. The Statutory rape law in majority of the jurisdiction stipulates 16 years as the age of consent. In 1990's, statutory rape law has been increasingly used in the United States to deter sexual behaviour, reduce sexually transmitted diseases, prevent teen pregnancy and reduce the number of single parent families and the resultant dependance on welfare support (Donovan, 1997).

However, lately in the 21st century the Statutory rape laws have come under immense scrutiny for injudicious application of same statutes and punishments to teen romances as are applicable to sexual offenders. Similarly, the Sexual Offences Act, 2003 of England which criminalizes all forms of consensual sexual activity between children is seen as excessively broad, ill-defined and illegitimate criminal law (Tadros, 2003; Ashworth, 2004; Smith, 2004). The usage of statutory rape laws to control the adolescence sexual curiosity and reduce teen pregnancies by criminalizing adolescent sexual experimentation has undergone transformation with the introduction of Romeo-Juliet laws in some states of USA.

Romeo-Juliet laws drawing its name from the epic Shakespearean story of "star-crossed, teenaged lovers" acts as an antidote to the overcriminalization caused by the statutory rape law while dealing with consensual relations. Romeo-Juliet laws also known as close-in age exemption protects young people from criminal prosecution for engaging in consensual sexual conduct with others close to their own age. The age differential for close-in age exemption just like age of consent varies from State to State.

2.2   Age of Consent in India

The Age of consent as it exists today can be traced back to the Indian Penal Code, 1860 drafted by Thomas Babington Macaulay. The rationale behind having age of consent is that the young girls consent to certain acts without understanding its nature, significance and consequences thus such consent is no consent in real sense to be recognized by the law (Arnest, 1998). It is seen as a means to regulate (Chalmers, 2011)/control the sexuality of young girls to serve the larger dominant puritanical "social interest" of preserving the chastity of young girls and simultaneously respecting the father's interest in his daughter's chastity (Oberman, 2000; Chalmers, 2011).

The causal link between the increase in age of marriage and the age of consent cannot be overlooked in a society where marriage is seen as a means to legitimize sexual relations and any pre-marital sexual relationship particularly for a girl is decried. The age of marriage was initially pegged at 14 years by the Sarda Act, 1929 and later increased to 15 years (Child Marriage Restraint Act, 1929. amend. 1949) and then 18 years (Child Marriage Restraint Act, 1929. amend. 1978) to delay sexual activity and the resultant teenage pregnancies. Thus, States in its capacity of *parens patriae* has simultaneously increased the age of consent to accord longer protection to girls from sexual aggression as well as to delay any sexual debut. The age of consent which was adopted from the English legal code was fixed at 10 years back then and has been subjected to increase more than once. It was increased from 12 years (Age of Consent

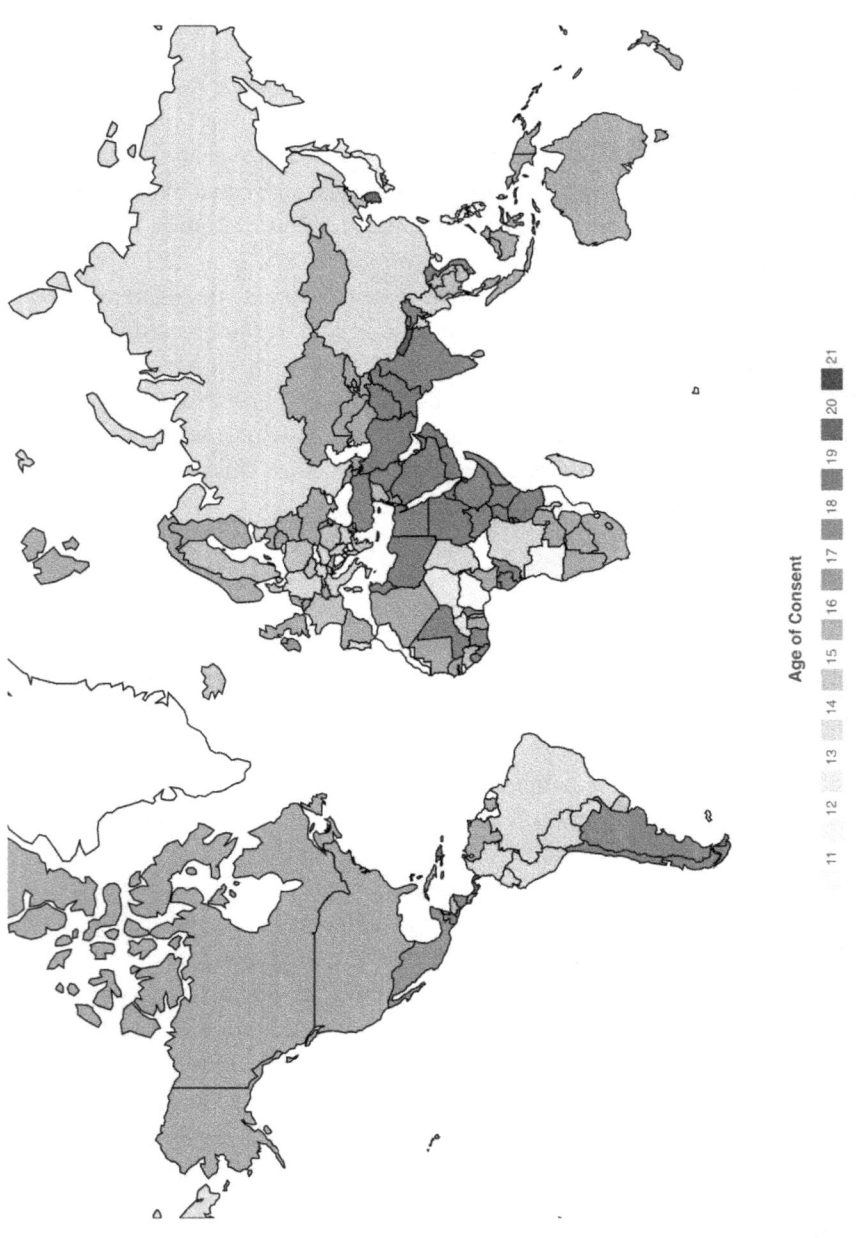

FIGURE 1.1 Age of consent by country, 2023
SOURCE: WORLD POPULATION REVIEW

Act, 1891) to 14 years (Indian Penal Code, 1860. amend. 1925) to 16 years (Indian Penal Code, 1860 and Child Marriage Restraint Act, 1929. amend. 1940) and finally to 18 years (Indian Penal Code, 2860. amend. 2013). While the age of consent for a girl to engage in sexual activities has always remained a contentious issue, the age of consent for a boy to do so is far from public discussion, let alone its reflection in the legal discourse. Unlike the United States, age of consent in India is gender-specific to females.

The age of consent underwent a major overhaul in the year 2013 under § 375 wherein it was increased from 16 to 18 years. The Criminal Law Amendment Act, 2013 which was predominantly based on the Justice Verma Committee recommendations, but contrarily refuted the latter on the recommendation of age of consent. Notably, Justice Verma committee recommended decreasing the age of consent under the Protection of Children from Sexual Offences Act 2012 from 18 to 16 years, in order to bring it in conformity with the Indian Penal code 1860(§ 375, Explanation 2) and the Art. 34 of the United Convention on the Rights of the Child (UNCRC) as mentioned in the Report of the Committee on Amendments to Criminal Law (2013).

The said recommendation was put forth in the backdrop of India being a signatory to the UNCRC, which primarily aims to protect children from sexual assault and abuse and not to criminalize consensual sex between two individuals even if they are below eighteen years of age. It is worth mentioning here that the possibility of consensual sexual activity was also factored in by the POCSO Bill, 2011 and the Ministry of Women and Child Development. But the same was withdrawn due to the concerns of the parliamentary standing committee that giving consideration to consent in statutory rape cases will shift the focus on the conduct of the victim. The Criminal Law Amendment Act, 2013 thereby increased the age of consent from 16 to 18 years in order to bring the IPC in conformity with the newly enacted special law POCSO which completely disregards the possibility of consensual sexual activity amongst adolescents.

Further, in the original Indian Penal Code, the age of consent differed for a married and an unmarried girl. For married women it was 15 years and remained unaltered whereas for an unmarried woman it was 16 years which was increased to 18 years in 2013. The aforesaid distinction created an ambiguity regarding applicability of POCSO Act to married women which doesn't distinguish between a married and an unmarried child. The said contradiction was reconciled by the Supreme court in *Independent Thought v Union of India, 2017* wherein the applicability of the POCSO was interpreted in favor of married underage females also. This appeared to be a progressive and practical approach, however contrary to the expectation, it wreaked havoc in a country where according to the NFHS-5 report, 23.3% of girls get married before turning 18 years. Over 2000 arrests under POCSO Act and the Child Marriage Act, across the State of Assam to crack down on child marriages is the manifestation of the unrest created due to conflicting social practice and legal measure (Baruah, 2023). The aftermath of *Independent Thought* has resulted in criminalization of sexual relations with a wife who is under 18 years of age (irrespective of consent) as mentioned by Gautam & Das (2023).

The age of consent by conflating consensual and non-consensual intercourse, acts as a double-edged sword by stigmatizing the girl (under the garb of protection) and by(harshly) criminalizing the male involved for an innocuous act. The plight of adolescent girls and how she is embroiled in a complex legal imbroglio has been elaborately discussed in the succeeding section.

3   Adolescent Sexuality: Socio-legal Framework

The Indian legal framework persecutes adolescent sexuality by seeming to be oblivious to adolescent female sexuality on one hand and by criminalizing the young males for consensual sexual exploration and labeling them as sex offenders. The impact of criminalization on young males has been discussed in the succeeding section i.e., Part IV. This part primarily focuses on the existing socio-cultural realities, the gap between the realities of adolescent sexuality and the legal framework and the consequent impact of the existing socio-legal envelope on the adolescent females.

3.1   *Socio-cultural Realities*

The sexuality of adolescent females (under 18 years of age) is fundamentally governed by the Indian Penal Code, 1860 in conjunction with the Protection of Children from Sexual Offences Act, 2012. These laws in order to protect an adolescent girl from sexual abuse negates their sexual agency. The denial of adolescent sexuality by the legal framework is however contradicted by the socio-cultural realities of our country- where 23.3% of girls get married before turning 18 years (Figure 1.2) with States like West Bengal (41.6%), Bihar (40.8%) and Tripura (40.1%) recording much higher numbers of child marriages than the national average.

Apart from the married cohort, NFHS-5 also testifies that sexual activity amongst unmarried adolescent girls in the age group 15–19 years with 45% of them having reported using contraceptives (any method) thus contradicting the basic premise of the legal framework.

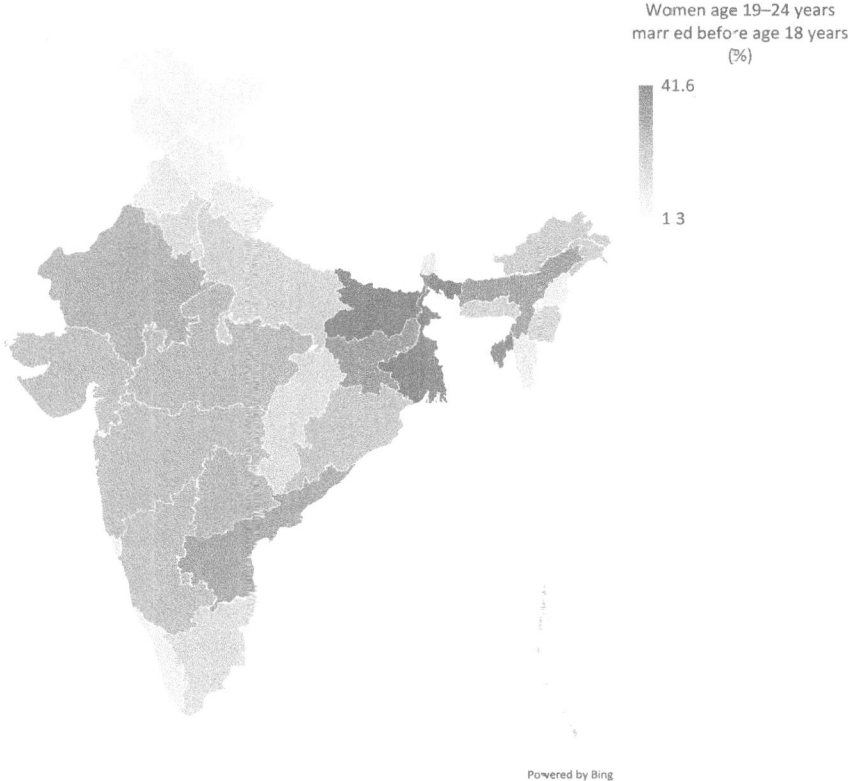

FIGURE 1.2   Women aged 19–24 years who got married before age 18 years
SOURCE: NFHS-5 (2019–20)

NFHS-5 also reports 6.8% of girls aged between 15–19 years being pregnant or have already become a mother. It is pertinent to note that teenage pregnancy further jeopardizes adolescent girls in terms of health indicators- such as high anemia, Infant mortality rate, Maternal mortality rate, poor nutritional levels (Das et al., 2022) and diminishes their chances of getting employment.

The partner/husband of these sexually active unmarried/married girls/ pregnant girls are at the risk of or are already caught in the clutches of the criminal justice machinery owing to the criminalization of consensual relations below the age of consent.

3.2   *Intersection of Laws*

Medical termination of pregnancy has been selectively legalized (Medical Termination of Pregnancy Act, 1971 § 3) in India. Its accessibility in general

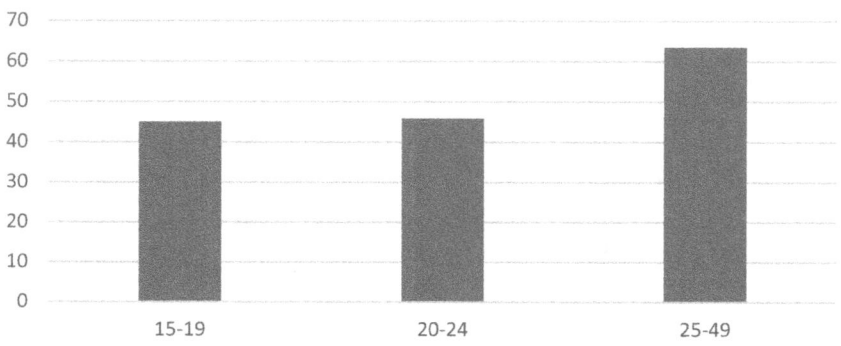

FIGURE 1.3   Contraceptive use (any method) amongst sexually active unmarried women (age-group wise)
SOURCE: NATIONAL FAMILY HEALTH SURVEY-5

and in particular to the sexually active unmarried adolescents has been a subject matter of frequent deliberation by the Courts in India (*X v. State (NCT) of Delhi, 2023*). The mandatory requirement of guardian's consent in event of termination of pregnancy of a minor coupled with the other mandates adversely affects the bodily integrity, privacy, equality and autonomy of the minors thereby violating their reproductive rights. This complex web of legal framework i.e. the mandatory consent from guardians under MTP Act for termination of pregnancy and the fear of initiation of police investigation due to mandatory reporting under POCSO Act is a discouraging factor towards safe termination of pregnancy. The POCSO Act, 2012 while criminalizing any sexual activity involving a minor girl, mandates reporting of commission of such offence by everyone including the doctors attending them. The mandatory requirement of consent of guardian under MTP Act for the termination of pregnancy and the mandatory reporting under POCSO Act which is in complete conflict with the confidentiality clause under the MTP Act, has posed a dilemma for not only the medical healthcare provider but also for minors who fear for their privacy and initiation of police investigation, before seeking professional help. The World Health Organization in its document titled *Safe abortion: technical and policy guidance for health systems* (2012) has also pointed that the constant fear of being exposed by the medical practitioner, the ostracization and stigmatization deters several girls from taking safe and legal abortion services, professional advice about sexual health and pregnancy, thereby coercing the girls to take unsafe procedures to terminate pregnancy (Gautam & Sharma, 2021).

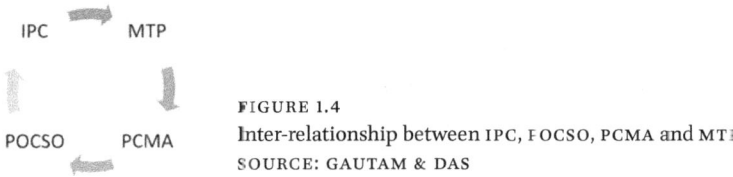

FIGURE 1.4
Inter-relationship between IPC, POCSO, PCMA and MTP
SOURCE: GAUTAM & DAS

The intersection of laws ends up controlling the sexuality of minor girls(married/unmarried) (by negating it) in the garb of protection. This is also manifested by the excessive usage of the provisions of the Indian Penal Code, 1860 (dealing with kidnapping (Indian Penal Code, 1860 § 363), kidnapping, abducting or inducing woman to compel her marriage (Indian Penal Code, 1860 § 363), procuration of minor girl (Indian Penal Code, 1860, § 366A)) by the parents of the girl in the event of her eloping with her lover. As depicted in Figure 1.5, 38% of cases of kidnapping were for the purpose of marriage, illicit intercourse and elopement/love relationship.

Thus, adolescent girls are faced by the double whammy of jeopardized health and well-being, on one hand and the brunt of criminalization on the other. The married adolescent girls are pushed to destitution due to criminalization of child marriage (under PCMA, 2006) and her sexual relation with her husband (criminalized by the combined reading of the Protection of Children from Sexual Offences Act, 2012 and the Supreme Court's decision in *Independent Thought v. Union of India*, 2017 has also criminalized sexual relations between a man and his wife, if the wife is under 18 years of age). The plight of child brides is further exacerbated by the complex medley of laws- MTP Act, 1971 and POCSO Act, 2012 as discussed above.

The systematic analysis of the socio-legal framework reveals that the adolescents are unreasonably exposed to the rigors of the justice system, with young males being labeled as sex offenders for manifesting 'developmentally normative sexual conduct". The legislative regime criminalizing consensual sexual activity amongst or involving a child has been termed as an abuse of the criminal law and is indicative of an overbearing state unaware of the social realities (Gautam et at., 2022)

4   Pre-trial Incarceration vis-à-vis Overcriminalization: Tracing the Judicial Discourse in Bail

Even though the prima facie aims of the legal framework discussed above is to protect all children under 18 years from sexual aggression, however in reality it ends up depriving the liberty of young people in consensual relationships. The accused men and boys are predominantly charged with non-bailable offences such as rape and penetrative sexual assault (Ramakrishnan & Raha, 2022), and are inevitably taken into custody. The cardinal principle of arrest is laid down in *Arnesh Kumar,* 2014 that arrest should not be made merely because the offence is non-bailable and cognizable, but should be made after complying with the mandate of § 41 and 41A, Code of Criminal Procedure, 1973 and only if there exists a necessity of the same. However, the burgeoning number of undertrials questions the observance of the requirements prescribed under *Arnesh Kumar,* even though the courts have time and again reprimanded the lower courts, punished the police and released the accused on bail in event of non-observance of the mandate of *Arnesh Kumar,* 2014.

The matters under POCSO are indiscriminately termed as serious, thereby diminishing the chances of bail further, even though POCSO being a special legislation does not impose any special prohibition on grant of bail (*Pratap v. State of Himachal Pradesh,* 2022). The matters of bail and bond under the POCSO Act is governed by the provisions of Code of Criminal Procedure, 1973 (Protection of Children from Sexual Offences Act, 2012, § 31). Bail, an indispensable part of a criminal justice machinery, upholds the liberty of the accused while ensuring their availability and presence before the court. Pre-conviction custody or detention is generally considered unnecessary and unwarranted owing to the principle *ei incumbit probatio qui dicit, non qui negat* i.e a (wo)

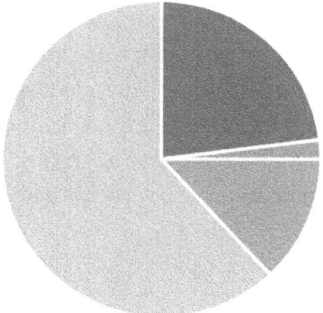

■ For marriage   ■ For illicit intercourse   ■ Elopement/Love relationship   ■ Others

FIGURE 1.5   Purpose of kidnapping
SOURCE: CRIME IN INDIA 2021, NATIONAL CRIME RECORD BUREAU

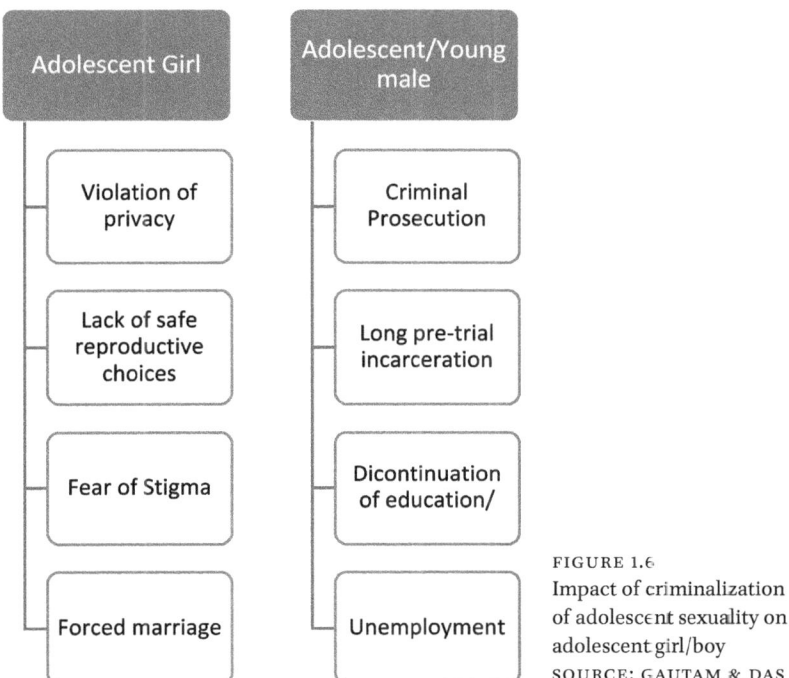

FIGURE 1.6
Impact of criminalization of adolescent sexuality on adolescent girl/boy
SOURCE: GAUTAM & DAS

man is presumed innocent until proven guilty.[3] Pre-trial incarceration exposes the accused to mental and physical deprivations, generally under more stringent conditions than the incarcerated convicts. The burden of this detention is borne by the innocent family members (*Moti Ram v. State of M. P,* 1975).

The rising number of "love-affair" cases (Figure 1.7), high pendency (Figure 1.8) coupled with *long* pre-trial incarceration/denial of bail and wrongful prosecution (acquittals- Figure) under the POCSO Act add to the plight of 'innocent' lovers caught in the act of love. This unprincipled criminalization of romantic love pushing the young lover in the wheels of (in)justice amounts to overcriminalization. This overcriminalization is caused at the instance of the entire criminal justice machinery particularly the police (while arresting/denying bail) and the courts (while denying bail/sentencing). In matters of sentencing (*Mohd. Azad Ahmed Ali Khan v. State of Maharashtra,* 2018; *Aaditya v. State of Maharashtra,* 2020), the courts have no discretion but to award the

---

3 Universal Declaration of Human Rights. (1948). Art. 11, S 1; European Convention for the Protection of Human Rights and Fundamental Freedoms. (1953). Art. 6, S 2; United Nations International Covenant on Civil and Political Rights. (1966). Art. 114, S 2.

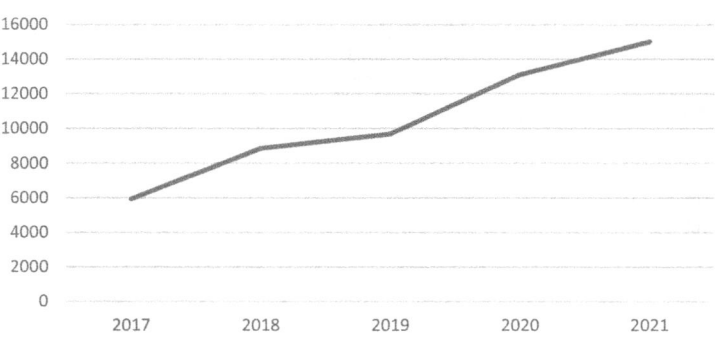

FIGURE 1.7 Offender relation with victim under POCSO Act, 2012 – friends/online friends/live-in partner on pretext of marriage
SOURCE: CRIME IN INDIA 2017–21, NCRB

minimum sentence prescribed under the penal code[4] i.e 7 years and the discretion to award a sentence below 7 years has been taken away by the Criminal Law Amendment Act, 2013, however they still enjoy vast discretionary power in granting bail.

The discretionary power is a double-edged sword, on one hand it allows the court to tailor-make the sentence/bail suiting the gravity of the case and on the other, it can also result in treating two similar cases differently. This section presents the systematic analysis of the approach of the court in bail matters of romantic love cases.

The Courts have a dichotomous approach while handling matters of bail in romantic cases. In some cases, the courts have strictly denied the bail on the grounds that the consent of the minor[4] Criminal Law Amendment Act 2013 took away the discretion of the Courts to pass a sentence below the mandatory minimum.

A girl is not valid in the eyes of the law and the act even though consensual amounts to statutory rape (*Smt Ephina Khonglah v. State of Meghalaya, 2021*; *Amit Raso v. State of Maharashtra, 2020*). The Courts have been increasingly adopting a strict approach and denying bail in such cases in the aftermath of Nirbhaya case (*Sunil Mahadev Patil v. State of Maharashtra, 2015*). The State of U.P has also made the provision for denying anticipatory bail in all the POCSO matters. In a study of cases of three states (West Bengal, Maharashtra and Assam), it was found that the accused was denied bail and remained in jail till the end of the trial in 15.2% romantic cases. For instance in *Rama @ Bande Rama v. State, 2022, a* 20-year-old accused in a "romantic" case was in judicial custody for 18 months.

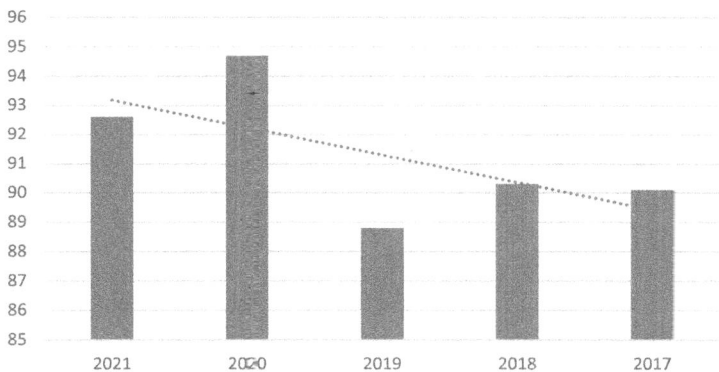

FIGURE 1.8   Pendency percentage in courts of cases under POCSO
SOURCE: CRIME IN INDIA 2017–21, NATIONAL CRIME RECORD BUREAU

Similarly in cases of elopement, courts generally drop the charges under § 363/366 where the girl had joined the company of the accused on her own free will (*Varsharajan, Bhagwat Maujabhai Hoge v. State of Maharashtra*, 2019; *Mohd. Azad Ahmed Ali Khan v. State of Maharashtra*, 2018) however the charges under § 376 are still maintained. Elopement out of free will often results in granting of bail (*Sanjeev Dhruv Varma v. State of Maharashtra*, 2020; *Jayantibhai Babulbhai Alani v. State of Gujarat*, 2018), though there exists a contrary outcome as well (*Aadityav.State of Maharashtra*, 2020). However, in cases of a love affair with a minor girl gone bad, courts are reluctant to grant bail (*X(Minor) v. State of Jharkhand*, 2022).

On the contrary, several High Courts have recognised the normalcy of adolescent relationships and criminalization thereof affects both the parties and is not in keeping with the objectives of the POCSO Act (*Kajal v State of Uttar Pradesh*, 2019; *Atul Mishra v. State of UP*, 2021; *Sunil Mahadev Patil v. State of Maharashtra*, 2015; *Vijayalakshmi v. State Rep, The Inspector of Police*, 2021; *Kuldeepv.State of Himachal Pradesh*, 2019; *Chander Vir Kaundalv.State of H.P*, 2017, *Aarti v. State of U.P*, 2018; *Sunilkumar Dilipbhai Patel v. State of Gujarat*, 2020; *Shembhalang Rynghang v. State of Meghalaya*, 2021; *Sknemborlang Suting v. State of Meghalaya*, 2021; *Sabarinathan v. The Inspector of Police*, 2019; *Xxxxx v. The State*, 2019) and therefore have granted the bail (*SunilMahadevPatilv. State of Maharashtra*, 2015; *Anhant Janardan Sunatkari v. State of Maharashtra*, 2021; *Vishnu Sitaram Sarode v. State of Maharashtra*, 2021). Courts have categorically granted bails where the accused and victim have gotten married and begot a child following a love affair (*AK v. State Govt. NCT of Delhi*, 2022; *Atul Mishrav. State of UP*, 2022; *Vijayalakshmi v.State*, 2021).

In the times when victim participation (*Jagjeet Singh v. Ashish Mishra*, 2022) in matter of bail is being hailed as an indispensable part of criminal process (Gautam & Das, 2022), the courts have granted bail on the grounds that "victim" girl did not want to pursue the case against her friend and did not have any objection to grant of bail (*Praduman v. State (NCT) of Delhi*, 2021) or that the victim girl, now the wife of the accused has stood as a surety (*X v. GNCTD*, 2023).

In contrast to the mechanical approach of the courts in matters of bail, the Delhi High Court in *Dharmendra Singh v. State Govt. of NCT*, 2020 has laid down the cardinal real-life considerations to be factored in while deciding bail in consensual relationship cases, to avert the perversity of justice. These relevant considerations include- the age of the victim; age of the accused; difference between the age of the victim and the accused; familial relationship; threat, intimidation, violence and/or brutality; conduct of the accused after the offence; repeated offence; easy access to victim; comparative social standing of the victim and the accused; innocent yet unholy physical alliance; tacit approval-in-fact; etc. Lesser the difference between the age of the victim and the accused, lesser the gravity is based on the western idea of Romeo-Juliet law for the statutory offences. Romeo-Juliet law in statutory offences provides a degree of protection to the offender where the age difference is within the prescribed limit.

"Romantic" cases take up notable judicial time, as most of the cases generally take more than a year to be disposed off thereby prolonging the detention of some accused persons by denying them bail, even though the matter eventually resulted in an acquittal. In a case the accused was acquitted after serving long pre-trial incarceration for lack of evidence (*Shri Wasim v. State of Karnataka Criminal Appeal No. 2632*, 2008). Similarly, where consensual

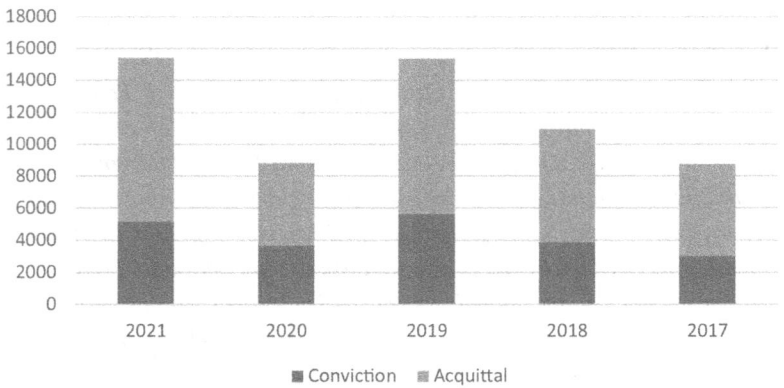

FIGURE 1.9   Trial outcomes under POCSO act: 2017–21
SOURCE: CRIME IN INDIA 2017–21, NATIONAL CRIME RECORD BUREAU

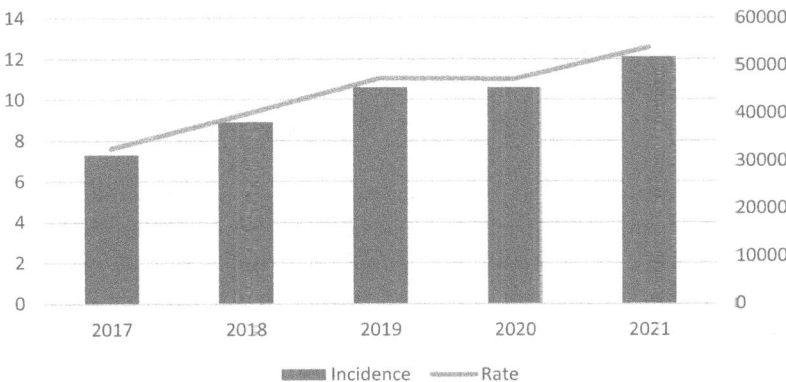

FIGURE 1.10 POCSO Act: incidence and rate
SOURCE: CRIME IN INDIA REPORT 2017–21, NATIONAL CRIME RECORD BUREAU

physical relations seem probable and the prosecutor's version does not inspire confidence, the proceedings are quashed (*Suraj v. State of Maharashtra*, 2021).

The criminalization of romantic relationships, the ensuing criminal process inflicts pain on the parties. The NCRB data reveals that the most likely trial outcome is that of acquittal (Figure 1.9). Securing a subsequent acquittal cannot compensate for the harm caused as the "sword of crime has already torn the soul of the accused." (*Bade Rama v. State of Karnataka Criminal petition No. 6214*, 2022).

The recent decisions of some High Courts showing 'flexibility' in granting bail in love-affair cases comes as a breath of fresh air. However, the Crime statistics reveals a worrisome increase in the incidence and rate of cases under POCSO Act in the last 5 years (Figure 1.10) out of which 25% cases are of romantic relations.

The dynamism of courts can do little to undo the 'overcriminalization' impact of criminalizing romantic cases. It can definitely protect the liberty of the accused but the fear of arrest, victimization by the system will subsist due to the banal and wretched practice of police filing POCSO cases at the behest of the family of a girl objecting to her romantic involvement with her paramour. This amounts to misapplication and subsequent misuse of law.

5   Conclusion and the Way Forward

The spiralling number of romantic cases (25%) in the criminal justice system raises concerns about overcriminalization and overburdening the criminal justice and child protection systems with cases that do not even include elements of "rape" or exploitation. The overflowing of the courts with criminal underage sexual activity cases for the sake of legal formalism (Phillis, 2011) calls for a nuanced investigation into the dormant question of unprincipled criminalization.

The statutory rape provision prima facie protects the girl against her sexual aggressor by doing away with the defense of 'consent'. However, blinded by the paternalistic attitude of protecting(*regulating*) the sexuality of underage girls, the State has mistakenly (*or not*) conflated the distinction between exploitative sexual practice and the general sexual expression by an adolescent. This paternalistic attitude of the State overlooks the socio-cultural realities of the society- manifested by incidents of romantic love, elopement, marriage and pregnancies amongst adolescent girls.

Criminalization of consensual relations with an underaged girl under the veil of protecting her, needs to be tested on the touchstone of *Mill's* harm principle. The Mill's harm principle puts fetters on the operation of criminal law as it desists State from criminalizing morally reprehensible conduct if the same is not baleful to others (Mill, 1991). Thereby the State cannot exercise its authority to violate individual liberty in the garb of legal paternalism. Moreover, the harm (if any) caused by consensual relations with an underaged girl is innumerably outweighed by the harm caused due to criminalization of such relations.

Therefore, to ensure dignity and protection of adolescents, the solution is not the police and the courts, rather it is prolonging years of education, providing counseling, reproductive health services and promoting economic empowerment (Das et al., 2022).

Bibliography

Aaditya v. State of Maharashtra, (2020). SCC OnLine Bom 2540.
Aarti v. State of U.P., (2018). Misc. Bench No. 5503.
Age of Consent Act. (1891).
AK v. State Govt. NCT of Delhi. (2022). Bail Application 2729.
Amit Rasao Patil v. State of Maharashtra. (2020). SCC OnLine Bom 917.
Anhant Janardan Sunatkari v. State of Maharashtra. (2021). SCC OnLine Bom 136.
Arnesh Kumar v. State of Bihar. (2014). 8 SCC 273.
Arnest, L. H. (1998). *Children, young adults and the law: A dictionary*. London: Bloomsbury Publishing.
Ashworth, A. (2004). Criminal Justice Act, 2003: part 2. *Criminal Law Review*, 516–527.

Atul Mishra v. State of UP. (2021). Criminal Misc. Bail Application No. 53947.
Atul Mishra v. State of UP. (2022). Criminal Appeal No. 4907.
Bade Rama v. State of Karnataka. (2022). Criminal petition No. 6214.
Baruah, S. (2023, February 5). Assam cracks down on child marriages, over 2000 arrested across the state. *The Indian Express*. Retrieved from https://indianexpress.com/article/political-pulse/assam-child-marriages-arrested-state-8423179/.
Bullough, V. (2005). Age of Consent. *Journal of Psychology & Human Sexuality*, 16, 25–42.
Chalmers, J. (2011). Regulating adolescent sexuality: English and Scottish approaches compared. *Child and Family Law Quarterly*, 23(4), 450.
Chander Vir Kaundal v. State of H.P. (2017). SCC OnLine HP 95.
Chandra, J. (2022, December 21). No plan to revise age of consent, Centre tells Rajya Sabha. *The Hindu*. Retrieved from https://www.thehindu.com/news/national/no-plans-to-reduce-age-of-consent-for-relationships-centre/article66288969.ece.
Child Marriage Restraint Act. (1929).
Cohen, M. (2008). No child left behind bars: The need to combat cruel and unusual punishment of statutory rape laws. *Journal of Law and Policy*, 16, 717–729.
Cornford, A. (2015). Preventive Criminalization. *New Criminal Law Review*, 18(1), 1–34.
Das, P., Gautam, U., & Tewari, D. B. (2022). Health and well-being of adolescent mothers and mortality status of infants in India: Mapping the socio-economic correlates. *International Journal of Health Sciences*, 6(S5), 10162–10178.
Dharmander Singh v. State. (2020). Bail Application 1559.
Donovan, P. (1997). Can statutory rape laws be effective in preventing adolescent pregnancy? *Family Planning Perspectives*, 29(1), 30–34.
Eidson, R. (1980). The constitutionality of statutory rape laws. *UCLA Law Review*, 27, 757–815.
European Convention for the Protection of Human Rights. (1953). Council of Europe.
Express News Service. (2022, September 24). UP Assembly passes bill against anticipatory bail to accused in rape, POCSO offences. *The Indian Express*. Retrieved from https://indianexpress.com/article/political-pulse/uttar-pradesh-amendment-bill-denying-anticipatory-bail-to-rape-accused-passed-8169586.
Friedlaender, L. H. (1913). *Roman life and manners under the early empire*. London: Routledge.
Gautam, U., & Das, P. (2022, April 29). Making room for the victim in the criminal justice system. *The Indian Express*. Retrieved from https://indianexpress.com/article/opinion/columns/making-room-for-the-victim-in-the-criminal-justice-system-7892293/.
Gautam, U., & Das, P. (2023). 'Child Marriage' in a legal quagmire: Unravelling the chimera of Prohibition of Child Marriage (Amendment) Bill 2021. *CPJ Law Journal*, 13, 472.

Gautam, U. & Sharma, S. (2021). Deconstructing the intersection between Medical Termination of Pregnancy Act and the Protection of Children from Sexual Offences Act: An Endless Battle. Rajpurohit, G.S & Singh, A. (2021). *Crimes against children in India: Preventive and Protective Laws.* Thomson Reuters.

Gautam, U., Tewari, D. B., & Das, P. (2022, December 24). Why CJI is right to express concern on age of consent: Criminalization of adolescents under POCSO Act shows an overbearing state unaware of social change. *The Indian Express.* Retrieved from https://indianexpress.com/article/opinion/columns/cji-right-to-express-concern-age-of-consent-criminalisation-adolescents-pocso-act-8340931/.

Gopika Jayan & Anr. v. Faisal M.A. (2022). *LiveLaw (Ker)* 308.

Graupner, H. (2000). Sexual consent: The criminal law in Europe and overseas. *Archives of Sexual Behavior,* 29(5), 415–461.

Hirschfeld, M. (2000). *The homosexuality of men and women* (M. Lombardi-Nash, Trans.). Amherst, NY: Prometheus Books. (Original work published 1914).

Independent Thought v. Union of India. (2017). 10 SCC 800.

Indian Penal Code. (1860).

Jagjeet Singh v. Ashish Mishra. (2022). Criminal Appeal No. 632.

Jayantibhai Babulbhai Alani v. State of Gujarat. (2018). SCC OnLine Guj 1223.

Kajal v State of Uttar Pradesh. (2019). SCC OnLine All 3909.

Kuldeep v. State of Himachal Pradesh. (2019). SCC OnLine HP 2659.

Lacey, W. K. (1968). *The family in classical Greece.* Ithaca, NY: Cornell University Press.

Medical Termination of Pregnancy Act. (1971).

Mill, J. S. (1991). *On liberty and other essays.* Oxford, UK: Oxford University Press.

Ministry of Health and Family Welfare. (2019–2021). *NFHS-5.*

Mohd. Azad Ahmed Ali Khan v. State of Maharashtra. (2018). SCC OnLine Bom 1093.

Moti Ram v. State of M.P. (1978). AIR SC 1594.

Muhammed Rafi v. Satheesh Kumar M.V. (2022). *LiveLaw (Ker)* 386.

National Crime Record Bureau. (2017–2021). *Crime in India.*

Oberman, M. (2000). Regulating consensual sex with minors: Defining a role for statutory rape. *Buffalo Law Review,* 18, 703.

Oberman, M. (2001). Girls in the master's house: Of protection, patriarchy, and the potential for using the master's tools to reconfigure statutory rape law. *DePaul Law Review,* 50, 799–802.

Oberman, M. (2004). Turning girls into women: Re-evaluating modern statutory rape law. *DePaul Journal of Health Care Law,* 8(1), 109.

Phillis, N. (2011). When sixteen ain't so sweet: Rethinking the regulation of adolescent sexuality. *Michigan Journal of Gender & Law,* 17(2), 271.

Praduman v. State (NCT) of Delhi. (2021). Bail Application No. 2380.

Purohit, G. S., & Singh, A. (2021). *Crimes against children in India: Preventive and protective laws.* Thomson Reuters.

Rakesh Kumar v. Vijayanta Arya (DCP) & Ors. (2022). *LiveLaw (Del)* 1.

Ramakrishnan S., & Raha S. (2022). 'Romantic' cases under the POCSO Act: An analysis of judgments of special courts in Assam, Maharashtra, and West Bengal. Enfold Proactive Health Trust. Retrieved from https://www.girlsnotbrides.org/documents/1951/Romantic-cases-under-the-POCSO-Act_wUNsbKC.pdf.

Sabarinathan v. The Inspector of Police. (2019). (3) MLJ (Crl) 110.

Sanjeev Dhruv Varma v. State of Maharashtra. (2020). SCC OnLine Bom 3813.

Shembhalang Rynghang v. State of Meghalaya. (2021). Crl. Petn. No. 64.

Shri Wasim v. State of Karnataka. (2008). Criminal Appeal No. 2632.

Skhemborlang Suting v. State of Meghalaya. (2021). Criminal Petition No. 63.

Smith, A. T. H. (2004). Criminal law: The future. *Criminal Law Review*, 971–976.

Smti. Ephina Khonglah v. State of Meghalaya. (2021). B.A No. 14.

Sunil Kumar Antil v. CBI. (2022). *LiveLaw (SC)* 577.

Sunil Mahadev Patil v. State of Maharashtra. (2015). Bail Application No. 1036.

Suraj v. State of Maharashtra. (2021). SCC OnLine Bom 325.

Tadros, V. (2003). Crimes and security. *MLR*, 71, 940.

United Nations International Covenant on Civil and Political Rights. (1966).

Universal Declaration of Human Rights. (1948).

Vardharajan; Bhagwat Munjabhai Hoge v. State of Maharashtra. (2019). SCC OnLine Bom 929.

Verma, J. S., Seth, L., & Subramanium, G. (2013). Report of the committee on amendments to criminal law.

Vijayalakshmi v. State Rep, The Inspector of Police. (2021). Crl.O.P.No. 232.

Vishnu Sitaram Sarode v. State of Maharashtra. (2021). SCC OnLine Bom 2389.

Vishwanath, A. (2022, December 12). 25% of POCSO cases are romantic relations: Study. *The Indian Express*. Retrieved from https://indianexpress.com/article/india/study-of-court-orders-in-three-states-2016-2020-25-of-pocso-cases-are-romantic-relations-8319269/.

X (minor) v. State of Jharkhand. (2022). *LiveLaw (SC)* 194.

X v. GNCTD. (2023). *LiveLaw (Del)* 94.

Xxxxx v. The State. (2019). Crl.O.P.(MD)No.18064.

CHAPTER 2

The Collateral Consequence of Over-criminalization: Analyzing the Effects of Parental Incarceration on Children

Ira Rana and Anurag Deep

1 Introduction

The heavy use, by the government, of the criminal justice machinery to keep the masses in control is evident from the Prison Statistics India Report – 2021 (NCRB, 2021 b). According to the study, 18,06,823 convicts were admitted nationwide in jails during 2021, an increase of 10.8% from 2020. 5,54,034 inmates were lodged in prisons across India as of 2021, Dec. 31. 4,27,165 of these 5,54,034 inmates were awaiting trial, making up 77.1% of the total jail population. 11,490 prisoners who were part of the population of undertrials were detained for five years or more. Convicts, detenues, and other prisoners made up the remaining jail population, making up 22.2%, 0.6%, and 0.1%, respectively. The figures released by National Crime Records Bureau (NCRB) not only indicated the overuse of prison machinery but also demonstrated the excessive exercise of arresting powers and elongated trials. According to the Crime in India Report – 2021 (NCRB, 2021 a), there were 58,09,380 arrests made overall in 2021. With 27,20,265 cases receiving a charge sheet, the percentage of charge sheets for offences under the Indian Penal Code was 72.3%. At the trial level, conviction rates for instances involving the Indian Penal Code and Special & Local Laws were 57.0% and 78.7%, respectively. Out of 2,33,43,551 ongoing trials, it was found that 20,21,771 cases had been pending for between three and five years, and 27,15,557 cases had been outstanding for five years or more.

The researcher's contention is that by giving in to punitive populism and assuming that any mention of the public's sense of justice translates to pushing for a tough-on-crime agenda, the government completely ignores a demographic frequently likely to suffer more than the perpetrator herself. The cohort, as mentioned above, includes the relatives of offenders, especially the children of incarcerated individuals. Here, it is crucial to recognize that children of incarcerated parents are not a small minority but a sizable population that outnumbers those behind bars. The present chapter concerns this segment, i.e., the children of incarcerated parents.

The chapter aims to demonstrate to the readers the subtleties of a child's journey once her parent(s) is incarcerated. Four sections make up the chapter. The phrase "children of incarcerated parents" is defined in the first part. The second section discusses the statistical breakdown of children in India facing parental incarceration is discussed after this. The third section touches upon the state's indifference towards the children facing parental incarceration. In conclusion, the researcher has proposed ways to safeguard the interests of these children.

2   Children of Incarcerated Parents: Meaning and Statistical Representation

Children, incarceration, and parents are the three components that make up the phrase "children of incarcerated parents." Thus, we must comprehend these three ideas to understand who all may be referred to as the offspring of incarcerated individuals. A *child*, according to common usage, is a person who is under the age of eighteen.

Black's Law Dictionary defines *incarceration* as "imprisonment; confinement in a jail or penitentiary". The meaning of incarceration, according to the Cambridge English Dictionary, is "to put or keep someone in prison or in a place used as a prison" (Cambridge Dictionary, 2023). Similarly, the Oxford Dictionary defines incarceration as "an act of putting somebody in prison or in another place from which they cannot escape" (Oxford Learner's Dictionaries, 2023). In light of these definitions, it is possible to define incarceration as "any type of custody of a parent by the criminal justice system, with the exception of only being imprisoned overnight." However, the researchers contend that, from the child's viewpoint, it is accurate to argue that parental incarceration starts the minute a child has been stripped away from her parent(s) – the exact moment a parent is arrested. As a result, it is possible to conceptualize parental incarceration as occurring in a series of stages, including arrest, inquiry, pre-trial, trial, sentencing, and imprisonment.

The term *parent* commonly refers to a person's biological or adoptive parent. According to this definition, a child is considered to be the offspring of an incarcerated parent if either her biological or adoptive parent is incarcerated. Nonetheless, a child can depend on someone outside her biological or adoptive parent; in such a case, this constrained definition of the term parent will exclude those children. According to the researchers, a restrictive definition of parent is unworkable in the context of the diversified family structures of the modern world as evident from the findings of the United Nations

Report (Progress of Women World, 2019–2020) and the fact that the majority proportion of offenders come from dysfunctional families. Considering this, the researchers suggest that the term "parent" be defined as a person who, *via* reciprocity and contact, regularly satisfies the child's physical and psychological needs for a parent (Goldstein, et al, 1996). According to this definition, a person can still qualify as a parent even if he or she is not the child's biological or adoptive parent, better reflecting the child's circumstances and potential interests.

Combining these three definitions, we can say a person may be said to be a child of an incarcerated parent if he/she under eighteen years of age experiences arrest, pre-trial, trial, sentencing, or imprisonment of the person who, *via* reciprocity and contact, regularly satisfy her/his physical and psychological needs for a parent.

3   Statistical Representation of the Children of Incarcerated Parents

It is important to note at the outset of the discussion about the quantitative portrayal of children of incarcerated parents that since no data about the children of arrestees is available, the findings of this section will be limited to the children of prisoners. Second, the numbers presented are an estimate based on a formula used to determine the number of children of incarcerated parents in many international studies. This is because the National Crime Records Bureau, the organization in charge of maintaining a data repository on crime and criminals, only collects information about a small portion of this cohort, i.e., the children accompanying their mothers inside the prison complex. Thus, the only information we have about this cohort is that as of 2021, Dec. 31 we had 1,867 children living in various jails across India (NCRB, 2021b).

According to the formula mentioned in the above paragraph, a sample of the prison population is surveyed. Each prisoner is asked to complete a questionnaire indicating if they have children and, if so, how many. Based on these responses, the average number of prisoners with children is determined. Applying this formula to the population of Indian prisons and using the data provided by the Maharashtra jail administration in *High Court on its Motion v. State of Maharashtra,* 2016 (High Court on its Motion v. State of Maharashtra, 2016) as a representative sample, where it was reported that the women inmates in Maharashtra had 846 children as of 2016, Feb. 11. Also, assuming that there were 330 female prisoners in Maharashtra as of 2016, Feb. 11 which is equivalent to the number mentioned in the Prison Statistics India Report-2015, we may estimate that an inmate in India has 2.56 children on average.

Based on these numbers, it may be deduced that, as of 2021, Dec. 31 Indian convicts were parents to 14,18,327 children. Taking note of the numbers arrived, it can be concluded that the population of the children of prisoners outnumbers the actual prison population, i.e., 5,54,034 as of 2021, Dec. 31.

It is to be noted that these figures can only provide us point prevalence (how many children have a parent in prison at one point of time) (Murray & Farrington 2008, p. 137) and not the cumulative prevalence (the proportion of children who experience parental imprisonment at some stage between their birth and their eighteenth birthday) (Murray & Farrington 2008, p. 137).

4   State's Apathy towards the Children of Incarcerated Parents

When a person is incarcerated, the state serves the public by reinstating their sense of justice. However, while fixating on "serving justice," the state overlooks the wrong being done to these incarcerated individuals' families (particularly children). Thus, instead of pondering over some fundamental questions such as the relevance of the longstanding means of punishment, i.e., imprisonment (Smith, 2014, p. 82) having the potential of ruining families or about the unbounded pain inflicted upon the individuals due to the mal-functioning of our criminal justice machinery, the state chooses to restore the society's fundamental notions of justice and guilt by giving in to penal-populism, assuming (in the absence of any scientific studies) that public's moral values and sense of justice are invariably tilted towards harsh sentences (Balvig et al., 2015, p. 345). The state ignores the fact that by doing this, it forces the children of incarcerated parents to see the criminal justice system as a sort of upside-down universe where the official representatives of society turn out to be this child's adversaries rather than allies (Foster, H. & Hagan, J., 2015). The state easily ignores the fact that when one regularly identifies children of prisoners who suffer more from their parent's sentence than did the original victim of the offence in many cases or the parent herself, the very foundation of justice and punishment crumbles. This section of the chapter attempts to illustrate to readers the hardships a child encounters due to his or her parent's incarceration.

The police often being the first "system" representatives through the door (Bernstein 2005, p. 17), mark the starting point of the child's secondary incarceration. Researchers worldwide believe that the parent's arrest is the most tender spot of the journey of parental incarceration, potentially setting the tone of the child's subsequent relationship with the agents of justice machinery. In the words of Nell Bernstein, "arrest, reimagined, could be an opportunity to make that vulnerable child and her family visible; to make a bad situation better rather than worse" (Murray, J. & Farrington, D. P., 2008). However, the operations of the Indian police functionary narrate an opposite story where the police functionaries, instead of reaching out to the children, communicate to her, most explicitly, how little she will matter within the system and institutions that lay claim to her parent (Goldstein J. et al. 1996). Research conducted in Rajasthan's two central jails by Dr. Asha Bhandari demonstrates this (Bhandari 2016, p. 357–359). Seventy per cent of the women interviewed in this study reported that the authorities were unbothered with their children's presence at the time of their arrest. The paper cites instances of police officers subjecting mothers to assault in front of their children. The mothers described being pulled by their hair or having their children forcibly removed from them (TISS, 2002). A video of a firework seller's arrest that recently went viral adds to the evidence. In this video, a young girl (the seller's daughter) can be seen appealing to police officers not to arrest her father. The girl was so upset by her father's arrest that she began bashing her head against the police van (IBTI, 2020). On another occasion, two police officers were observed severely punching a man while his tiny nephew begged them to leave his uncle alone (Tribune, 2019). Another viral video shows Uttar Pradesh police violently smashing a man carrying a toddler in his arms (India Today, 2021).

Along with seeing their parent's defenselessness, these children witness their home and possessions, including their personal items, being relentlessly searched, taken away, or destroyed by law enforcement personnel. Further, research reveals that, despite the legislation allowing children under the age of six to accompany their mothers inside police stations and jails, the arrestees are often not informed of this provision. Thus, babies as young as a few months old are left without a mother upon the mother's arrest (IBTimes India, 2020, November, 14). These children, upon their parent(s) arrest, are placed informally with relatives or neighbors (Myers B. et al. 2004) or left unattended and forgotten about by the authorities. Even when the mothers are permitted to take the babies with them, everything happens so quickly that they do not have time to prepare the child. A mother stated in a survey, "My younger one was just in his underwear. It was cold, and I had to take him to the police station just like that" (IBTimes India, 2020, November, 14). These unprepared babies are then placed in police detention facilities deprived of even the most basic amenities, (Human Rights Watch, 1991) where they witness their parent's abuse and torture (CHRI, 2019).

The law requires that within twenty-four hours of arrest, the police shall present the accused before a magistrate (Art. 22 (2), COI, 1948). It should be emphasized that no provision in our legislation requires this magistrate, before whom the arrestee is produced, to inquire if the arrestee's children require any assistance. Hence, it is entirely up to the individual magistrate's conscience whether she wishes to initiate such enquiries either *suo moto* or in response to a request made by the arrestee regarding her children. It is worth noting that, despite the importance of this stage, which symbolizes the family's admission into the justice system, it is carried out in a routine fashion.

The matter then moves on to the trial stage. In the absence of any legal knowledge, the families face the trial with a lot of confusion and anxiety. Delhi National Law University's Death Penalty Report outlines incidents in which families of defendants facing undertrial proceedings reported that they did not comprehend much of the trial and were met with resistance from counsel when they sought to seek information about the day's events (DPRP,2016). There were occasions when the family would visit trial courts and wait outside the courtroom because they could not comprehend what was going on or because court officials would not let them in. The Report elaborates on the grounds for this denial of participation to implicated family members. It reads (DPRP,2016):

Clearly there are structural reasons and institutional practices that prevent family members from being meaningful participants in the trial proceedings. The opaqueness of legal processes with multiple levels of impediments in accessing information about the progress in cases only adds to the frustration and disenchantment with the criminal justice system.

It is crucial to emphasize that the Death Penalty Report does not explicitly discuss the accused's children. Nevertheless, one can imagine if this situation affects the adults so adversely, how must it affect the child whose primary care giver is embroiled in this predicament and who is destined to watch the entire drama develop, clueless of what is going on.

The second problem the families experience at the court premises is the need for infrastructure amenities to be available. Young mothers nursing their new-born in the open or in the absence of appropriate seating, youngsters sleeping or playing on filthy floors, are therefore familiar sights in court corridors. It is also typical to see police officers misbehave with family members while the members of the family attempt to approach the accused.

It is vital to note that no legal provision in India mandates the trial judge to consider the accused's children both at the stage of trial or sentencing. Nevertheless, because the legislature has granted our court broad discretion, a judge may take note of these children or make proper provisions for them if necessary. As a result during the trial, it remains customary for the accused to petition the hearing judge for assistance with her child(ren). However, given the prevalence of ignorance, lack of legal help, and illiteracy among offenders, how frequently this practice is used remains debatable. Although the judiciary, on several occasions, has raised its voice for the protection of these children, these attempts seem to dwindle when it comes to sentencing, particularly in the case of male convicts.

During the investigation, the researchers came across many instances which made them realize that trial judges (if sensitized) might play an essential part in the journey of children of incarcerated parents. The case which elaborates this point involves a fifteen-day-old daughter who lost her mother, and whose father was soon sentenced to ten years in jail for rape. In the absence of any relatives who could care for the child, the father carried her to jail with him, where she remained for five years in the women's section. In this case, the researchers believe both the jail system and the judiciary failed the child by failing to provide enough resources for her outside of the prison grounds. If there had been some coordination between the correctional and court systems, or if the trial judge had inquired about the convict's children on his initiative, this child could have been given a far better environment to thrive. On another occasion, a session judge in Ghaziabad sentenced both parents to life in jail. The couple had three children aged between two to six years at the time of arrest, who were quickly admitted into an orphanage by their relatives. The children were ten, eight, and six years old when the session judge sentenced them to life in jail. According to the researchers, if the case had been expedited, at least one child may have been young enough for adoption or instead, the sentence may have been written in such a way that at least one parent is accessible for the children at any given moment. The destiny of these children would have been different if there had been a process mandating judges to consider the children's welfare throughout the trial and then again during sentencing. However, that would have required our judges to prioritize the child's best interests in court procedures, which is still unusual in our legal system.

Prison is the third essential criminal justice agency that interacts with the accused and their families. Prisons are particularly important since perpetrators spend most of their time in jail, either as under trials or convicts. Researchers worldwide believe that the better the quality of visitation throughout a prisoner's incarceration, the better the effects on the prisoner, his or her post-release adjustment, the family of the prisoner and the community (Bernstein N., 2005).

Children, according to research, are most impacted due to parental imprisonment. Studies relate parental imprisonment to a number of short-term and long-term detrimental outcomes for children (Gaston, 2016, p. 1056). They include behavioral issues (Foster & Hagan, 2015, p. 387–429), deteriorating physical health (Sukhramani, N. & Gupta, S., 2020), stigmatization (Arditti et al., 2003, p- 195–204), diminished chances (Myers B. et al., 2004), criminality (Trice & Brewster, 2004), low academic performance (Trice & Brewster, 2004), school drop-out (Raghavan, V. & Nair R., 2011), family upheaval (Snyder et al., 2001), monetary troubles (Sukhramani, N. & Gupta, S. 2020), and so on. It is impossible to envisage a situation in which a parent's imprisonment is not upsetting for a child. Yet, constant, ongoing communication between the parent and the child throughout parental imprisonment may alleviate these difficulties and sorrows. According to research, constant, ongoing contact between family members reduces the stress of separation, lowers recidivism, and is the single most crucial factor in determining whether a family will rejoin after a jail sentence (Bernstein, 2005).

Bearing in mind the significance of preserving inmates' touch with the outside world, our Indian jail system provides each convict with four channels of communication: interviews, telephones (if accessible), letters, parole and furlough. The insufficiency of the most preferred form of communication (i.e., interviews or *mulaqat*) has been discussed in the paragraphs that follow. The primary issues that have been addressed include: (i) if the physical setting of the visiting area allows the child to have a meaningful interaction with the parent and (ii) whether the length of these visits is conducive to developing or maintaining strong relationships.

Depending on the amenities offered by the jail where the subject is being held, there are primarily two sorts of settings in India in which interviews are conducted. The interview area in one situation is partitioned into small cubicles. Each cubicle includes an intercom system and a glassed fibre wall. In the alternative sort of setup, communication between the interviewer and the interviewee occurs *via* a small window divided by barbed wire or an iron grill. The majority of jails in India have a barbed wire setting. An Indian politician Rajesh Ranjan described the quality of communication permitted by this kind of *mulaqat* as follows:

It was everyone altogether shouting over each other to be heard across the iron mesh that would serve as a partition between the prisoner and their visitors. Children, unable to meet their fathers in custody, would often start crying, making the atmosphere even more desperate. 'They start hustling you even before you have started speaking to your families'. In Purnea ... there were just two windows for all the visitors who had come to meet the inmates. Two windows for hundred or more people! In that small place, people would try to exchange food, they'd try to talk, they'd try to exchange crucial information- can you imagine what's that like? The same hand would search everyone, the same hand would receive the food and the same hand would give the food.

This does not imply that the first variant of *mulaqat*, which includes the installed intercoms, is trouble-free. In this kind of setting, a wall of glass can elicit feelings of deprivation and humiliation in both parties, each of whom will likely experience herself as walled off, walled-in-jailed (Bernstein, N., 2005). In his book, Nell Bernstein quotes Dr Barbara Howard as saying (Bernstein, N., 2005):

For babies and small children, window visits (with fiber glass) are more than unsatisfying; they are largely incomprehensible. Touch is more than just a nice thing for a relationship. It is basic to the nurturing process. If you are talking about children under a year of age, your main means of communication is touch. A baby looking through a plate of glass at his incarcerated mother would really be looking at his reflection in the window, not making a connection with the parent at all.

The troubles associated with the interviews *via* intercom were recounted by the wife of one of the detainees. "How much you would talk would depend on your luck", she explained. "Sometimes the intercom is not functioning correctly, and the room is so noisy that you can scarcely hear what the other person is saying. The intercom will automatically disconnect after a maximum of fifteen minutes. Sometimes we even struggle to say goodbye properly." The ratio between the number of convicts and available intercoms is another issue in this scenario. Just three intercoms serve around 138 convicts at Sub Jail-Kannod.

The quantitative factor is another aspect of any visitation policy that decides its effectiveness. The number of visits allowed in Indian jails ranges from just one visit to sixteen per month. However, a more thorough analysis of the visiting regulations shows that more visits do not always imply more fruitful communication. For instance, while Sub Jail-Jaleswar permits sixteen visits each month, the time permitted for these visits has been limited to only eight minutes, depriving the parent and child of the opportunity for any substantive dialogue. Similarly, just ten and ten-fifteen minutes are allowed for each of the eight monthly visits permitted by Central Jail-Thrissur and Sub Jail-Yelamanchili, repectively.

It was observed during the research that an essential factor that prevented children from visiting their parents was the disruption of their daily activities owing to the timings fixed for *mulaqats*. Examples are Central Jail-Tihar, Central Jail-Mandoli, Central Jail-Rohini, Women Jail-Mandoli, and Women Jail-Tihar. The *mulaqats* are held in these prisons Monday through Friday from 8:30 AM to 1:30 PM. So, if we look at the hour and the days established, it is evident that such visitation practices would increase the difficulties faced by the children visiting their detained parents.

5 Conclusion

The discourse above demonstrates the slip of children from one criminal justice agency to another in the absence of any child-friendly provisions. A plausible explanation for the legal system's failure to appreciate its responsibility towards these children might be that the justice agents do not consider these children their responsibility at all. The researchers believe that the root cause of the justice authorities' failure to recognize their obligation to these children lies in the way we are accustomed to understanding crime. *Crime* is referred to as anti-social conduct to which the state intentionally responds by causing suffering (Schwendinger et al. 2013, p. 123–157). It is described as "the breach of a legal duty treated as the subject matter of a criminal proceeding" in Black's Law dictionary. Merriam Webster Dictionary describes crime as "an illegal act for which someone can be punished by the government" (Merriam-Webster Dictionary, 2023). With these definitions in mind, it can be concluded that the criminal justice system's agents are the defendants of order who are primarily focused on the crime, the victim, and the criminal (McShane & Williams, 1992, p. 258–271). However, if we approach crime from the standpoint of rights, we may claim that it is not sufficient to defend and respect merely the rights of the offender and victim, as is the case with the current judicial system. This is because crime affects not only the rights of the perpetrator and victim but also those of their families. With the shift in trend, the victims' families are beginning to gain the limelight in justice systems globally. However, the families of offenders are still the collateral costs of the functioning of justice machinery. Sometimes the prisoner's rights to privacy and reproduction are considered in conjunction with the rights of spouses and partners (McShane & Williams, 1992, p. 82). Nonetheless, the children of the prisoners are still mainly invisible. The researchers contend that to improve this situation, we must have a comprehensive understanding of the effects of crime. Put another way, we need to define "victim" more broadly. Because the issue is more complex than just incidence, the impact is a vital second dimension (Foster, H., & Hagan, J., 2015). Thus, we should identify victims based on the "impact" a certain incident had on a person rather than making distinctions based on "how" someone got to be a victim. This implies that instead of adopting the conventional definition of the term victim, such as the one provided in the Criminal Procedural Code (CrPC), we should adopt a more inclusive definition of a victim. Thus, a crime victim should be defined as 'a person who has suffered bodily or mental harm as a consequence of the crime, a person who regularly cares for such a person, or a person who is deprived, bereaved, or disadvantaged as a result of crime'. The term "deprived, bereaved, and disadvantaged" should be broadly construed to include not only the families of the victims and those who have suffered harm while intervening to assist victims in need or stop victimization but also the families of the perpetrators, who also suffer losses as a result of the crime. This inclusive definition of 'victim' will bring the – spouses, children, parents, other dependents of the offender and the caretakers of the offender's dependents -within its ambit. The researcher would want to stress, however, that being regarded as a victim does not indicate that children of incarcerated parents should be treated in the same way as the victim or the victim's family. We must remember that each victim category has unique requirements that must be met in a unique way.

Bibliography

Arditti, J. A., Lambert-Shute, J., & Joest, K. (2003). Saturday morning at the jail: Implications of incarceration for families and children. *Family Relations, 52*(3), 195–204.

Balvig, F., Hoeffding, A., & Lolle, H. (2015). The public sense of justice in Scandinavia: A study of attitudes towards punishments. *European Journal of Criminology, 12*(3), 345.

Bernstein, N. (2005). *All Alone in the World: Children of Incarcerated*, 14.

Bhandari, A. (2016). Women prisoners and their dependent children: A study of Jaipur and Jodhpur Central Jails in Rajasthan. *Sociological Bulletin, 65*(3), 357–379. https://www.jstor.org/stable/26369541.

Cambridge Dictionary. (2023). Incarceration. In *Cambridge Dictionary | English Dictionary, Translations & Thesaurus*. Retrieved from INCARCERATION | English meaning – Cambridge Dictionary (Accessed on Feb. 25, 2023).

Commonwealth Human Rights Initiative (CHRI). (2019). Inside Haryana Prisons. *Justice Hub.* https://www.nationalheraldindia.com/india/commonwealth-human-rights-initiative-report-suggests-haryana-prisons-are-problematic Constitution of India. (1950).

Death Penalty Research Project (DPRP). (2016). The Death Penalty Report. *ISSUU.* https://www.project39a.com/dpir.

Foster, H., & Hagan, J. (2015). Maternal and paternal imprisonment and children's social exclusion in young adulthood. *The Journal of Criminal Law and Criminology (1973-), 105*(2), 387–429. Retrieved from https://scholarlycommons.law.northwestern.edu/cgi/viewcontent.cgi?referer=&httpsredir=1&article=7560&context=jclc.

Gaston, S. (2016). The long-term effects of parental incarceration: Does parental incarceration in childhood or adolescence predict depressive symptoms in adulthood? *Criminal Justice and Behavior, 43*(8), 1056.

Goldstein, J., Freud, A., Solnit, A. J., & Goldstein, S. (1996). *Beyond the Best Interests of the Child: The Least Detrimental Alternative*. Free Press.

High Court on its Motion v. State of Maharashtra, MANU/MH/1886/2016.

Human Rights Watch. (1991). Report on prison conditions in India. *Prison Conditions in India 1991 report by Human Rights Watch*. Retrieved from https://www.hrw.org/reports/INDIA914.pdf.

IBTimes India. (2020, November 14). *Daughter grieves as police arrest firecracker seller in UP, administration comforts girl*. Retrieved from https://www.youtube.com/watch?v=Wibxz5KjQLI.

India Today. (2021, December, 10). (204) UP: *Kanpur Cop Suspended For Mercilessly Thrashing Man With Child, India Today | NewsMo – YouTube*. Retrieved from https://www.indiatoday.in/india/video/video-kanpur-cops-slap-businessman-grab-his-collar-for-filming-them-2478784-2023-12-21.

McShane, M. D., & Williams, F. P. (1992). Radical victimology: A critique of the concept of victim in traditional victimology. *Crime & Delinquency, 38*(2), 258–271.

Merriam-Webster Dictionary. (2023). Crime. In *Dictionary by Merriam-Webster: America's most-trusted online dictionary*. Retrieved from https://www.merriam-webster.com/.

Murray, J., & Farrington, D. P. (2008). The effects of parental imprisonment on children. *Crime and Justice, 37*, 137.

Myers, B., Smarsh, T. M., & Amlund-Hagen, K. (2004). Children of incarcerated mothers. *Journal of Child and Family Studies, 13*(1), 11–25.

National Crime Records Bureau (NCRB). (2021a). *Crime in India Report – 2021*. https://ruralindiaonline.org/bn/library/resource/crime-in-india-2021-volume-ii/#:~:text=In%202021%2C%20the%20country%20registered,(Prevention)%20Act%2C%201967.

National Crime Records Bureau (NCRB). (2021b). *Prison Statistics India Report – 2021*. https://ncrb.gov.in/sites/default/files/PSI-2021/PSI_2021_as_on_31-12-2021.pdf.

Raghavan, V., & Nair, R. (2011). A study of the socio-economic profile and rehabilitation needs of Muslim community in prisons in Maharashtra. *Centre for Criminology and Justice School of Social Work, Tata Institute of Social Sciences, Mumbai*.

Schwendinger, H., & Schwendinger, J. (2013). Defenders of order or guardians of human rights. *Issues in Criminology, 5*(2), 123–157.

Smith, P. S. (2014). *When the innocent are punished: Children of imprisoned parents* (p. 82). Palgrave Macmillan.

Snyder, S. M., Dwyer, W. O., Miller, M. K., & Omori, M. (2001). Parenting from prison: An examination of a children's visitation program at a women's correctional facility. *Marriage and Family Review, 32*, 33–61.

Sukhramani, N., & Gupta, S. (2020). Children of incarcerated parents. *Indian Pediatrics, 57*(3), 199–203.

Tata Institute of Social Sciences (TISS). (2002). *Forced Separation: Children of imprisoned mothers (An exploration in two cities)*. Retrieved from https://www.tiss.edu/uploads/files/Dharmadikari.pdf.

The Constitution of India, art. 22 (2).

Tribune Web Desk. (2019, September 13). *UP Police thrash man mercilessly, nephew watches, begs forgiveness*. Retrieved from https://www.youtube.com/watch?v=IwXWnF5fLT0.

Trice, A. D., & Brewster, J. (2004). The effects of maternal incarceration on adolescent children. *Journal of Police and Criminal Psychology, 19*, 27–35.

(Progress of the Women World, 2019–2020). *Progress of the World's Women 2019–2020: Families in a Changing World*. Retrieved from https://www.unwomen.org/en/digital-library/publications/2019/06/progress-of-the-worlds-women-2019-2020#:~:text=Publication%20year%3A%202019&text=Families%20can%20be%20%E2%80%9Cmake%20or,and%20where%20gender%20inequality%20prevails.

CHAPTER 3

Policing Homosexuality post the Transgender Persons (Protection of Rights) Act, 2019: A Critical Legal-Victimological Analysis

Debarati Halder and Rupesh Rizal

1   Introduction

Indian history, mythology and culture are well connected with the concept of transgender and gender fluidity since time immemorial. Mohini, the female avatar of Lord Vishnu is considered as the first epic character who represented the concept of transwoman: as per the ancient epics, Lord Vishnu appeared in a female form to distribute the elixir of immortality to the gods saving the same from the demons (Monks, 2022). Vishnu Purana also mentioned about Mohini's role in curtailing the blessings of Lord Siva on Bhasmasura who, empowered by the latter, was able to destroy anyone by touching the head of the said person (Monks, 2022). The epic of Mahabharata also mentions the existence of two trans characters Shikhandi and Bruhannala, who played significant roles in the great war of Kurukhsetra (Monks, 2022). Born as Amba, daughter of the king of Kashi, she was abducted by Bhisma to be married to the latter's half-brother Vichitryavirya, the king of Kauravas. Amba was in love with another man who refused to marry her as she was abducted by Bhishma. The former then requested the latter to marry her. But Bhisma refused as Amba was supposed to be the bride of his brother and he was practicing celibacy. Angered by this, Amba vowed to be the reason for the death of Bhishma and committed suicide. In her next birth she was born as a daughter named Shikhandini to King Drupad. But with her penance she was able to change her gender to that of a male named Shikhandi who became the reason for the defeat of Bhishma (Srinivasan, S. P., & Chandrasekaran, S. 2020). Bruhannala on the other hand is the male to female transformed version of Arjuna who became so due to the curse of Urvashi (Agoramoorthy, G., & Hsu, M. J., 2015). These epics may show that Indian transgenders since the ancient era were not criminalized for being different from the normal heterosexual people. The ancient legal texts like the Arthashastra also recognize the legal identity of the transgenders (Sutradhar, R. 2022). As such, in the ancient Hindu period, the Sutrakaras or the law makers did not consider criminalizing transgender identity of individuals unless the said person/s had committed certain acts which were morally and socially wrong. Quite the same understanding prevailed during the Mughal era as well (Agoramoorthy, G., & Hsu, M. J. 2015).

Colonial era in India brought in a different perspective for the legal treatment of the transgender people. The colonial British rulers, who were heavily influenced by moral and religious Christian norms, did not accept the legal existence of third gender people who lived with a gender identity that was different from that assigned by birth. The colonial rulers felt the existence of the transgender people was threatening to the social and moral norms especially because it was believed they were having a parallel powerful socio-cultural-religious influential system that may heavily influence the natives. British colonial rulers brought in an uniform criminal law by the name of Indian Penal Code (Indian Penal Code, 1860) which was enacted on 16th October, 1860. This to a large extent brought an end to several social crimes including Sati (bride burning), *narabali* (sacrifice of human beings including children in the name of religious rituals) etc. This statute also touched upon certain offences which seemed unnatural and immoral to the colonial law makers: this included bestiality, homosexuality etc. S.377 of the Indian Penal Code therefore criminalized unnatural offence which was explained and penalized as below:

> Whoever voluntarily has carnal intercourse against the order of nature with any man, woman or animal, shall be punished with imprisonment for life, or with imprisonment of either description for a term which may extend to ten years, and shall also be liable to fine.

Explanation attached to the said provision further emphasized that penetration is sufficient to constitute the offence of carnal intercourse (Indian Penal Code, 1860 § 377). S.377 of the Indian Penal Code offers three divisions to be understood as unnatural offence: (a) voluntary carnal intercourse with any man, woman; (b) voluntary carnal intercourse with male, female children; (c) voluntary carnal intercourse with animal. We will concentrate on the first two points for this chapter. A clear reading of the provision would suggest that the law prescribes punishment for that who *has* carnival intercourse *voluntarily*. The wordings do not suggest that punishment would be applicable if any man or woman has a mere interest for same sex relationships but has not committed sexual intercourse. The provision was constituted with a futuristic approach which presumes that if any man or woman expresses interest to grow a same sex relationship that would definitely end in carnal intercourse which is morally wrong. In order to control this consequence, the provision was applied by the lawmakers to empower the police to treat such behavior of growing interest in homosexual people for the purpose of sexual connection as a criminal offence which is cognizable in nature. Here we have to understand that several people who may develop homosexual attitudes may or may not transform into trans men or trans women (holistically known as transgender). There may be gay men, lesbian women, or people with gender fluidity or cross dressers who may not prefer to undergo gender changing surgeries to become trans woman or trans man. Transgender people were considered criminals themselves because it was assumed by the colonial rulers that changing gender assigned by birth is against the nature and moral laws and this will create an extremely bad example for mankind as a whole. The famous expression of Jean-Louis de Lolme, the creator of Constitution de l'Angleterre (Constitution of England, 1771) which says *"Parliament can do everything but make a woman a man and a man a woman,"* probably is the best self-explanatory statement to support our above argument.

Policing homosexuality with the aid of S.377 of the Indian Penal Code therefore became a significant issue whereby the police officers could get almost unfettered power to detain, arrest, torture, violate and harass anybody who may explicitly show homosexual attitude in colonial British India. Interestingly, even though several researches have researched on the plight of members of LGBT (especially transgender people) from holistic human rights approaches, not many researches can be found on the issue of policing homosexuality post the Transgender Persons (Protection of Rights) Act, 2019. This chapter aims to fill this particular gap. This chapter is divided into three parts including the introduction as the first part. The second part discusses types of police brutality against homosexuals post the Transgender Persons (Protection of Rights) Act, 2019 and the third part is the conclusion.

2   Understanding the Key Features of the Transgender Persons (Protection of Rights) Act, 2019

In 2014 the Supreme Court of India in the landmark case of National Legal Services Authority (NALSA) v. Union of India, (NALSA v. UOI) found that the transgender persons in India lack constitutional recognition as human beings. This finding led the court to suggest to the parliament about creating a statute for providing specific protection to the transgender persons to exercise their fundamental rights. resultantly the Transgender Persons (Protection of Rights) Act was brought into existence in 2019. The statute has certain key features which include definitions of transgender person and person with intersex variation: the latter is defined as "a person who at birth shows variation in his or her primary sexual characteristics, external genitalia, chromosomes or hormones from normative standard of male or female body" (The transgender persons (Protection of Rights) Act, 2019, § 2(i)). The former is defined as "a person whose gender does not match with the gender assigned to that person at birth and includes trans-man or trans-woman (whether or not such person has undergone Sex Reassignment Surgery or hormone therapy or laser therapy or such other therapy), person with intersex variations, genderqueer and person having such socio-cultural identities as *kinner, hijra, aravani* and *jogta*" (The transgender persons (Protection of Rights) Act, 2019, Sec 2 (k)). As such, this statute extends legal recognition of the transgender persons in India for the purpose of enjoying right to life, right to education, right to shelter, right to health, right to work, right against discrimination, rights including right to own properties and rights against any discrimination that has been prohibited by Constitutions of India as well as by other statutes protecting the rights of the people belonging to minority communities in India (The Transgender Persons (Protection of RightsAct, 2019). The Act has emphasized on certain discriminatory and degrading practices targeting the transgender persons and has made such actions prohibitory and criminal activities: these include forcing the transgender persons to act as forced laborers, denying usage of public places, forcefully removing them from households and villages where they may have been staying as natural family members or they may have legally occupied the premises, sexually, physically and emotionally harassing and assaulting the transgender people etc. The Act has also established a National Council for transgender persons specifically for advising the government for formulating policies for the holistic welfare of the transgender people, monitoring the execution of the policies, reviewing the activities of the stakeholders in providing proper justice to the transgender persons (The transgender Persons (Protection of Rights) Act, 2019 § 18). But on many occasions this Act has proved to be a paper tiger and could not provide proper justice to the transgender individuals. The below mentioned examples of police brutalities, social ostracization and transphobia may support the above-mentioned argument of these authors:

Case example no. 1: In January 2022, four transgender people were arrested by the police in Tripura allegedly on the issue of their gender identity. They were reportedly forced to strip down to physically prove their gender in the police station (Deb, 2022).

Case example no. 2: In Maharashtra almost regularly during the festival period traders in busy trading areas file police cases against transgender beggars who routinely visit the shops begging and sometimes demanding money. The October 2022 newspaper report suggested that festival periods like the

Diwali and pre-diwali periods are the peak times for the transgender people to visit the busy commercial areas to collect money by way of begging for a living (B.Dheeraj, 2023).

Case example no. 3: In January, 2022 a trans man was forcefully taken to a police station from a government aided shelter home in Delhi. The report suggested that the police from the nearby police station broke open the shelter home as they had received a missing complaint from the family members of the concerned transman. While the other members of the shelter home went to the said police station to resist the alleged forceful taking away of the transman, they were also physically harassed and traumatized (Singh Asuthosh, 2022).

Case example no. 4: As published in the Times of India news channel web portal, R. Nazriya, a transwoman police constable had submitted her resignation letter due to alleged harassment by her superior police officers who used to harass her due to her gender and caste harassment (TNN, 2023). The news report suggests counter allegations of workplace misconduct by Nazriya as well. But this news report also shows how trans women may be subjected to harassment at the workplace.

The above-mentioned case examples can be taken as representative examples to understand how transgender people continue to be victimized due to police harassment and social discrimination. The second case however clearly shows that transgender people may still be subjected to harassment because they may not get a job in the job market due to the social perceptions or due to lack of proper training and education. This may happen due to several reasons including lack of family support, community support and long process of changing name and identity in the government papers that may delay admission process to selected institutions etc. The first example however may show that even though the Transgender Persons (Protection of Rights) Act, 2019 prohibits discrimination of transgender people in the workplace, educational institutes etc., in practice the said discrimination and trans phobia still exist and this may encourage the police to harass and humiliate members of the trans community in the name of prevention of nuisance and possible unnatural offences by them (even if the 'accused' may not have committed any such thing). The third example may show a growing intolerance in families about gender transformation of their adult children and how the said emotions may be misused by certain police officials to abuse people from trans gender communities. At this point it becomes necessary to understand about the powers of police as granted by various statutes in India and its limitations as set out by the courts.

3 Powers of the Police in India and Its Limitations under the Indian Laws

There are three main statutes in India that regulate the powers of the police: these are Criminal Procedure Code (Cr.P.C), The Police Act, 1861 and the Constitution of India. Cr.P.C provides unfettered powers to the police for investigation. But this does not mean that the investigation can be done by misusing and abusing the laws. Section 151 of the CrPC grants powers to the police to arrest any person without the orders of the magistrate and without any arrest warrant to prevent commission of cognizable offence only when the said officer knows that the arrestee has designed to commit an offence and there is no other way to prevent such commission of offence unless the later be arrested. But this section prevents the arrestee from being detained in the police custody for a longer period. It states that the police officer must get the proper authorization to keep the arrestee under detention beyond 24 hours and the said authorization must be justified (CrPC, 1973, § 151). The rules laid down in this provision regarding using the police intelligence to arrest for preventing the happening of a cognizable offence is further reflected in S.156 of the CrPC which speaks about power of the police officer to arrest in cognizable cases. It says an officer in charge of a police station may investigate any cognizable offence within the local limits of the station for which he has received the information. The provision further says that investigation procedure and powers of the police officer to carry forward the investigation in such cases must not be questioned as this may disrupt the process of fact finding. But the provision does not however leave this reason and process of investigation completely at the individual whims of the investigating officer. The investigating officer is bound to provide the preliminary report of the investigation to the court who has jurisdiction over the region and the police station as has been mentioned under Sections 157 (CrPC, 1973, § 157) (discusses about the procedure for investigation) (CrPC, 1973, § 157) and 158(discusses as how the report should be submitted) (CrPC, 1973, § 158) of the Cr.P.C.

As can be seen from the above, detention and arrest can be made by the police officer using the provisions of the Cr.P.C before the investigation and without the order of the magistrate in certain cases if the officer in charge has credible information that the concerned accused may cause more damage to the victim, to the evidences and may pose as a threat to the national security (Halder Debarati, 2021) But every such action by the police must be within the framework of the guidelines as has been laid down by the Supreme Court of India in Joginder Kumar v. the State of U.P. (1994) (Joginder Kumar v. the State of U.P., 1994). The Supreme Court of India in this case held as follows:

No arrest can be made in a routine manner on a mere allegation of commission of an offence made against a person. It would be prudent for a Police Officer in the interest of protection of the constitutional rights of a citizen and perhaps in his own interest that no arrest should be made without a reasonable satisfaction reached after some investigation as to the genuineness and bonafides of a complaint and a reasonable belief both as to the person's complicity and even so as to the need to effect arrest. Denying a person of his liberty is a serious matter. The recommendations of the Police Commission merely reflect the constitutional concomitants of the fundamental right to personal liberty and freedom. A person is not liable to arrest merely on the suspicion of complicity in an offence. There must be some reasonable justification in the opinion of the Officer effecting the arrest that such arrest is necessary and justified. Except in heinous offences, an arrest must be avoided if a police officer issues notice to a person to attend the Station House and not to leave Station without permission.

Joginder Kumar v. the State of U.P., 1994

This observation was made specifically on the basis of constitutional provisions against arbitrary arrest and detention of accused persons and rights of the accused persons that are available in Article 21(right to life) (India Constitution Art. 21), Article 22(discussing protection against arrest and detention in certain cases), (India Const. Art. 19), etc.

The Police Act, 1869 on the other hand discusses the police administration and disciplinary rules for the police officers in India. This statute provides that police officers cannot go overboard their statutory duties and constitutional obligations to inflict unwanted harm on others. They have to mandatorily maintain diaries for arrests etc. and they may also be liable for punishment for negligence in their duties etc. (Police Act, 1861)

4 Powers and Responsibilities of the Police and Criminal Justice Machinery towards Transgender Persons

Interestingly the Transgender Person Protection of Rights Act also has also mentions that the police officers are duty bound to protect the transgender persons from any harm etc., and provide them immediate relief in case any person from the transgender community reaches out to the police with a plea for protection against physical and mental abuse and harm, discrimination, forceful eviction from a lawful occupancy in any premises by the transgender person etc. (Transgender Persons (Protection and Rights) Act, 2019, §. 18). Even though we have not found any specific resource which may suggest that transgender people may have assistance from the police force which may consist only transgender police officers, India has several junior level police officers who are transgender persons. But the number is less. As such if any transgender person may become victim of physical and mental abuse, women police officers may be engaged to provide immediate first aid, rescue etc. This is also evident from the Government of India's advisory on the treatment and care of the transgender persons in the prison (MHA, 2022). The advisory states that every prison must have infrastructure for accommodating transgender persons. In case of search of such persons, liberty must be given to choose the gender of the officer concerned and search must be conducted adhering to the constitutional guidelines respecting the gender identity of the transgender person. The advisory further states that the transgender persons may be kept in separate cells but that should not mean that they are kept in complete isolation. Correctional administration system must see that every transgender prisoner must get chances for rehabilitation with dignity and respect. The advisory guideline also suggests that transgender persons must be subjected to health check-ups and such medical check-ups must not violate their basic rights, self-respect and gender identity (MHA, 2022).

4.1 The Act and Its Scheme

The law puts a complete ban on intoxicants. Section 13 states that no person shall manufacture, bottle, distribute, transport, collect, store, possess, purchase, sell or consume any intoxicant or liquor. Thus, the ban is complete or overarching in terms of any activity pertaining to intoxicants or liquor. The manufacturer, distributor, transporter or seller is likely to face criminal sanction, as is a mere possessor or consumer of such intoxicant. The definition of intoxicant is also very wide [Bihar Excise and Prohibition Act, 2016: S.2(40 and 41)] and it includes other substitutes and drugs, which are covered under the Narcotics and Psychotropic Substances Act (NDPS), 1985.

Chapter 6 of the Act, 2016 deals with offences and penalties in particular. Section 30 of the Act states that "Whoever, in contravention of provision of this – (a) manufactures, possesses, buys, sells, distributes, collects, bottles, imports, exports, transports or removes any intoxicant or liquor" shall be punished with imprisonment for a term may extend to life and with fine which may extend to ten lakh rupees. The section further states that punishment for the first offence shall not be less than five years, while for the second and subsequent offences, shall not be less than ten years rigorous imprisonment and fine of not less than five lakh rupees. Herein, for 'possession' of such intoxicants or liquor, the Act introduces a reversal of burden of proof. It states that people in possession of such contrabands have to account for those and "in the event of a failure to offer a satisfactory explanation", there shall be a presumption that the accused person is guilty of the commission of such offence, unless proved otherwise [Bihar Excise and Prohibition Act, 2016: S. 32(2)]. It is further mentioned that any animal, vessel, cart, vehicle, conveyance or any premises involved in the offence would be liable for confiscation [Bihar Excise and Prohibition Act, 2016: S. 32(3)].

Section 33 of the Act, 2016 makes it an offence if one prepares an intoxicating drink out of denatured spirit fit for drinking. The law says that any such alteration or attempt of alteration of the drink would attract a mandatory minimum sentence of ten years which may extend up to life imprisonment along with fine extending from one lakh to ten lakhs. Section 34 may further be highlighted due to its serious penal consequences. The provision bans mixing noxious substances with liquor (See also, S.36). It is interesting to note that the amendment brought in 2018 [Bihar Excise and Prohibition (Amendment) Act, 2018], imposed penalties depending upon consequential damage following such an act. If upon consumption any person succumbs to such noxious substance, the punishment shall be either death or life imprisonment and fine [S.34(b)(i)]. Likewise, if the consequences lead to disability or grievous hurt, he shall be incarcerated for not less than ten years or up to life imprisonment along with substantive fines [S.34(b)(ii)]. In case of any other consequential injury, mandatory punishment is not less than eight years which may extend to life imprisonment [S.34(b)(iii)]. It has been further added that even if there is no consequential damage, imprisonment shall be not less than eight years and may extend to ten years along with monetary penalties [S.34(b)(iv)].

Section 37 [Bihar Excise and Prohibition (Amendment) Act, 2022] of the Act attempts to penalise the local population for consumption of liquor. It provides a penalty for consumption and allows for arrest and production before appointed executive magistrates if found intoxicated, for securing bail. The release is, however, available upon payment of stipulated penalty but not available as a matter of right. The old provision (Bihar Excise and Prohibition Act, 2016 S. 37) mandated Rs. 50000/- fine or three months imprisonment for first time offenders, which increased to one year imprisonment extendable till five years, along with one lakh fine, in case of repeat offenders. The particular section has been under constant scrutiny and criticism and has seen repeated amendments in the last few years.

Section 41 imposes a penalty for import, export, manufacture, transport, sale or possession by one person on account of another, with knowledge, and is punishable with imprisonment ranging from eight to ten years along with fine. Section 45 penalises assault and obstruction in discharge of official duty of excise officers. Furthermore, section 48 criminalises 'attempt' to commit any offence under the Act with half of the punishment prescribed for that offence. Section 54 imposes onus on the occupier of any premises to disclose information of unlicensed manufacture or cultivation or consumption of liquor or intoxicant. In case of any failure to disclose, the person is liable for imprisonment. The legislation makes the offences under the Act non-compoundable in nature.

Section 73 deals with power to inspect, search and seize. It lists specific personnel who would be empowered to function under this provision. These authorities may, without warrant, but subject to such restrictions as may be prescribed by the State Government, enter, inspect, search any place at any time, day or night, and seize any document, sample, equipment, conveyance, animal, commodity, intoxicant, material, raw material or any other item of concern and may effectuate arrest of any person, vehicle, animal etc. at any time of day and night under Section 74.

The above scheme of the legislation indicates its severity and is a classic example of over criminalization. While the manufacture, sale, distribution etc. of intoxicants, identified as 'narcotic' and 'psychotropic', is the subject matter of another Central legislation, the NDPS Act, 1985, this Act is specifically targeted towards intake of liquor and its consequent addiction. The Government has proposed to deal with the habit of the common masses with sternness, using the highest level of deterrence to dissuade the people, with serious consequences. The provisions for incarcerating people for various offences under the Act, ranging from five years to life imprisonment or even death, do not conform to the basic principles of criminal jurisprudence; neither do they correspond with the legal structures of a modern legal democracy. As commented by the Chief Justice of the High Court of Patna, on the initial legislation (Confederation of Indian Alcoholic Beverage Companies v. State of Bihar, 2016):

The submission is that though the legislature has the right to provide for punishments for contravention of provisions of Acts made by the legislature, the procedure and the punishment has to be fair and not draconian, for, that would be violative of Article 21 of the Constitution. The punishment cannot be disproportionate to the offence. ... it is submitted that virtually, the punishment for any offence has been prescribed as not less than ten years, which may extend to imprisonment for life and with fine, which shall not be less than Rs. one lakh but may extend to Rs. ten lakhs. ... It is highly disproportionate and can be termed as draconian.

The law is not merely disproportional and encourages overcriminalization, but additionally, it has ignored other basic notions of criminal law. Section 32 of the Act is designed to presume every accused guilty until proven otherwise. There is no application of the presumption of innocence, a fundamental principle which provides a safe cover to the accused in a criminal case, till the State proves his guilt. The Court hence remarked., (Confederation of Indian Alcoholic Beverage Companies v. State of Bihar, 2016) This provision reverses the criminal jurisprudence of prosecution having the liability to prove the guilt beyond reasonable doubt. Here, a person is presumed to be guilty unless he proves to the contrary. The presumption of innocence is totally taken away and the burden of proof thereof is put on the accused. For any reason, if he fails to prove his innocence, he would straightway be liable to punishment, which would be of minimum 10 years imprisonment with an astronomical fine and would lose his entire property by virtue of confiscation and the Courts are rendered helpless in the matter even though there may be mitigating circumstances.

Again, sections 73 and 74 give right to the concerned authorities to enter, inspect and search any place without a warrant and also arrest any person at any time day or night. The impugned law fails to take into consideration Sec 41A of the Code of Criminal Procedure (CrPC), 1973, which mandates notice of appearance in lieu of arrest; or Sec 165 CrPC, 1973 which requires the officer conducting a search to record in writing the reasons for doing so without warrant, and sending a report forthwith to the Magistrate. The provision also discards the rule of basic decorum and propriety as laid down in Section 46(4) CrPC, 1973 where it is expressly mentioned that "no woman shall be arrested after sunset and before sunrise".

The fallibility of the Act, passed in haste and in complete disregard of fundamental principles, has witnessed repeated amendments over the last few years. Since its inception, the law has already witnessed two amendments [Bihar Prohibition & Excise (Amendment) Act, 2018 and Bihar Prohibition & Excise (Amendment) Act, 2022] along with additional changes made via introduction of Bihar Excise and Prohibition Rules [The Bihar Prohibition and Excise Rules, 2021 and Notification no. – 2458 Amendment of Bihar Prohibition Excise Rules, 2021] which have also gone through necessary amendments in order to remove the rigors of the penal provisions as also introduce fairness in its procedures. These amendments are testimony to the fact that the legislation is ill-conceived and fails to further any legitimate purpose of the State.

4.2 Patterns of Police Brutality over Transgender People

The above discussion may show general powers of the police and how this may be misused. Patterns of harassment of transgender people may not differ much from the general patterns of police brutality over general individuals. But identifying the patterns of police brutality on transgender people may help us to understand the key reasons behind policing transgender post the Transgender Persons (Protection of Rights) Act, 2019.

Police brutality in simple words can be explained as unwarranted use of force by police against people, and the misuse of the powers vested upon them for a specific purpose. Police brutality has not been categorized or defined under any law, but with evident and rampant acts of atrocities against people by the police, we have an understanding of this term on our own. Police brutality can also be termed as abuse of power by police.

The following can be understood as types of police brutality over transgender people;

a. *False imprisonment*: One of the common forms of police harassment and brutality over the transgender persons in India may be false imprisonment on frivolous charges and allegations. In the case of *Bhim Singh v. State of Jammu and Kashmir* (Bhim Singh v. State of Jammu and Kashmir, 1986), the court held that the police cannot arbitrarily restrain a person as it violates his right to freedom under Article 19. This is no exception for the transgender people as well. The case examples provided in the above may suggest that transgender people may also be subjected to false imprisonment by the police on frivolous allegations. The reasons can be numerous. It may include charge for committing public nuisance, attempt to kidnap children, false allegation of forcefully influencing young adults to change their gender or to act like gays or lesbians etc. such allegations may also be motivated due to socio-economic reasons whereby general individuals may be extremely irritated or annoyed due to the begging behaviour or forceful extraction of money from them by the transgender people in the name of auspicious occasions like child birth, marriage etc. the transgender people who may be living on such types of incomes may not get opportunities for empowerment and even if they do, there may be various hidden socio-economic reasons which may force them to be engaged in such types of works rather than getting engaged in self-help group programs or other kinds of empowerment programs. Unfortunately, they may not even be supported for bail. Resultant they may have to stay in extremely degrading situations in the prisons. Here we have to have a panoramic understanding of public nuisance which is considered as major reason for false imprisonment of transgender persons, gays, lesbians and queer group people.

S.268 of the Indian Penal Code defines the term as follows:

A person is guilty of a public nuisance who does any act or is guilty of an illegal omission which causes any common injury, danger or annoyance to the public or to the people in general who dwell or occupy property in the vicinity, or which must necessarily cause injury, obstruction, danger or annoyance to persons who may have occasion to use any public right. A common nuisance is not excused on the ground that it causes some convenience or advantage.

It may be seen that the concept of 'annoyance' or 'danger' to the public is the common cause that is used to apply false imprisonment charges on people belonging to LGBTQ people, especially transgender people. Unfortunately, before such people may access their lawyers or even free legal aid services provided by the district or state legal services authorities, the police may have already violated their basic fundamental rights.

b. *Excessive use of force:* The Cr.P.C and the Constitution of India prohibits any usage of excessive force that may cause acquit physical harm, mental trauma, public humiliation of the individual for detention, prevention of any illegal activities etc. unless the same is utterly necessary for preventing danger to the security of the nation and the same may be authorized by the higher authority of the police force. Even in such cases also the constitutional provisions prohibit usage of excessive amounts of force as it violates the citizens' right to life and personal liberty guaranteed under Article 21 of Indian Constitution. But Section 46 of the Indian Penal Code however allows the police to use force while making an arrest by stating as follows:

(1) In making an arrest the police officer or other person making the same shall actually touch or confine the body of the person to be arrested, unless there be a submission to the custody by word or action.

(2) If such person forcibly resists the endeavor to arrest him, or attempts to evade the arrest, such police officer or other person may use all means necessary to effect the arrest.

(3) Nothing in this section gives a right to cause the death of a person who is not accused of an offence punishable with death or with imprisonment for life.

Here the words "use necessary means to" in Clause 2 of the above Section, must not be interpreted as arbitrary use of force on the accused to cause irreparable damage to the body of the person. But unfortunately, such guidelines are not properly used by the police, especially for the arrest of transgender persons or homosexual persons who may be alleged to be engaged in public display of activities which may cause public nuisance. Excessive force against the transgender people by the police may also include pulling their hair, forcefully disrobing them to prove their gender identity, physical pushing and beating, verbal bullying for degrading their reputation etc.

c. *Custodial torture including Rape*: In the cases of *Nilbati Behra v. the State of Orissa*, (Nilbati Behra v. the State of Orissa, 1993) *Joginder Singh v. State of U.P.*, (Joginder Singh v. State of U.P., 1994) and *Dk Basu v. State of West Bengal* (D K Basu v. State of West Bengal, 1997) the Supreme Court of India has laid down several principles to ensure the rights of the accused including prevention of custodial torture. While transgender people may be forced to undergo custodial torture including the infamous third-degree methods by the police to extract information and also to forcefully submit accused statements, custodial rapes of transgender people is an issue which needs high attention from the stakeholders now. Custodial rape in this context means the rape of a woman in police custody. Section 376 C of the IPC deals with sexual intercourse by a person in authority and also penalises such crime with at least 10 years of rigorous imprisonment which may extend up to life imprisonment along with fine. However, such instances are barely reported because of numerous reasons. In March 25, 2021, a transgender jail inmate from Nagpur alleged custodial rape in the prison. The matter was taken up by the Nagpur bench of Bombay High court which directed the concerned prison administration to produce the transgender woman before the local police station to lodge an FIR so that the investigation on the alleged rape may begin as per the rules laid down by Cr.P.C (Bose.S., 2021). This case example can be taken to understand how custodial rapes may be used by the police as a tool gratify sexual interest without charging the police officers and fellow prison inmates who may be involved in such heinous incidences. It is ironical to note that while The Transgender Persons (Protection of Rights) Act, 2019 prohibits sexual offences against transgender persons, Indian Penal Code is silent about rape of transgender persons. The only solace is S.18 of the Transgender Persons (Protection and Rights) Act, 2019 which discusses offences and penalties against the transgender persons. Sections 377 of the Indian Penal Code may be used very narrowly to punish offenders for committing non-consensual homosexual activities especially if the commission of the act is interpreted as unnatural offence and non-consensual sexual intercourse between two men one of the whom (the victim) has undergone medical procedure of sex change to become a transwoman. But even this argument may not be firmly established if the court sees the victim as a transwoman only.

d. *Online victimization of the transgender persons and police apathy:* It is significant to note that transgender persons undergo acute victimization in cyberspace as well. They are trolled, their privacy is violated and they are victimized by stalking, voyeurism, making sexually colored remarks, forcefully showing pornography etc. (Halder & Jaishankar, 2016) Indian Penal Code offers a general solution for such kinds of victimization through Ss. 354D (punishment for stalking), 354C (punishment for voyeurism), S. 354A (sexual harassment and punishment for the same), S. 507(criminal intimidation by anonymous communication) etc. But transgender people hardly get any response from the police in this regard. If any transgender person prefers to register any complaint, they may be met with verbal bullying, victim blaming, physical harassment at the police stations. There are possibilities that their online humiliations may further be re-shared for fun sake and involvement of the police personnel who may have been in charge of registering their complaints may not be overruled. (Halder & Jaishankar, 2016)

4.3 Possible Reasons for Police Brutality on Transgender People and Police Apathy

There may be several reasons for police brutality and police apathy over the crime victimization of transgender people in India. These may include the followings:

a. *Lack of awareness about the Transgender Persons (Protection of Rights) Act, 2019:* Police brutality and apathy towards victims of different kinds of abuses may occur due to the lack of awareness about, The Transgender Persons (Protection of Rights) Act, 2019 and punishments provided for physical and mental harassment of transgender persons. Police officials, constables and head constables posted in the remote areas of the country, in urban places and semi-rural places may have the same negative feelings about the transgender persons as the majority of society members may have. They may neither have proper training to deal with the transgender crime victims, medical necessities of such persons and need for psychological counselling for such persons.[1] Further there is a lack of awareness among the transgender people about their rights, about the National Council for Transgender Persons where they may reach out against police brutality and police apathy.

b. *The issue of social bias:* Even though The Transgender Persons (Protection of Rights) Act, 2019 came into existence unfortunately it could not eradicate social bias against the transgender people from the minds of general people. As has been mentioned above, transgender people are still considered a public nuisance especially since many of them make their living by begging and forceful extraction of money from people in social occasions. Such people may not be educated enough to get a job in mainstream societies or they may be under the influence of social goons including transgender goons who may be using them to make money for a living. Police brutality may be caused by such social reasons as well (Brahmbhatt S. & Shali S.K., 2017).

c. *Lack of stringent laws to address custodial rapes and torture targeting the transgender people:* There are no strict laws that can hold the police accountable for custodial rape and torture of transgender people. As such even if the existing laws offer extremely narrow solutions for the same, no police station may register any case in this regard and the transgender people may not have funds to hire lawyers to go ahead for filing court cases directly. Even though some law practitioners are supporting the causes of transgender people in this regard, the majority of people from such communities may have to stay as muted victims.

d. *Legal twists in creating new gender identity for transgender persons:* Even though the present governance system has made the gender and name changing simplified for the transgender persons, due to lack of awareness about the system and paucity of funds many transgender people may not get proper help for their gender identity. Resultant they may need to reach out to local police stations and politicians for getting necessary documents and certificates which may prove to be a herculean task as they may not be supported by their families and they may neither be properly educated under the system. They might be ridiculed in the

---

1 This information was shared by experts in the Module Course on 'Proclivity of Gender: Socio – Legal Approach to LGBTQ Community' on September 09, 2019 held in Karnavati University, Gujarat. https://karnavatiuniversity.edu.in/events/proclivity-of-gender-socio-legal-approach-to-lgbtq-community-2/ The authors argue that the above-mentioned reasons may enhance police brutality against the transgender people.

banks and in the government offices which may further consider their presence as a nuisance.

5 Conclusion and Suggestions

As the above discussion may suggest, policing transgender people in India may have been addressed for achieving positive goals. But in fact, the situation presents a grim reality. Unwanted bad policing on transgender people still exists and the patterns of such police brutality, police apathy and harassment and the reasons for the same are self-explanatory. Even if the Transgender Persons (Protection of Rights) Act, 2019 was brought into existence by the Indian parliament, police officials in many pockets of India may not be aware of the rights of the transgender persons and their duties towards the members of the transgender community. It is also necessary to find out how the national council for transgender people are working towards the upliftment of the status of the transgender people: it is interesting to note that Department of Social Justice and empowerment has initiated national portal for transgender persons in the name of "Support for marginalized individuals for Livelihood & enterprise" and the portal is available at https://transgender.dosje.gov.in/. But it must be found out how many transgender persons all across the country have knowledge about the same and how many of them are using the portal for holistic positive welfare. It is also necessary to know whether the police units in the districts and villages are aware of the same and are helping the transgender persons to access the said portal for general welfare. Many transgender persons may not be knowing about such portals, and even if some of them may know, due to lack of access to the internet and awareness about the facilities available in such portals, they may not be able to use or access such portals. Further, policing in the contemporary world has become welfare policing shredding its old profile of agent of torture and human right violation. As such, police officials must be trained about the rights of the transgender persons, their rights as have been established by the constitution and courts in India and their plights due to socio-economic challenges. These authors suggest that the government may consider appointing more police officers from the transgender community so that the police unit may have officers with practical knowledge and awareness about the rights of the transgender people. There are women police officers and all women police stations to handle women crime victims including victims of domestic violence, sex trafficking etc. Indian laws have also accommodated the special juvenile police units to address the needs of children in conflict with law and children in need of care and protection. These authors strongly suggest that the government must consider establishing transgender police cells in every district or sessions division to address the needs of transgender persons who are crime victims or who may have been affected by social atrocities. If the police force in its entirety is involved in protecting the rights of all individuals including the rights of transgender people, unnecessary criminalization of the transgender people solely because of their gender may be reduced.

Bibliography

Agoramoorthy, G., & Hsu, M. J. (2015). Living on the societal edge: India's transgender realities. *Journal of Religion and Health, 54*(4), 1451–1459. https://doi.org/10.1007/s10943-015-0034-9.

Bengrut, D. (2022). Traders' association lodges complaint against transgender beggars. *Hindustan Times*. Retrieved from https://www.hindustantimes.com/cities/pune-news/traders-association-lodges-complaint-against-transgender-beggars-101666466422881.html.

Bhim Singh v. State of Jammu and Kashmir, AIR 1986 SC 494.

Bose, S. (2021, March 25). Transgender alleges rape in jail, moves HC. *The Times of India*. Retrieved from https://timesofindia.indiatimes.com/articleshow/81676465.cms.

Brahmbhatt, S., & Shali, S. K. (2017). Empirical study on transgender identity: Socio-legal position in the district of Gandhinagar. Retrieved from https://dx.doi.org/10.2139/ssrn.3408351.

Code of Criminal Procedure. (1973).

Constitution of India. (1950).

D. K. Basu v. State of West Bengal, AIR 1997 SC 610.

Deb, D. (2022, January 11). 'We were forced to strip to prove our identity': Transgenders arrested in Tripura file complaint. *The Indian Express*. Retrieved from https://indianexpress.com/article/north-east-india/tripura/tripura-transgenders-forced-to-strip-police-complaint-7717450/.

Dheeraj, B. (2023) Traders' association lodges complaint against transgender beggars. *Hindustan Times*. Retreived from https://www.hindustantimes.com/cities/pune-news/traders-association-lodges-complaint-against-transgender-beggars-101666466422881.html.

Halder, D. (2021). Charge sheet to charging: A comparative analysis of case management by police and prosecution between India and the UK with special reference to cybercrime. In M. Pittaro (Ed.), *Global Perspectives on Reforming the Criminal Justice System* (pp. 1–324). IGI Global. https://doi.org/10.4018/978-1-7998-6884-2.

Halder, D., & Jaishankar, K. (2016). *Cyber crimes against women in India.* Sage Publications.

Indian Penal Code. (1860).

Joginder Kumar v. State of Uttar Pradesh, (1994) 4 SCC 260.

Karnavati University. (2019, September 9). Proclivity of gender: Socio-legal approach to LGBTQ community. Retrieved from https://karnavatiuniversity.edu.in/events/proclivity-of-gender-socio-legal-approach-to-lgbtq-community-2/.

Monks, S. (2022). A Vishnu-come-lately: John Bacon's monument to William Jones (1799). *Journal of Victorian Culture, 28*(1), 21--31.

MHA (2022). Advisory for protection of transgender persons. retrieved from //efaidnbmnnnibpcajpcglclefndmkaj/https://www.mha.gov.in/sites/default/files/2022-09/Advisory_TransgenderPersonsinPrisons_10012022%5B1%5D.PDF.

National Legal Services Authority (NALSA) v. Union of India, AIR 2014 SC 1863.

Nilbati Behra v. State of Orissa, 1993 AIR 1960, 1993 SCR (2) 581.

Police Act. (1861).

Singh, A. (2022, July 23). Trans man forcibly picked up from Delhi shelter, assaulted by police: Activists. *The Quint.* Retrieved from https://www.thequint.com/gender/transgender-persons-garima-griha-mitra-trust-delhi-dwarka-up-police-assault.

Srinivasan, S. P., & Chandrasekaran, S. (2020). Transsexualism in Hindu mythology. *Indian Journal of Endocrinology and Metabolism, 24*(3), 235.

Sutradhar, R. (2022). Contradiction and concurrence of castration and the fertile phallus: A transgender reading of ancient Indian literature and contemporary hijra experience. In D. A. Vakoch (Ed.), *Transgender India* (pp. 1–15). Springer, Cham. https://doi.org/10.1007/978-3-030-96386-6_5.

The Transgender Persons (Protection of Rights) Act. (2019).

TNN. (2023, March 19). Transwoman cop tenders resignation in Coimbatore. *Times of India.* Retrieved from http://timesofindia.indiatimes.com/articleshow/98764860.cms.

CHAPTER 4

Criminalization of Addiction – Analyzing the Bihar Liquor Prohibition Law

Dipa Dube and Shekhar Kumar

1   Introduction

Criminal law, as an instrument of social control, has been used since long to suppress anti-social, pernicious and harmful behaviour in society. It works on the principle that any harm perpetrated on an individual does not remain limited as such, but generates panic and insecurity in the surroundings. The state has the duty and obligation to maintain order to establish civility. Such civility is achieved through the instrument of criminal law which penalizes specific acts or conduct of individuals and prescribes punishment for the same. In fact, exerting punishments have been an intrinsic part of every society, long before the existence of formal states. The states have only contributed to it by making it robust and formalized.

However, the point which remains somewhat contentious is what conduct ought to be 'criminal'. In other words, while referring to acts of individuals which cause harm, thereby falling within the scope of criminal law, one needs to delve into the factors that are determinant therein. Most of the contemporary criminal legislations are based on the notion of 'harm'; but there are certain intricacies attached to it. What is harm? What is the extent and dimension of such harm? Is it good practice to advance grounds other than harm to criminally prosecute? These are some of the pertinent questions which need to be clarified before a conduct is criminalized. Looking at the expansion of contemporary criminal law, it is clear that 'harm' is not the only principle the states are looking to adapt. Kleinig (Kleinig, 2009), while discussing Douglas Husak's work (Husak, 2008) comprehensively refers to the seven constraints on the scope of criminal law. Husak divides them into internal as well as external constraints. The internal constraints comprise of (1) The conduct criminalized must be a non-trivial harm or evil; (2) The conduct must be wrong; (3) The conduct criminalized must warrant punishment; and (4) The burden of proof falls on those justifying criminalization. The three external constraints are (1) The state must have a substantial interest in pursuing the objective that the legislation is designed to pursue; (2) The said law must reflect such interest;

and (3) The law must be extensive to the extent it serves its purpose. The said constraints are comprehensive and provide a basic framework for the purpose of legislation.

In this context, the problem of liquor addiction and its criminalization may be looked into. Few states of the country have declared themselves as 'dry', thereby prohibiting any sale, distribution, consumption etc. of liquor in the state. Prior to the assembly elections of 2015, the ruling party in Bihar announced a blanket ban on the consumption of liquor in the state. This decision was made in response to the demands by a considerable section of the female population, owing to domestic problems arising out of such intoxication. After the electoral victory, the government announced total prohibition of intoxicants in Bihar with effect from 1st April, 2016. While this ban was received with much aplomb and applause amongst the voting population, strengthening the resolve of the government to implement the prohibition with an iron hand (Kumar, 2021) the blanket ban generated a lot of controversy owing to its indiscriminate deposition of penal power in the hands of authorities. The question which arose was whether a legislation of this nature necessitates the use of criminal law or was it a blatant example of 'overcriminalization'?

The chapter is divided into two broad sections; the first examines the basic principles governing criminalization, while the next section analyses the provisions of the Bihar legislation. The paper argues that while the state needs to regulate the manufacture and sale of alcohol, its policy to penalize alcohol consumption is flawed and fraught with several limitations. Most importantly, it is an example of excessive use of power by the State through the use of criminal laws.

2   Criminalization of Conduct – The Harm and Offence Principle

Joel Fienberg, a prominent theorist, states that only two considerations should be kept in view while declaring a conduct within the criminal sphere – 'Harm' principle as well as 'Offence' principle. He explained both the doctrines in the following manner (Fienberg, 1984: 26):

a.   *The Harm Principle:* It is always a good reason in support of penal legislation that it would probably be effective in preventing (eliminating or reducing) harm to persons other than the actor (the one prohibited from acting) and there is probably no other means that is equally effective at no greater cost to other values.

b.   *The Offence Principle:* It is always a good reason in support of a proposed criminal prohibition that it is probably necessary to prevent serious offence to persons other than the actor and would probably be an effective means to that end if enacted.

The harm principle is considered to be the most accepted doctrine, one that can be given the status of 'master principle' for criminalization of conduct (Duff, 2018; Ashworth, 2006). It simply means that once there is harm or injury in a conduct, it must come within the purview of criminality. But it is more easily said than understood. The term 'harm' possesses in itself a very comprehensive meaning and latitude. As stated by J.S Mill (1859: 14), "the only purpose for which power can be rightfully exercised over any member of a civilized community, against his will, is to prevent harm to others". Mill talks about harm principle as a political principle and justifies check on community or government from coercing individuals on illogical grounds. The pertinent intention at his end was to eradicate all foul, illogical and wrong reasons which put liberty in restriction. He was against paternalistic governance, where liberty can be curtailed on the ground of self-good and moralistic reasons.

Harm may be classified into 'individual harm' and 'collective harm'. The legislations drafted in contemporary civilized states take into account both the classes. Feinberg elaborates on 'individual' harm as a detriment or defeating of an individual's interest (Fienberg, 1984). Joseph Raz mentions that the conduct that inherently affects one's future wellbeing can be treated as harmful (Raz, J, 1986). These takes on harm are concerned with lost interest and adverse effect on future well-being (Dworkin, 1999). Collective harm is somewhere akin to 'collective moral harm' where states criminalize moral conduct and curtail liberty of the individuals in the name of collective protection.

The 'offence' principle of criminalization takes in concern the collective well-being. The principle proposes that those conducts which belittle the conscience of the general public must be criminalized. Simester and Hirsch have critically analyzed Fienberg's statement and put forth certain major concerns (Hornle, 2016). How far it is justified to decide based on people's emotions is questionable as it strongly varies and criminal wrongdoing does not find a significant and independent place. Hornle argues that the appropriate role of law is to regulate interpersonal conduct rather than taking into account the emotions around it to function more objectively and efficiently.

The Offence principle paves a path for intrusion of morality in the legal sphere. It is the most complicated topic of criminalization where segregation has to be made between moral and legal wrong. Behaviours such as alcoholism, visiting bars, going to night clubs etc. are largely criticized within social affairs, but are legal in nature. Imposing morality and criminalizing in the name of good or bad is a direct strike on the freedom of individual to make free choice which is guaranteed by the constitution. It is difficult to recognize these moral rights within the legal rights.

We must mention here that Devlin debated against decriminalization of homosexuality not on the ground of being morally wrong, but that the state is free and should criminalize acts which are widely regarded as 'wrongs' in order to protect the social fabric (Stewart, 2010). According to Stewart, Devlin was of the view that legal moralism tends to be detrimental to the interest of liberal democracies as it indicates rejection of application of floating emotions and morality of individuals to decide upon the merit of the conduct. The 'wrong' that should be taken in consideration must be contravention of legal rules framed by the appropriate legislature.

The states must act as an ideal guardian and show some faith in the individual citizenry to let them exercise their rights autonomously. It is a popular saying that people learn from their own mistakes and the government must not exercise coercion to reverse the process. States must not endeavor to penalize citizens in the name of protecting their interests. Such laws are bad in public taste and put significant restrictions on public choice and autonomy (Larkin, 2013).

3 Overcriminalization – What Is?

The term 'overcriminalization' itself suggests having an abundance of laws which consolidates its obedience using criminal law as sanction. When the state over utilizes this weapon to mend the citizenry, the phenomenon is called 'overcriminalization'. It is, of course, difficult to make such claims without a normative baseline-an idea of what constitutes the 'right' number of criminal laws-and such a baseline is elusive at best (Smith, 2012). While critically examining, we must not miss the intent behind such overuse, which is 'collective good'. The state has responsibility to provide security to its citizens and in its endeavor to do so, it prefers to use the instrument of criminal law. Mill's argument seems to have been diluted and weakened in modern law making through appropriate legislatures. Our ideas about 'harm' have become sufficiently capacious to take in almost anything legislators wish to criminalize. It has been vehemently argued that overcriminalization tends to diminish dignity of the criminal law which no faction, either the retributivists or utilitarian, desires (Smith, 2005).

A pertinent question here is why are democratic nations so fascinated by overcriminalization? Nations claiming to be welfare states and heralding democratic values are rapidly attracted towards criminalizing conduct of variable nature. This may be seen in various perspectives and there may be numerous reasons attributed for such global preference. We may try to summarize the causes under the following headings:

- *Enforcement of morals:* It has been widely observed that laws are increasingly being made to enforce moral norms in the society. There has been a longstanding debate of law and morality since the early development of contemporary laws. Smith (2005) discusses that the tussle between natural law school and positive school over this issue has been going on, but thinkers like Hart and John Stuart Mill disagreed with the reasoning of J. Stephen and Lord Devlin. In the context of India, the apex court has affirmed its position regarding regulation of morality by the law (Joseph Shine v. Union of India, 2018). In the aforementioned judgement, the court held that treating adultery as an offence would be tantamount to state entering into the most private realm of a citizen's life, and it did not appear to be in good taste. In similar lines, as stated in the famous Wolfenden report, "Unless a deliberate attempt is to be made by society, acting through the agency of the law, to equate the sphere of crime with that of sin, there must remain a realm of private morality and immorality which is, in brief and crude terms, not the law's business" (The Report of the Committee on Homosexual Offences and Prostitution, 1885). We must realize that religion was society's regulator prior to the formation of the legal structure. Religion is nothing, but a code of moral values and teachings which guides human behaviour. Religious notions of good and evil provided the original grounds for criminalizing behaviour, such as drug and alcohol use, gambling, prostitution, and a variety of consensual, non-commercial sexual activities (Henkin, 1963). The contemporary legislations tend to enforce criminal sanctions against such moral violations on the ground of protection of 'social fabric'.
- *Sense of Crises:* Another reason behind the surge in overcriminalization is democracy itself. The elected legislators represent the will of the people and are accountable to them.

There are occasions where legislation is just enacted to portray a certain message among the public or to please them. In these kinds of 'crises', legislation is passed without due research and implications (Larkin, 2013). For instance, the Criminal Law Amendment Act, 2013 and 2018 are direct consequences of the unfortunate Nirbhaya rape case (Mukesh v. State, 2017) and Kathua rape case (Mohd. Akhtar v. The State of Jammu And Kashmir, 2018) respectively. Both these brutal rape and murder cases led to massive public discontentment on account of the failure of criminal justice system leading to crisis among the government. Such victims of brutal offences are considered powerful non-governmental interest groups in the criminal

and political processes (Gewirtz, 1996). Larkin further elucidates that such groups see themselves as warriors in a battle of good versus evil. "Motivated by moral concerns not susceptible to compromise, special interest groups throw their weight behind like-minded politicians regardless of their stance on other issues, and those politicians attempt to repay their supporters with favorable legislation' (Larkin, 2013: 741–742)
- *Similar and Overlapping Statutes*: The passage of similar statutes or overlapping legislations is one of the means adopted by governments. In India, we may observe passage of criminal laws by individual states, regarding offences which are sufficiently dealt with by federal laws. For instance, the state of Uttar Pradesh passed the Uttar Pradesh Control on Gunda Act, 1970 and The Uttar Pradesh Gangsters and Anti-Social Activities (Prevention) Act, 1986 creating offences which were already covered under the provisions of the Indian Penal Code, 1860. These laws create special offences out of general crimes leading to stereotyping and enhanced punishments. As a rule, lawmakers have a strong incentive to add new offences and enhanced penalties, which offer ready-made publicity stunts, but face no countervailing political pressure to scale back the criminal justice system (Robinson and Cahill, 2003). Such specific legislations are never backed by scientific evidence and consequently may prove counterproductive or lead to abuse.
- *Politics:* The foremost duty of any state is to protect its citizens from unwanted harm and provide them with a sense of security. The fear of harm which is deeply rooted in the minds of the people is exploited by the political and powerful class (Luna, 1998). Conventional politics and wisdom suggest that depicting oneself harsh on crimes and criminals could gain electoral victory (Luna, 2005). He further argues that there is no such political campaign where the politicians vouch for reduction of punishment or any sort of decriminalization. In India, we see politicians creating fear of increasing crime in the society during election campaigns and promising additional criminal laws or enhanced punishments without providing actual scientific basis for it (Omar, 2021).

There are several other ways to look at the reasons for overcriminalization other than above mentioned factors. George and Stigler (1971) have even taken into account the theory of special interest groups forcing governments to legislate in order to fulfil selfish objectives. These groups are powerful enough to influence the legislative process largely related to industries and labor unions. "It is important to recognize, however, that overcriminalization has qualitative dimensions that may be even more significant to the integrity and efficacy of the criminal law than its better-known quantitative aspects" (Smith, 2012: 540).

4 Bihar Prohibition and Excise Act, 2016

4.1 *The Background*

Prior to the Bihar assembly elections of 2015, the sitting ruling party of Bihar announced a blanket ban on consumption of intoxicants in the state. This decision was a popular stunt, rather than a well-deliberated idea. It was primarily made in response to the demands by a section of the female population of the state. It was alleged that intoxication led to considerable increase in domestic violence cases and women had to bear the brunt of such violence, affecting family lives as well as education of children. After the electoral victory and formation of the government, the government announced total prohibition of intoxicants in Bihar. This ban was received with much enthusiasm amongst the voting population, strengthening the resolve of the government to implement the prohibition with an iron hand.

The legislation, however, generated controversy since its inception. The High Court of Patna initially struck down the whole legislation on the ground of unconstitutionality as it was considered highly arbitrary. Chief Justice Ansari ruled that "reasonable restriction on consumption of alcohol, or complete prohibition on consumption of alcohol, can be imposed by the state in order to carry forward the goal set by the Constitution in form of Directive Principles of State Policy, but such implementation of policy shall be in accordance with law and not in violation thereof" (Singh, 2016). The Court also directed the Government to cater to constitutional values while formulating alternative legislation. On appeal, the Supreme Court of India, however, stayed the judgement of the Patna High Court. The division bench of Dipak Misra J. and U. U. Lalit J. observed that "ban on liquor and fundamental rights do not go together" while quashing the order which declared the law ultra vires the Constitution (PTI, 2016).

There was a sense of reprisal when the government came up with stricter ironclad law which struck down all boundaries of contemporary critical criminal laws. The idea of criminalization of addiction led to the formulation of a draconian law in the form of Bihar Excise and Prohibition Act, 2016. The law on liquor prohibition in Bihar is not novel, as several other states such as Gujarat, Mizoram, and Nagaland have passed similar legislations in the past. The issue with the legislation of Bihar is, however, its rigidity, overcriminalization, and disproportional use of penal sanction.

5 Analyzing the Use of Criminal Law to Ensure Compliance

It has been a trend in the past century to rely upon criminalization in order to extract desired behaviour in the name of maintaining social order (Haley,

2019). However, there are other factors as well which function as a medium of social control. Haley (2019) argues that, we live in a society where consensus and stigma related to any act may work as an efficient control mechanism; social disapproval is one of the factors to ensure obligation from the populace. John Braithwaite argues that society is effective in controlling crime when it actively participates in shaming and boycotting the offenders through collective participation (Braithwaite, 1989). Crime is nothing but a designated label used to identify certain undesirable acts which have the potential to harm the community. Hence, we can say that criminalization occurs when the community together seeks formal adherence to its consensus. As far as Bihar's liquor prohibition policy is concerned, neither the means of its prevention, nor the implications of punitive ban were discussed elaborately or debated. Even the possibility of an alternative approach to the use of criminal laws was not considered. There are certain activities in the society which are deemed wrong or deviant, but they do not carry such degree of social disapprobation as to necessitate the use of penal laws. Consumption of alcohol, smoking etc. fall in this category- they are generally frowned upon by society as deviant or morally wrong, but do not stand on such a degree of disapproval as other violent crimes.

Thus, attaching the same degree of seriousness to such regulatory offences may undermine the efficacy of social disapproval attached to several other heinous offences (Langbein, 1974). In other words, we need to keep criminalization as a serious process and must not advance it casually. John Haley has summed up the whole phenomena interestingly. He remarks, "Neither the threat nor the imposition of the penalty itself has much effect if the offender is free from any stigma of having committed the offence or having been involved in a criminal proceeding. Consequently, before any conduct is deemed 'criminal,' there should be social consensus on both sociological and ethical grounds that such stigma is justified". Otherwise, the process will be difficult to invoke, and a conviction will be difficult to sustain, by those who have discretion (complainants, prosecutors, or judges, or any combination thereof). If the criminal process tends to initiate without popular public consensus, it gradually erodes legitimacy as well as gravity of the criminal process (Haley 1984: 480).

Furthermore, does intrusion of criminal law in such a sphere as alcohol prohibition seem fair as far as consumption is concerned? The seriousness in case of illegal manufacturing of alcohol is beyond question, but individual responsibility for possession or consumption may need serious reconsideration. The manufacturing, sale, distribution of liquor needs to be segregated from activities such as consumption. While the former are formalized activities of networks or groups for profit, intending to spread the addiction across the state and beyond, the latter are predominantly individual actors who may or may not have the necessary criminal intent. For them, it is simply a matter of pleasure or habit. By criminalizing habits of individual beings in society, can a State really regulate the same? Interestingly, if one goes through the efficacy of the laws for the past six years since its inception, it provides a baffling picture. Recent reports suggest that the rate of consumption of alcohol in Bihar is greater than that of states like Uttar Pradesh, Rajasthan, and Maharashtra, despite the blanket ban, unlike other states. In Bihar, more than 15% of males aged 15 and above are estimated to be alcohol consumers, while the numbers for Rajasthan, Maharashtra, and Uttar Pradesh stand at 11%, 13.9%, and 14.5% respectively (Mishra, M. 2022). This is therefore an indicator of the fact that mere criminalization cannot regulate the behaviour of individuals, unless there is a consensus over the same. Generating strong condemnation for such behaviour amongst the community, creation of self-help groups, early education and awareness amongst the adolescents, as also regulating the widespread availability of alcohol may be ways to restrict the problem.

The issue of domestic violence, which appears to be the principal cause behind the legislation, may be addressed in a similar fashion. Domestic violence is a universal problem with women from all sections of society falling victims to it. The United Nations estimates that one in every three women is subjected to physical and/or sexual violence by their partners (UN Women, 2021) and the same is true for India. The penal law has enacted provisions for criminalizing acts of domestic violence in specific circumstances (Indian Penal Code 1860, S. 498A). Furthermore, the Protection of Women from Domestic Violence Act 2005 provides remedies to women who are faced with difficult situations. So, the law has provided means for women to act against such violence.

Furthermore, moderate alcohol consumption does not cause problems, but its dependence over continued and unregulated usage creates disorders, which may create familial disruptions and violence (APA, 2012). The Association is of the view that such disorders call for clinical therapeutic interventions, rather than penal sanction to address the problem. Long term incarcerations will neither improve the familial bond, nor ensure responsibilities towards self and family. If we look at figures, the National Family Health Survey (NFHS-4, 2015–16) reveals that, in Bihar, around 30% of men between the ages of 15–49 consumed alcohol. 40% of married women faced physical, sexual or mental violence by their drunken husbands, while 25% percent of the women faced such violence, despite sobriety. The National Family Health Survey conducted in 2019–2021 (NFHS-5, 2019–21), after the ban is brought to effect, suggests that Bihar has one of the highest instances of reported domestic violence cases (40%), despite the ban, while Himachal Pradesh, without any such ban, has the lowest spousal violence complaints (8.6%). 34% of women are subjected to spousal violence, without any reference to alcoholism whatsoever (Tewari, 2020).

This brings us to the next point of deliberation which is punishment. As may be seen, the Bihar legislation has deployed stringent punishments to contain the acts. Such punishments are grossly disproportionate to the offences and their consequent effects on society. Probably, the government has acted on the principle that severe punishments would discourage people from engaging in criminal acts. There are definitely studies which support the plea. Researchers like Waldo and Chiricos (1972) provide examples of how deterrence may be useful in controlling behaviour of the people. According to the data collected by them, 26% of respondents who never smoked marijuana revealed that they would have smoked it if the laws were not severe enough (Tittle and Rowe, 1973). However, a contradictory stand is that people refrain from committing offences not so much for fear of punishment but because of the norms they have internalized (Andenaes, 1952). Deterrence has very little effect on rate or incidence of crime. "It would be unwarranted to conclude that 'stiffer' sentences could reduce" the crime rates (Gibbs, 1968: 530). In fact, increasing the risk of apprehension and conviction is more influential in reducing crime than raising the expected severity of punishment (Bun et. al., 2019). Thus, disproportionately severe sentences ranging from eight years to life imprisonment is not the answer to the problem. It will only lead to increased arrests and prosecutions, thereby overwhelming the criminal justice system of the state. It will also lead to long-term incarcerations of people with no identifiable outcome, while at the same time, creating space for unchecked expansion of the illegal liquor market in the state (Zumbish, 2019).

6 Conclusion

"Most people who think seriously about the criminal law think that there should be less of it" (Tadros, 2009: 74). It should be used by the State only when all other instruments fail to achieve the desired end and criminal law appears to be the sole means to contain a specific 'harm'. However, if one looks into the ways in which use of criminal law is expanding, it barely seems to be the case. The Bihar liquor prohibition seems to be a classic example aimed at preventing 'collective harm', identified in the plight of women suffering from increasing instances of domestic violence in the hands of their husbands. It is presumed that alcoholism is the primary factor for spousal violence, especially amongst the lower income households. Accordingly, the Government criminalized all activities pertaining to intoxicating substances, thereby creating new offences which are likely to interfere with the habits of common people and cause immense hardship in the long run. Such legislation, unfortunately, does not correlate to the object sought to be achieved, viz. reducing instances of domestic violence in the state, as may be seen from statistics. Rather, the legislation interferes in the domain of individual autonomy. It dictates the code of conduct for individuals in society and is based on the notion that the lawmakers are the best judges to decide on the lives of subjects (Stone, 2011).

As a result of the ban, about half a million people have been incarcerated in the past six years clogging the justice delivery system (Tripathi, 2022). Innocent people who are mere consumers of alcohol, either for pleasure or habit, have now turned into criminals and are being arrested and prosecuted by the system. The Supreme Court of India expressed displeasure over the same, as evident from the remark of the then Chief Justice of India, N.V. Ramanna:

> You know how much impact this law has created in the working of Patna High Court and it is taking one year to get a matter listed there and all the courts are choked with the liquor bail matters ... I have been told that 14–15 high court judges are hearing these bail matters every day and no other matters are being taken up.
>
> Express News Service, 2022

Interestingly, after the rap by the apex court, the government of Bihar has somewhat retracted from its earlier position, reducing sentences and appointing executive magistrates under the recent Bihar Prohibition and Excise (Amendment) Act, 2022. Section 37 which deals with penalty over consumption has been substituted and provides for arrest and production before executive magistrates. Bail is, however, discretionary, upon payment of stipulated penalty, not as a matter of right. Interestingly, the Bihar government has come up with a rule to avoid jail term in individual liquor consumption cases which again seem contentious. The people who are caught drinking will have to expose the name and place of liquor mafia and raids will be conducted based on such information. If the information proves to be useful for the authorities, the arrested person can walk free (Jha, 2022). The person who is passing such crucial information may be subjected to life risk at the hands of a strong liquor mafia operating in the state. There is no rationale in involving common masses in such intricate tasks and putting him or her in harm's way. Such unreasonable and unwarranted orders need to be avoided by the authorities who must work in a more concerted manner to regulate the availability of liquor in the state.

To conclude, criminal law as a tool has tremendous capability to enforce rules and maintain civility in the society, but excessive use of this weapon through overcriminalization of conduct may prove unproductive. It is generally said that excess of everything is bad and it fits well in the particular circumstance as well. There are several ways of taking potential offenders to task sans incarceration in modern liberal democracies. States must not frame legislation which could later prove detrimental to the purpose of legislation itself. The impugned Act is gradually going through drastic amendments, and it appears that the government may soon consider alternative means and strategies to address the issues, instead of criminalizing its citizens.

Bibliography

American Psychological Association. (2012.). *Understanding Alcohol Use Disorders and their treatment*. AmericanPsychologicalAssociation. Retrieved from https://www.apa.org/topics/substance-use-abuse-addiction/alcohol-disorders.

Andenaes, J. (1952). General prevention: Illusion or reality? *The Journal of Criminal Law, Criminology, and Police Science, 43*(2), 176. https://doi.org/10.2307/1139261.

Ashworth, A. (2006). *Principles of Criminal Law*. Oxford University Press. https://doi.org/10.1093/he/9780138777663.001.0001.

Braithwaite, J. (1989). *Crime, Shame and Reintegration*. Cambridge University Press. https://doi.org/10.1017/CBO9780511804618.

Bun, M. J. G., Kelaher, R., Sarafidis, V., & Weatherburn, D. (2019). Crime, deterrence and punishment revisited. *Empirical Economics, 59*(5), 2303–2333. https://doi.org/10.1007/s00181-019-01758-6.

Duff, R. A. (2018). *The Realm of Criminal Law*. Oxford University Press. https://doi.org/10.1093/oso/9780199570195.001.0001.

Dworkin, J. (1999). Devlin was right: Law and the enforcement of morality. *William and Mary Law Review, 40*, 927–930. https://scholarship.law.wm.edu/wmlr/vol40/iss3/11.

Express News service. (2022, February 15). Bihar anti-liquor law: SC issues notice, transfers pleas to itself. *The Indian Express*. Retrieved from https://indianexpress.com/article/india/bihar-anti-liquor-law-sc-issues-notice-transfers-pleas-to-itself-7774217/.

Feinberg, J. (1984). *The Moral Limits of Criminal Laws: Harm to Others*. Oxford University Press. https://doi.org/10.1093/0195046641.001.0001.

Gewirtz, P. (1995–1996) Victims and voyeurs at the criminal trial. *Northwestern University Law Review. 90*(3), 863–897. Retrieved from http://hdl.handle.net/20.500.13051/957.

Gibbs, J. P. (1968). Crime, punishment and deterrence. *The Southwestern Social Science Quarterly, 48*(4), 515–530. https://doi.org/10.1007/s00181-019-01758-6.

Great Britain Committee on Homosexual Offences and Prostitution. (1957). Report, Command No. 247 (Wolfenden Report), Paras. 61 and 62.

Haley, J. (2019). Rethinking criminalization: Aims, attributes, and alternative approaches. *Willamette Journal of International Law and Dispute Resolution, 26*(1–2), 1–41. Retrieved from https://www.jstor.org/stable/26915362.

Hart, H. L. (1963). *Law, Liberty and Morality.* Stanford University Press. https://doi.org/10.2307/1141219.

Henkin, L. (1963). Morals and the constitution: The sin of obscenity. *Columbia Law Review, 63*(3), 391–414. https://doi.org/10.2307/1120595.

Hornle, T. (2016). Theories of criminalization. *Criminal Law and Philosophy, 10*(2), 301–314. https://doi.org/10.1007/s11572-014-9307-4.

Hornle, T. (2020). One master principle of criminalization – or several principles? *Law, Ethics and Philosophy,* 208–220. https://doi.org/10.31009/LEAP.2019.V7.12.

Husak, D. (2008). *Overcriminalization: The Limits of the Criminal Law.* Oxford University Press. https://doi.org/10.1093/acprof:oso/9780195328714.001.0001.

Indian Alcoholic Beverage Companies v. State of Bihar (2016). SCC Online Pat 4806. Retrieved from https://www.scconline.com/blog/post/tag/bihar-liquor-ban/.

Jha, S. (2022, February 28). No Jail if caught drinking: Here's what Bihar's new order says. *India Today.* Retrieved from https://www.indiatoday.in/india/story/bihar-prohibition-law-caught-drinking-alcohol-no-jail-time-1918969-2022-02-28.

John, O. Haley. (1984). Antitrust sanctions and remedies: A comparative study of German and Japanese law. *Washington Law Review, 59*(3), 471. Retrieved from https://digitalcommons.law.uw.edu/wlr/vol59/iss3/2.

Joseph Shine v. Union of India (2018). SCC Online SC 1676. Retrieved from https://www.scconline.com/blog/post/tag/joseph-shine/.

Kleinig, J. (2009). Douglas Husak, *Overcriminalization: The Limits of the Criminal Law. Criminal Justice Ethics, 28*(1), 25–26. Retrieved from https://doi.org/10.1080/07311290902833736.

Kumar, M. (2021, November 17). Ensure liquor ban with an iron hand: Bihar CM to officials. *The Times of India.* Retrieved from https://timesofindia.indiatimes.com/city/patna/ensure-liquor-ban-with-an-iron-hand-nitish-to-officials/articleshow/87745121.cms.

Langbein, J. H. (1974). Controlling prosecutorial discretion in Germany. *The University of Chicago Law Review, 41*(3), 439–467. https://doi.org/10.2307/1599175.

Larkin, P. (2013). Public choice theory and overcriminalization. *Harvard Journal of Law & Public Policy, 36*(2), 715–794. Retrieved from https://www.harvard-jlpp.com/wp-content/uploads/sites/21/2013/04/36_2_715_Larkin.pdf.

Luna, E. (1998). Foreword: Three strikes in nutshell. *Thomas Jefferson Law Review, 20*(1), 1–96. Retrieved From https://www.proquest.com/trade-journals/foreword-three-strikes-nutshell/docview/198131878/se-2.

Luna, E. (2005). The overcriminalization phenomenon. *American University Law Review, 54*(3), 703–746. Retrieved from http://digitalcommons.wcl.american.edu/aulr/vol54/iss3/5.

Mill, J. S. (1859). *On Liberty*. Cambridge University Press. https://doi.org/10.1017/CBO9781139149785.

Mishra, M. (2022, May 17). Dry Bihar still on high: Consumption of alcohol greater than, Uttar Pradesh, Rajasthan and Maharashtra. *India Today*. Retrieved from https://www.indiatoday.in/diu/story/consumption-of-alcohol-higher-in-bihar-than-up-rajasthan-maharashtra-1950625-2022-05-17.

Mohd. Akhtar v. The State of Jammu and Kashmir (2018). *8 SCCJ 265*. Retrieved from https://www.scconline.com/blog/post/tag/kathua/.

Mukesh v. State (NCT of Delhi) (2017) *6 SCC 1*. Retrieved from https://www.tcconline.com/blog/post/tag/nirbhaya/.

Omar, R. (2021, November 28). Yogi Adityanath vows to put in place tough law against 'love Jihad'. The Hindu. Retrieved from https://www.thehindu.com/news/national/other-states/yogi-adityanath-vows-tough-law-against-love-jihad/article61711959.ece.

Pal, G. (2015). Measures for rehabilitating drug abusers and alcoholics: A study conducted in Haldwani, Uttarakhand. *International Journal of Sociology and Anthropology, 7*(8), 173–188.

Pranjal, K. (2019, August 12). Criminalization of 'nothing': India cannot afford any more criminal provisions. *Business Standard*. Retrieved from https://www.business-standard.com/article/economy-policy/can-india-afford-more-criminal-provisions-the-answer-is-a-resounding-no-119081200145_1.html.

Press Trust of India. (2016, October 7). Supreme Court stays Patna High Court order quashing Bihar liquor ban law. The Indian Express. Retrieved from https://indianexpress.com/article/india/india-news-india/supreme-court-stays-patna-high-court-order-quashing-bihar-liquor-ban-law-3070309/.

Priyadarshini, D., & Pal, G. (2016). Connotation of relocated slums towards drug abuse, alcoholism: A sociological study conducted in Delhi. *International Journal of Advanced Research, 2*(7), 428–438.

Raz, J. (1986). *The Morality of Freedom*. Oxford: Clarendon Press. https://doi.org/10.1093/0198248075.001.0001.

Robinson, P. H., & Cahill, M. T. (2003). Can model penal code second save the states from themselves. *Ohio State Journal of Criminal Law, 1*(1), 169–178. Retrieved from https://scholarship.law.upenn.edu/faculty_scholarship/42.

Singh, S. (2016, October 1). Patna High Court strikes down Nitish Kumar's total prohibition plan, terms it illegal. *The Economic Times*. Retrieved from https://economictimes.indiatimes.com/news/politics-and-nation/patna-high-court-strikes-down-nitish-kumars-total-prohibition-plan-terms-it-illegal/articleshow/54602261.cms.

Smith, S. F. (2005). Proportionality and federalization. *Virginia Law Review, 91*(4), 879–952. Retrieved from http://www.jstor.org/stable/3649448.

Smith, S. F. (2012). Overcoming overcriminalization. *Journal of Criminal Law and Criminology, 102*(3), 537–592. Retrieved from http://www.jstor.org/stable/23416055.

Stearns, A. (1936). Evolution of punishment. *Journal of the American Institute of Criminal Law and Criminology, 27*(2), 219–230. https://doi.org/10.2307/1135604.

Stewart, H. (2010). The limits of the harm principle. *Criminal Law and Philosophy, 4*(1), 17–36. https://doi.org/10.1007/s11572-009-9082-9.

Stigler, G. J. (1971). The Theory of Economic Regulation. *The Bell Journal of Economics and Management Science, 2*(1), 3–21. https://doi.org/10.2307/3003160.

Stone, S. A. (2011). Harm Principle. *Encyclopedia of Global Justice*, 472–474. https://doi.org/10.1007/978-1-4020-9160-5_288.

Tadros, V. (2009). The architecture of criminalization. *Criminal Justice Ethics, 28*(1), 74–88.

Tewari, A. (2020, December 17). In dry Bihar, '84% of women face spousal violence when husbands get drunk often', finds NFHS-5. *The Hindu*. Retrieved from https://www.thehindu.com/news/national/other-states/in-dry-bihar-84-of-women-face-spousal-violence-when-husbands-get-drunk-often-finds-nfhs-5/article37973242.ece.

Tittle, C. R., & Rowe, A. R. (1973). Moral appeal, sanction threat, and Deviance: An experimental test. *Social Problems, 20*(4), 488–498. https://doi.org/10.2307/799710.

Tripathi, P. (2022, April 7). Over 4.5 lakh people were arrested in Bihar in 6 years for violating liquor law. *The Times of India*. Retrieved from https://timesofindia.indiatimes.com/city/patna/over-4-5l-arrested-in-state-in-6-yrs-for-violating-liquor-law/articleshow/90695175.cms.

UN Women. (2021). Facts and Figures: Ending violence against women. Retrieved from https://www.unwomen.org/en/what-we-do/ending-violence-against-women/facts-and-figures.

Waldo, G. P., & Chiricos, T. G. (1972). Perceived penal sanction and self-reported criminality: A neglected approach to deterrence research. *Social Problems, 19*(4), 522–540. https://doi.org/10.2307/799929.

Zumbish. (2019, April 24). 'Dry' Bihar is losing its battle against the bottle. *The Wire*. Retrieved from https://thewire.in/law/dry-bihar-is-losing-the-battle-against-the-bottle.

CHAPTER 5

Decolonization of India's Legal System through Transformative Constitutionalism

Contemporary Legislative and Judicial Developments towards Indianization

Arvind Tiwari and Sonali Kusum

1   Introduction

"Colonialism" is described as the establishment of a colony in one territory by a political power from another territory and the subsequent maintenance expansion of that colony by that ruling power (Mudane H., 2020). Whereas the term "decolonization" is synonymous with "political independence," "self-determination, national liberation movements, state's independence". The law lexicon defines decolonization as "the process by which a colonial power divests itself of sovereignty over a colony – whether a territory, a protectorate or a trust territory so that the colony is granted autonomy and eventually attains independence"(Elias, 1954). Decolonization, is a political and demonstrative process that refers to the withdrawal of the colonizer from the oppressed country (Jaswal C., 2022).

The Black's Law Dictionary (eighth edition), defines the term, "Colonial Laws" refers to "the body of laws, regulations in force in the colonies before the Independence, as in America, colonial law designates law in force in thirteen original colonies before the Declaration of Independence"(Black's law dictionary, 2004). In England, the "colonial Laws" signifies the laws enacted by Canada and the other present British colonies (Campbell H., 1991).

The term "Colonial law" applies to or applied in the colonies. The "colonial law " refers to laws applied to all those dependent territories of the British Crown commonly described as colonies, protectorates, and trust territories. Some of the common illustrations are as follows: "Orders in Council, Queen's and King's Regulations, Government Ordinance, Imperial Acts of Parliament and Indian Acts" among others. (Elias, T. O. 1954). In other words, colonial law encompasses "the totality of the legal norms and research which related to the governance and administration of overseas regions conquered by western power" (Schmidhauser J. R., 1997).

The Supreme Court of India in M. v. *Elisabeth And Ors v. Harwan Investment And Trading, 1992,* "the Colonial statutes continue to remain in force by reason of Article 372 of the Constitution of India (Continuance in force of existing laws and their adaptation of pre-Independence laws including relevant provisions of Government of India Act, 1935), but that does not stultify the growth of law or blinker it's vision or fetter it's arms" (M.V. Elisabeth And Ors. v. Harwan Investment And Trading, 1993). The "legislation has always marched behind time, but it is the duty of the Court to expound and fashion the law for the present and the future to meet the ends of justice" (Choudhry Sujit, Khosla Madhav, et.al., 2016). Further, the Supreme Court in South India in *Corporation Pvt. Ltd. v. Secretary, Board of Revenue, Trivandrum and Anr.* (Corporation Pvt. Ltd. v. Secretary, Board of Revenue, Trivandrum and Anr., 1964) examined the issue of continuation and validity of the Pre-constitution laws and held that "Pre-constitutional law made by a competent authority, though it has lost its legislative competency under the Constitution, shall continue in force provided the law does not contravene other provisions of the Constitution". The Apex Court in *Amalgamated Coalfields Limited and Ors. v. Janapada Sabha Chhindwara* (Amalgamated Coalfields Limited and Ors. v. Janapada Sabha Chhindwara, 1961), held that the coal tax originally imposed under Central Provinces Local-self Government Act, 1920, was valid and continued to be valid after the Government of India Act, 1935 and the Constitution, by virtue of Article 372 of the Constitution of India.

2   Decolonization of the Indian Legal System

The formal process of decolonization in India was ushered in with the end of colonial rule and the grant of Independence in 1947, the enactment of the Constitution securing rights to the citizens, including the rights of the accused. Justice Abdul Nazeer, judge of the Supreme Court of India, in his speech on "Decolonization of Indian legal System" expounded upon the colonial takeover of the Indian legal system and the need for its decolonization. (Rajagopal, 2021) Justice Nazeer refers to the persistent "colonial psyche" in the administration of criminal justice with the use of words such as "my lords" and pleadings under the Indian legal system. This colonial legacy is being continued even today in a largely unchanged manner. Therefore, the proposal for "Indianization of legal system" draws its inspiration from the ancient Indian legal philosophies and getting rid of the "colonial psyche."

The Indianization of the legal system is traced from the indigenous treatise, epics, monographs, and other authoritative secondary sources. Under

Kautilya's Arthashashtra (322–298 BC), the indigenous legal system identified in India was the "Inquisitorial Legal System," not the "Adversarial legal system" as it was the duty of the King to do justice. Whereas at present, in India, there is a practice of an "Adversarial legal system" taken after the tradition of the common law system of adversarial litigation followed in England.

Under the purview of the Indianization of the legal system, great Indian jurists, including *Yajnavalkya, Brihaspati, Katyayana*, and their commentaries expounded on the Court, process, and procedures. There was much emphasis on the functioning of Law courts which were established at the meeting places of districts as Sangrahanas. There was a practice of alternative means of dispute resolution as well, as per *Brihaspati Smiritis*; there was a system of Family Courts and Family Arbitrators. The indigenous legal system of India included administrative units, which were categorized as *Sthaniya, Dronamukha, Khrvatika and Sangrahana* (the ancient equivalent of the modern districts, tehsils and parganas). Law courts were established in each Sangrahana. The Court consists of three jurists (*Dhramastha*) and three ministers (*Amtyas*). This was the scheme of an indigenous legal system that needed to be reinforced after doing away with the decolonization of the existing system.

3   Contemporary Relevance of Decolonization and Need for Reconsideration of Indian Colonial Laws

The Executive wing of the Government of India (GoI), represented by the Prime Minister of India, declared during his speech on the 75th anniversary of India's Independence Day, 15th August, 2022, from the Red Fort, addressed the nation to "remove any trace of a colonial mindset as part of his *panch pran* (five pledges)" to all the citizens of Indian Union. (Iyer. P.,2022, October 21).

Further, in *S.G. Vombatkere* v *Union of India, 2022* (S.G. Vombatkere v. Union of India, 2022), the Supreme Court of India quoted, the Prime Minister's words marking 'Azadi Ka Amrit Mahotsav' (75 years since Independence) "we as a nation, need to work harder to shed colonial baggage of outdated colonial laws and practices." It is stated that the "Government of India with assistance from the Law Commission of India has scrapped over 1500–2,000 outdated law since 2014–17 year" (PTI. 2022, October 10).

The Law Ministry, Government of India (GoI) mentioned "that the Indian Government would be repealing around 1,500 obscure, irrelevant legislations enacted during the British-colonial regime in the upcoming Parliament session" (Dasgupta S., 2022), as these laws have been rendered obsolete due these legislations having no purpose no place or being *non est* or non-functioning as these may not serve the needs of present modern-day society. The Law Ministry informed the Government of India that "around 1,200 laws have been relegated as redundant Acts that are subject to be repealed" (Nair H., 2017, June).

The Law Commission of India, in its successive reports, such as these, report no. 5 on British Statutes applicable to India, 1957, report no. 81 on Hindu Widows Remarriage Act, 1856, 1979, report no. 96 on Repeal of Certain Obsolete Central Acts 1984, report no. 148 on Repeal of Certain Pre-1947 Central Acts,1993, report no. 159 on Repeal and Amendment of Laws, 1998, report no. 248 on Obsolete Laws: Warranting Immediate Repeal (Interim Report), 2014, report no. 249 on Obsolete Laws: Warranting Immediate Repeal (Second Interim Report), 2014, report no. 250 on Obsolete Laws: Warranting Immediate Repeal (Third Interim Report) 2014, report no. 251 on Obsolete Laws: Warranting Immediate Repeal (Fourth Interim Report), 2014 have recommended repeal of colonial law.

It is stated that the Law Commission of India, in its aforementioned reports, has identified around 261 statutes identified for repeal. These outdated legislations have been recommended for repeal based on these parameters and accordingly grouped under these categories; "first, the subject matter of the law in question is outdated, and a law is no longer needed to govern that subject; second, the purpose of the law in question has been fulfilled, and it is no longer needed, and third, there is newer law or regulation governing the same subject matter" (248th Interim Report On Obsolete Laws, 2014).

One such law repealed in India post-independence is the Criminal Tribes' law. The Criminal Tribes Act Repeal Act 1952. In 1871, the British Government brought the Criminal Tribes Act. In 1876, the Criminal Tribes Act was extended to the Bengal Presidency. In 1911, the Criminal Tribes Act was extended to the Madras Presidency. The Criminal Tribes Act was revised and extended in 1924 all over to British India. This Act criminalized entire communities as habitual criminals, punishable with non-bailable offences. The Adults from these criminal tribes communities had to mandatorily report every week to their local police, and there were restrictions imposed on the movements of community members.

Communities notified under the Criminal Tribes Act were labeled as Criminal Tribes. Anyone born in these communities across the country was presumed to be born a criminal, irrespective of their criminal precedents. The police were entrusted with the power to arrest, monitor, and oversee their movements. The District Magistrates used to maintain records of all such criminal communities. In 1936, Pandit Jawaharlal Nehru expressed on the Criminal Tribes Act, "the monstrous provisions of the Criminal Tribes Act constitute a negation of civil liberty. No tribe is classed as criminal as such and the whole principle out of consonance with all civilized principles." In 1950, the Central

Government of India constituted a committee that issued the recommendation to "decriminalize" the same and to "repeal the Criminal Tribes Act accordingly the Criminal Tribes Act was repealed in 1952". However, The Habitual Offers Act,1958 is still stigmatizing and labeling Nomadic Tribes as Criminal Tribes.

The Government set up a National Commission for Denotified Nomadic and Semi-Nomadic Tribes in 2005, under the Chairmanship of Balkrishna Renke to identify the denotified nomadic tribes. The Social Justice and Empowerment Ministry, GoI seeks to formulate and implement a Scheme for the Economic Empowerment of Denotified Nomadic Tribes.

In *Shri Salek Chand Jain v. Ministry of Social Justice. 2022* (Shri Salek Chand Jain v Ministry of Social Justice, 2022)the Court reiterated that several Committees and Commissions like the Criminal Tribes Inquiry Committee, 1947; the Ayyangar Committee have been constituted for the improvement of the conditions of the members of these tribes. The Kalelkar Commission, which was constituted in 1953, gave its report in 1955; the Lokur Committee was formed in 1965; the Mandal Commission; Justice Venkatachaliah Commission etc. Further, the National Commission for Denotified, Nomadic, and Semi-Nomadic Tribes was also constituted on 14.03 2005 and gave its report on 30.06.2008 to ameliorate the hardships faced by the members of these tribes. But despite that, constitutional and legal rights, as guaranteed in the Constitution of India, have not been provided to the members belonging to these tribes. It is primarily observed that "the perception amongst people that members belonging to these tribes are criminals has yet not changed." This shows "the colonial era regressive mind-set prevalent in society". In view of this, the direction is sought from the Court that these tribes be included in the Scheduled Tribes so that they can avail their rights.

In *Priyanka Wd/O. Yogesh Rathod v The State of Maharashtra2020*, (Priyanka Wd/O. Yogesh Rathod v The State of Maharashtra, 2020) it was contended that the Banjara community is a scheduled tribe included in the Criminal Tribes Act, 1924 by the British Government. This Criminal Tribes Act of 1924, had a history of previous Acts like Criminal Tribes Act of 1858 as Banjara tribe was branded as a criminal tribe. It is stated that even after the freedom from British Rule, the tribe carried the stigma, and the authorities treated the people of this community as criminals, subjecting them to atrocities by the police officers and jail officers.

4 Colonial Continuity in Existing Indian Legal System

One of the most cardinal examples of colonial legacy in our existing legal framework is, the Constitution of India, which is viewed as a "continuation of colonial law, namely the Government of India Act, 1935", a colonial statute. Some of the eminent political leaders referred to the Constitution of India as an "anti-India Act;" calling it a "slave constitution" and a "charter of bondage" (B.B. Pande, 2010). The colonial legacy as colonial continuity is evident in Indian Penal Code (IPC), the British Royal Commission's 1843, English jurist Fitzjames Stephen observed that "the Indian Penal Code is described as the criminal law of England freed from all technicalities and superfluities, systematically arranged and modified in some few particulars to suit the circumstances of British India" (B.B. Pande, 2010).

One of the classic instances of colonial continuity is seen in the case of the enactment of IPC, its substantive content borrowed from the British colonial rule, and Gujarat High Court reiterates this in *Nimeshbhai Bharatbhai Desai v State of Gujarat, 2018* (Nimeshbhai Bharatbhai Desai v State of Gujarat, 2018), the Indian Penal Code was drafted by Lord Macaulay and was introduced in 1861 during the British's colonial rule over India. Thus, it has been largely influenced by British laws. "What was considered a crime in Britain at that time has also been made a crime under the IPC to a large extent. (Criminal Misc. Application, 2017)" (*Nimeshbhai Bharatbhai Desai v State of Gujarat, 2018*) Macaulay's draft of IPC was "not free from repressive elements". Under the mandate of IPC, "the acquiescence and compliance by the natives to British Rule was overridden by security to life and property, protection of the state". (B.B. Pande, 2010).

In the same vein, it is stated by Delhi High Court in *'Abul Hassan And National Legal v. Delhi Vidyut Board & Ors.,1999* (Abul Hassan And National Legal v. Delhi Vidyut Board & Ors.,1999), that "India has inherited a colonial legal system, it is of the Victorian era, which must undergo a metamorphosis to fit in with the changing times, the justice delivery system will crumble if innovative approaches are not resorted to."

The common law legal system followed in India of "Adversarial Litigation" but this may not be compatible with the rising number of petitioners seeking their grievance redressal and justice from the courts through the regular mode of litigation. "Adversarial litigation involves client representation through the advocates in trials before the Courts, this dependency on advocates causes the pendency of cases. Thus, at the time of drafting the IPC, Macaulay was guided by the considerations to suit the needs of firstly, the dominant colonial administration, which was following the common law system of Adversarial litigation, and secondly, the need to promote a stranded form of law- justice delivery system that was over and above all distinct religious groups, to legitimize their rule through a singular standard of justice that was superior to the existing Muslim, Hindu and Company Regulation laws. Overall, this notion of colonial continuity in its varied facets is illustrated through the conventions," Colonial Language, Shell Law, Colonial Relic mong other forms.

5 Colonial Inheritance of Laws

Colonial Inheritance in simple terms, means "the practices and regulations of the primitive colonial rulers who have originated under the colonial regime, but these instruments are continued or followed by the colonies within their existing system; as originally taken after the colonial law" (Arasanayagam, J., 1987).

In *Jayaswal Shipping Company v. The Owners And Parties, 1953* (Jayaswal Shipping Company v The Owners And Parties, 1953) the Calcutta High Court reiterated that "Admiralty Jurisdiction in this High Court is an ancient inheritance". The Calcutta High Court referred to the jurisdiction and power of High Courts, Supreme Courts in India taken after the "Admiralty Jurisdiction" set up under the Government of India Act, 1935. This also referred to the "Colonial Courts of Admiralty Act", 1890. Further, "the Charter of 1774 defines the Admiralty Jurisdiction of the Supreme Court, this made the Supreme Court of Judicature, at Port William in Bengal, the Court of Admiralty for the provinces, countries or districts, of Bengal, Behar and Orissa". This admiralty jurisdiction of the Supreme Court "is the same as used and exercised in that part of Great Britain called England; these provisions are preserved under the Government of India Act, 1935 which is the foundation for Constitution of India", 1950.

In *Rojer Mathew v. South Indian Bank Ltd. And Ors. Chief, 2019* (Rojer Mathew v. South Indian Bank Ltd. And Ors. Chief, 2019), the Supreme Court of India mentioned the existing Indian legal system inherited from the common law tradition of the colonial era or the inheritance of the colonial legal system. In this case, the Supreme Court enumerates the legal history of setting up Tribunals in India. The Supreme Court mentions the Justice Rankin Committee Report in 1924, recommending the setting up of a "tribunal system" for the first time. "This tribunal system is modeled after the then-existing system in England and Canada. The Supreme Court expressly states that in India, the establishment of tribunals was done in 1941 by the British Colonial Government. Post-Independence and tribunals were first created in the sphere of tax laws" (Choudhry, S., et al. (Eds.), 2016).

A series of legislations are primarily instances of the colonial inheritance of laws. Some of these are briefly mentioned as following:

5.1 Contempt of Court Act *(Contempt of Court Act, 1971)*
In *Re: Prashant Bhushan and Anr., 2020* (Re: Prashant Bhushan and Anr., 2020) before the Supreme Court of India, it was contended that the "contempt jurisdiction is vague and colonial". The Supreme Court referred to landmark international precedents as *R. v. Blackburn* (R. v. Blackburn, 1968), *R. v. Almon* (R. v. Almon 1965), *Mcleod v. St. Aubyn* (Mcleod v. St. Aubyn, 1899), wherein Lord Denning refused to convict or sentence for contempt.

5.2 Official Secrets Act *(Official Secrets Act, 1923)*
This law is an "offshoot against the movement of nationalism" in our country. This Act continues to prevail in India. This restricts, and abridges citizen's right to information about the Government. In *Registrar General v R. M. Subramanian, 2013* (Registrar General v R. M. Subramanian, 2013), the Madras High Court referred to "the Official Secrets Act, 1923" as "a colonial legacy".

5.3 Foreigner's Act *(Foreigner's Act, 1946)*
The Foreigners Act, 1946, is another piece of colonial law, drafted earlier to Independence for the purpose of identification of foreigners. The Act does not define the term "foreigner" but instead states that "any person who is not an Indian citizen is classified as a foreigner under this Act". The Act further states that the "individual will have to prove whether or not he or she is a foreigner". On the mere grounds of suspicion, a person may be identified as a "foreigner staying in India illegally for longer than permissible," such "a person is liable to report to the local police station within 24 hours of receiving the information".

5.4 Foreign Recruiting Act *(Foreign Recruiting Act, 1874)*
This Act empowered the Government to issue an order that prevented the recruitment of Indians by a foreign State. The Act confers a wide discretion on the Government to specify the conditions under which persons may be barred from being recruited by a foreign State. According to the Law Commission, in its 43rd Report on Offences Against National Security Act (1971), states that there is such a wide discretion might violate the constitutional guarantee to freedom of occupation under Article 19 of Indian Constitution. The 2nd Administrative Reforms Commission Report of 2006 observed this Act is outdated.

5.5 Colonial Conventions

The phrase "Colonial Conventions means unwritten governance, administrative regulations which are not legally enforceable, but universally observed as a commonly practiced for several years for effective administration and discharge of Governance functions." (Corbett Haselgrove-Spurin, 2004). Our Indian Court process and procedures follow the colonial conventions. In the colonial regime of the UK, the petition includes the terms as "prayed for relief", and "prayers", for this reason, it is often stated that "justice is not demanded but prayed" (Baxi U., 2018). In India, the public interest litigation, writ, civil, and criminal petition mentions "prayers" before the Court for appropriate reliefs.

The official dress code of present-generation advocates, including the mandatory "coat-and-gown dress code for lawyers," is prescribed under the then "Common Law System" by the British colonial rulers.

The use of the terms "Ladyships" and "Lordships" to refer to judges in the courts is a well-established colonial convention from the United Kingdom (Bar Council, Ch- IIIA3 2006). These demonstrate the visible effects of "British Colonial" rule in India The Bar Council of India in its resolution Gazette of India in the year 2006, issued the Bar Council Of India Rule Part VI, Chapter IIIA that prescribe the use of "Your Honour" or "Hon'ble Court" in Supreme Court & High Courts and "Sir" or equivalent words in the Subordinate Courts and Tribunals.

The explanation further states that the words "My Lord" and "Your Lordship" are relics of Colonial post; hence, it is open to the lawyers to address the Court as "Sir" or the equivalent word in respective regional languages. Accordingly, the Rajasthan High Court in the year 2019, issued notice to all counsels appearing before the Court to honor the mandate of the right to equality, the right to desist from using terms as Hon'ble Judges as "My Lord, My Ladyship." (Rajasthan High Court, 2019).

5.6 Colonial Relic

The colonial relics are the legislations, and statues, enacted under the East India Company which have become "anachronistic" as in state of chronologically out of place or outdated in the present context. For example, the Treasure Trove Act. It is an archaic Act that is at present a form of colonial relic. This needs to be amended Lok Sabha Debates (2015, December). The Treasure Trove Act, 1878 (Trove Act, 1878), provides for "anachronistic" provisions as "Treasure Trove" meaning "anything of any value hidden in the soil", provision for "suit by person claiming the treasure hidden within one hundred years before the date of the finding" (Indian Treasure- Trove Act, S. 2,8, 1873). It is reported that under the Treasure Trove Act the notion of "treasure trove" was originally developed during the colonial era as the property of the British crown, and the same is still in effect in India.

Under the Indian Civil Procedure Code, 1908, relevant provisions provide for auction, decree, and summons to be announced by beat of a drum at the behest of Government Officials (the Revenue officers, Lekhpal). These provisions, though being anachronistic, are not repealed as yet. In *Sunil Kisanrao Bagul, Nashik v. Assistant Commissioner of Income Tax, 2023* (Sunil Kisanrao Bagul, Nashik v. Assistant Commissioner of Income Tax, 2023) before the Income Tax Appellate Tribunal, Pune it was contended that under the *Maharashtra Land Revenue Record of Rights and Registers (Preparation and Maintenance) Rules, 1971*, the Talathi visits the field for maintaining entries and records on Crops, its particulars in the Government register of crops, "the Talathi shall fix a date of his visit to the village for the purpose at least seven days in advance and arrange to inform the villagers" by "beat of drum" (Maharashtra Land Rules, 1971). In *Rajesh Upadhyay v. The State of Bihar, 2023* (Rajesh Upadhyay v. The State of Bihar, 2023), before Patna High Court mentions about the "Proclamation of Sale by beating of drum".

5.7 *Colonial Mindset*

The term "colonial mind" refers to the "perception, understanding and internalization" of the attitude that the "colonial forces are superior" and that the "the colonies are inferior" and the colonies would be subordinated to the Colonial ruler (Letters, 2021). This colonial mindset entails a sense of "superiority of race, ethnicity, culture, life style, Governance regime of British colonial rulers" over the general population of Indian colonies. The colonial mindset is implicit with "notion of racial suppression, feeling of shame, inferiority" among colonies. A "sense of pride and glorification" is associated with the British Colonial rulers.

The Rule of "British Raj" includes the authority of colonial law enforcement agencies and administrative authorities as Indian Civil Service (ICS) and the police for suppression and maintaining control over the colonial State. During the British Raj, the Indian Civil Service (ICS), police were considered to be superior Government forces representing the imperial crown, that was responsible for suppression and subordination of the civil disobedience movements of 1930s, imposing stringent civil control measures in Indian colonial set up. The ICS reporting to the Viceroy or the Secretary of State was formulating the Government Policies which resulted in enforcing excesses on the political activities.

However, in the present times, the Government of India, the Ministry of External Affairs as well as the Prime Minister's Office (PMO) gave out a "clarion call" to the nation to cast away their 'colonial mindset' (Baskar B., 2023). This is to make the nation revisit and check the borrowing and emulating of Law, administrative, political regulations from the West. This also fosters the nation to reinvigorate and take pride in giving effect to its indigenous Indian legal, administrative tradition, practices from the past.

In *Anil Kumar Bhatt v. State of Uttarakhand, 2022* (Anil Kumar Bhatt v. State of Uttarakhand, 2022).The Uttarakhand High Court calls out against the "Colonial Set" among the Law Enforcement agencies as Police regarding the applicable rules of Corroboration under Section 161 Criminal Procedure Code. The Uttarakhand High Court held that "it is settled by plethora of judgment that, there is no law prohibiting the use of evidence led by the police officers especially when it is not shown that the police officer has any grudge against the appellant, When independent witness do not support the case of the prosecution which they have been confronted with the statement made under Section 161 of the Criminal Procedure Code. The Uttarakhand High Court states that "this colonial mindset of seeking corroboration to each statement made by the police officer has to be done away with". In *Shri Ishwar Singh v. Land and Building Department and Anr, 2018* (Shri Ishwar Singh v. Land and Building Department and Anr, 2018), the Delhi High Court contended that "this 'Babu' culture in the Indian bureaucracy is a symbol of colonial mindset and a major obstacle to development". In *Anil JS v. State of Kerala & Ors.,2010* (Anil JS v. State of Kerala & Ors.,2010)the Kerala High Court condemned the police force for using "derogatory terminologies" against the vulnerable sections of society, including elders, which exhibits the colonial mindset of police.

5.8   Shell Law

Shell laws are such statutes or legislations whose most substantive provisions have been done away with, but the statute itself has not been repealed. One such example is the Epidemic Diseases Act, 1897 (Epidemic Diseases Act, 1897) is still being enforced in India. India's 123-Year-old law was put to effect during the novel coronavirus pandemic COVID 19. The main objective of the Act is better prevention of the spread of Dangerous Epidemic Diseases. This Act is very small and has merely four (4) sections. Out of which many of its provisions have been repealed or amended. The Act has been repealed in its application to Bellary District by Mysore Act, 1955. It is also important to note that most of the provisions under the Act have been carried into effect through the provisions of Indian Penal Code of 1860.

The Epidemic Act was enacted during the Colonial era way back in 1897. The plague was identified in Bombay, Queen Victoria delivered a speech in which the British Parliament "directed the Government to take measures for eradication of plague." Post Victoria's address, the Epidemic Diseases Bill was introduced in the Council of the Governor-General of India in Calcutta, granting the power to the executive to draft a bill to this effect. Accordingly, the Epidemic Diseases Act was enacted (Kiran Kumbhar, 2022). Many provisions under the Act has been repealed, but the entire State Act has not been repealed, one such important illustration is the Legal Practitioner's Act 1879 (Legal Practitioner's Act 1879), seeks to consolidate and amend the Law relating to legal practitioners. This Act 1879, uses the terms like *"Vakils"*, "Attorney of any High Court", a pleader *"Mukhtar"*. However, these terms are replaced by using the uniform term "Advocate" under the Advocate's Act, 1961. The substantive part of the Act, 1879 including twenty around (21) sections out of forty-two (42) have been replaced yet the entire Act is still prevalent. Besides, throughout the country, among legal professionals, the Advocate's Act is still followed.

5.9 *Obsolete and Irrelevant Law for Repeal*
The Government of India, Law Commission Report no. 248th Interim Report on Obsolete Laws (248th Interim Report On Obsolete Laws, 2014) on "Identification of Obsolete Laws" undertaken by the 19th Law Commission *suo moto*. Previously, the 20th Law Commission also continued with the same project. In the past, the Law Commission has submitted various reports identifying a number of laws as obsolete which demanded repeal. The Law Commission's 18th and 81st Reports recommended the repeal of particular colonial Law. The 18th Report sought to repeal the 'Converts Marriage Dissolution Act', and the 81st Report recommended the repeal of 'Hindu Widows Remarriage Act'. The 96th Report recommended repeal of a substantial number of obsolete laws.

6 Role and Significance Government (Legislature, Executive, Judiciary) Initiative to Decolonize Indian Legal System

6.1 *Role of Legislature*
The legislature has enacted, "Repeal Act" and "Amendment Act or Bill" to expunge the colonial legacy from our existing Indian legal regime. There have been roughly four "Repealing and Amending Acts" in the year 2015, 2016, 2017, 2019 that have repealed around 76 colonial laws of pre pre-independence regime. From 2014 to August 2016, a total of 1,175 laws have been repealed through Repealing and Amending Acts. The Repealing and Amending (Third) Bill, 2015 was passed by Parliament in 2016 which repealed 294 laws and made minor amendments to two laws. In 2017, the Repealing and Amending Bill, 2017 was introduced in Lok Sabha which sought to repeal 104 Acts in whole,

partially amend one law, and make minor amendments to three laws (PRS India, 2017). The Lok Sabha enacted the Repealing and Amending Bill and the Repealing and Amending (Second) Bill in 2017, repealing 245 obsolete and archaic laws and identifying almost 1,800 laws.

For instance, the Motor Vehicles Act, 1914 of the colonial era, was redrafted as Motor Vehicles Act, 1939. Under the 1914 Act, archaic provisions were provided stating that "an inspector would have been disqualified if he or she had a flat feet or hammer toes". (India Today, 2017). Both these Acts are repealed. This Act was replaced with the Motor Vehicles Act, 1988 amended by The Motor Vehicles (Amendment) Act, 2019.

Another such instance is the "Dramatic Performance Act, 1876" (Dramatic Performance Act, 1876), originally enacted by the British to regulate theater to empower the Government to control, to prohibit dramatic public performances which are scandalous, defamatory, seditious or obscene (Dramatic Performance Act, 1876); This Act still prevails in India even seventy-six years after Independence until its repeal 2018 (Dramatic Performance Act, 1876).

Many states, with the exception of few states, though several states introduced and amended it post-Independence. States like Delhi and West Bengal have repealed it. At present, the Dramatic Performance (Delhi Repeal) Act 1963, is given effect. In *N. V. Sankaran Alias Gnani v. The State of Tamil Nadu, 2013* (N.V. Sankaran Alias Gnani v. The State of Tamil Nadu, 2013) it is recommended by the Court towards the existing criminal justice system to consider for repeal Dramatic Performances Act, the Act empowers the State Government to prohibit performances that are scandalous, defamatory or likely to excite feelings of disaffection. Disobeying such prohibitions attracts penalties. It was enacted during the colonial era and extensively used to curb nationalist sentiments propagated through dramatic performances. It has no place in a modern democratic society.

The Madras High Court in *N. V. Sankaran alias Gnani v. The State of Tamil Nadu, 2013* (N.V. Sankaran Alias Gnani v. The State of Tamil Nadu. 2013), held that relevant provisions of the Tamil Nadu Dramatic Performance Act, 1954 and Rules under the Tamil Nadu Dramatic Performances Rules, 1955 violate Articles 14 and 19 of the Constitution. These provisions should be considered for repeal on these grounds. "*The Tamil Nadu Dramatic Performance Act, 1954*" is a relic of colonial rule in India, taken after the "Dramatic Performance Act, 1876" to regulate theater performances, scenes, play, pantomime or any other drama in India, to impose restrictions, to prohibit public performances if the Government found any play to be of a scandalous nature or disrupting social values or felt that it might excite feelings of disaffection against the Government established by law or that it would corrupt persons, such person liable for the same would be issued prohibitory order, liable to be punished with either imprisonment for a term extending three months or fine or both in some cases. Under the Dramatic Performance Act, the law enforcement agencies, including police, were granted permission to enter, arrest and seize any persons, scenery, costumes, or articles whose use or intended use in the performance was prohibited under the Act.

This Act was an instrument of suppression by the colonial Government to curb or gag patriotic themes seeking freedom, Independence against the colonial powers. This sought to prohibit, and restrict drama promoting free speech, and expression.

Modifications, Amendments to Redress Colonial Legacy and Colonial Control in Statutes:

6.2 Arms Act Amendment

There are a series of existing legislations or statues subject to modification, and amendment to redress the colonial legacy, these are briefly discussed as following:

In *Hukum Chand v. State of U.P., 2012*, the Allahabad High Court observed that "the legislation relating to arms is a colonial legacy" as held by the Allahabad High Court, "the then Colonial Government considered it safe to disarm the native people for political and administrative reasons" to prevent any scope for protest, dissent (Hukum Chand v. State of U.P., 2012). However, post-independence, the people of India gave themselves the Constitution, an elected Government was formed, "a liberal policy was followed in the administration of Arms Act, 1959". The Arms Act was modified with the definition of "arms" and classified "firearm" in the category of "prohibited", "non-prohibited" etc. There have been four major amendments in Act, 1959 by Arms (Amendment) Act 55 of 1971, Arms (Amendment) Act 25 of 1983, Arms (Amendment) Act 39 of 1985, Arms (Amendment) Act 42 of 1988, (Arms Act, 1959).

Discussions on Draft Bills, Legislative Proceedings:

Lok Sabha Debates: Discussion on The Motion for Consideration of the Transgender Persons (Protection Of Rights) Bill, 2018 , It was deliberated that "with the advent of the British rule and there has been a practice of archaic "Victorian ideas of morality" on sexuality, sexual identities as opposed to the standards of homosexuality which has adversely impacted our mindset. This colonial concept of "Victorian ideas of morality" has adversely impacted transgender people. The plight of the Transgender Community has deteriorated following the adoption of the Criminal Tribes Act, 1871, which deemed the entire "transgender community as a criminal tribe". For the longest time until the path breaking judgment of *NALSA Vs Union of India, 2015* (NALSA Vs Union of India, 2015). Even after the enactment of Transgender Persons (Protection of Rights) Act, in the year 2019 (Transgender Persons Act, 2019), the transgender community is facing a negative British colonial legacy. Thus, the prejudice against the transgender community continues in this country. They are subjected to discrimination in all forms, subjected to mental and, physical abuse and sexual abuse, denied employment, and abandonment by their families. Whereas, in the UK, the UK Gender Recognition Act, 2004, has been enacted, this granted legal recognition to the third gender, the trans gender community and granted them legal rights.

In order to ameliorate the conditions of tribals, the National Human Rights Commission (NHRC) in its reports titled as issues of "Violation of Human Rights: Social Stigmatization De – Notified Tribes (DNTs)" (NHRC, 2020) and "Atrocities on SCs & STs," made a number of recommendations to concerned State Governments for redressing issues of de- notified tribes which are briefly reiterated as following:

The NHRC recommended to the Ministry of Social Justice & Empowerment & Ministry of Tribal Affairs, GoI to fund one NGO in each State in case of DNTs notified as STs for liaising with State agencies, providing necessary support to members of DNTs, providing legal assistance for DNTs in distress (Devy, 2007). Also, it recommended that the State to organize DNTs as a "collective" and themselves as a "society" to address grievances or common problems for redressal purposes with the various Governmental agencies, also members of each bustee of Denotified Tribes may be trained as a social worker. Further, it recommended the Local Panchayats, to sensitize the respective local jurisdiction on issues of DNTs in their respective area about changing peoples' attitudes towards the DNTs.

The NHRC also directed that a retired senior police officer of high rank be appointed in every state to oversee the "cases of atrocities against DNTs" in places of concentration or an old settlement with such tribals and a separate officer may be appointed at the district level. Finally, the NHRC directed the National Police Academy to impart training to police officers and reorient their syllabi. The Central and State Governments are directed to make proper enumeration of Denotified Communities. These measures seek to redress the criminality and stigma associated with denotified tribes.

6.3   Role of Executive

The Prime Minister has constituted a committee chaired by the Former Secretary Legislative Department to carry out a review to identify obsolete laws for repeal in the year 2014. This committee revisited the previous Union Government Committee Report on Review of Administrative Laws of the year

1998 and observed that out of the 1382 Acts recommended for repeal by that Committee of 1998 only 415 have been repealed so far. Hence, a focused and result-oriented exercise must be carried out to systematically repeal archaic laws and rules that have become obsolete within the last ten to fifteen years, such laws must be repealed.

6.4 Role of Judiciary in Decolonizing the Legislations through Transformative Constitutionalism

The term "transformative constitutionalism" is coined for the first time by an American Professor Karl Klare in South African Journal of Human Rights, 1998 as long-term goal of constitutional enactment, interpretation, and enforcement committed to transforming a country's political and social institutions and power relationships in a democratic, participatory and egalitarian direction (Rapatsa M., 2015). The concept of "transformative constitutionalism" owes its origin to the South African legal developments redressing unjust, racist society to normative egalitarian legal order.

This constitutional perspective of transformative constitutionalism finds consonance with Indian Constitution's Preamble setting forth the nature of Indian polity as the socialist, secular, democratic, republic. The Part fourth of the Indian Constitution, "Directive Principles of State Policy" enunciates "equality and justice in social -political -economic spheres among all"; part third of the Indian constitution, "Fundamental Rights," as "right to equality, freedom, liberty". In keeping with this constitutional mandate, the Indian judiciary through progressive and breaking interpretation has paved the way for "transformative constitutionalism" in Indian socio-legal context. As in *B.K. Pavitra v. Union of India, 2017* (B.K. Pavitra v. Union of India, 2017), the Court held that Indian society suffered from "deep structural inequalities" and the Constitution of India would serve as a "transformative document" to overcome them. In *Babulal s/o Bapurao Kodape v. Sau. Reshmabai Narayanrao, 2019* (Babulal s/o Bapurao Kodape v. Sau. Reshmabai Narayanrao, 2019), upheld the principle of "transformative constitutionalism" by placing upon the judicial arm of the State a duty to ensure and uphold "supremacy of the Constitution".

The Supreme Court by invoking the concept of "transformative constitutionalism" within the facet of the Article 21 of Indian Constitution, the SC through its interpretation, expanded the horizon of "right to privacy, personal liberty, identity, gender rights, minority rights, towards more egalitarian and liberal order" in several cases.

The recent cases, namely the *Navtej Singh Johar v. Union of India, 2017* (Navtej Singh Johar v. Union of India, 2017)and *Joseph Shine v. Union of India, 2018* (Joseph Shine v. Union of India), the Supreme Court (SC) observed that transformative constitutionalism is abhorrent to any kind of regressive approach, further in *Shrimati Sarala v. State of Chhattisgarh, 2021* (Shrimati Sarala v. State of Chhattisgarh, 2021) transformative constitutionalism dissuades from indulging in any form of "discrimination differentiation, discrimination, unequal treatment" is writ large, the limited implementation of judicial decisions.

This concept of "transformative constitutionalism" is applied by the Indian judiciary in redressing any colonial law, its consequent impacts, and colonial conventions. The Section 377 of Indian Penal Code (IPC) derives its origin from the Buggery Act of 1533. It is important to note here that this, law has not been amended by the Parliament ever since its enactment. This law is based on the "Judeo-Christian moral and ethical standards" which conceive of sex on purely functional terms, that is, for procreation and on this basis 'homosexuality is considered as unnatural and against the order of nature under Section 377 of IPC. The Acts of sodomy were penalized by hanging under the Buggery Act of 1533 which was re-enacted in 1563 by Queen Elizabeth I, after which it became the charter for the subsequent criminalization of sodomy in the British colonies".

7   Landmark Judgments on Transformative Constitutionalism

7.1   *Sodomy, Buggery under Section 377 of Indian Penal Code (IPC)*

Suresh Kumar Koushal & Anr, v. Naz Foundation & Ors., 2013 (Suresh Kumar Koushal & Anr, v. Naz Foundation & Ors., 2013)- The judiciary in a catena of cases has sought to break away from the colonial legacy, colonial mind set by progressive and transformational interpretation of laws. In *Suresh Kumar Koushal & Anr, v. Naz Foundation & Ors., 2013*, Section 377 under IPC is challenged post decolonization, as laws, institutions represent "colonial continuity", the fact that an institution or Law is a "colonial inheritance" is taken as a ground to challenge or annual or to repeal or to alter such law or its character. The concept of "colonial continuity" is incompatible with the free, liberal political ideologies (Sarkar, S., 2001).

One of the classic instances of colonial continuity is seen in the case of enactment of IPC, its substantive content borrowed from the British colonial rule, this is reiterated by Gujarat High Court in *Nimeshbhai Bharatbhai Desai v. State of Gujarat* on2 April, 2018 (Nimeshbhai Bharatbhai Desai v. State of Gujarat, 2018); The Indian Penal Code was drafted by Lord Macaulay and was introduced in 1861 during the British's colonial rule over India. Thus, it has been largely influenced by British laws. "What was considered a crime in

Britain at that time has also been made a crime under the IPC to a large extent" (Nimeshbhai Bharatbhai Desai v. State of Gujarat, 2018).

"Accordingly, the acts of sodomy were penalized by hanging under the Buggery Act of 1533 which was re-enacted in 1563 by Queen Elizabeth I, after which it became the charter for the subsequent criminalization of sodomy in the British colonies". Thus, Section 377 of Indian Penal Code derives its origin from the Buggery Act of 1533. It is important to note here that this Law has not been amended by the Parliament ever since its enactment. This Law is based on the "Judeo-Christian moral and ethical standards", " which conceive of sex on purely functional terms, that is, for procreation and on this basis "homosexuality is considered as unnatural and against the order of nature" (Nimeshbhai Bharatbhai Desai vs State of Gujarat, 2018). The Gujarat High Court in *Nimeshbhai case* observed that Section 377 of IPC uses the word 'against the order of nature' without any elaboration, and· leaves It for the courts to interpret.

In analyzing the same, the Supreme Court invoked transformative constitutionalism by seeking to do away with colonial notion of sexuality, Victorian era morality evident these cases, the Supreme Court has upheld the concept of "constitutional morality" in *Suresh Kumar Koushal & Anr, v.Naz Foundation & Ors, 2013* (Suresh Kumar Koushal & Anr, v. Naz Foundation & Ors, 2013), the Gujarat High Court in *Nimeshbhai Bharatbhai Desai v. State of Gujarat on 2 April, 2018* (Nimeshbhai Bharatbhai Desai v. State of Gujarat, 2018), it was held that "constitutional morality upholds and respects protection and preservation of fundamental rights, constitutionally ordained rights". This has to be distinguished from popular morality. It is quoted as "popular morality generally refers to public disapproval of certain acts is not a valid justification for restriction of the fundamental rights under Article 21". If there is any type of "morality" that can pass the test of compelling state interest, it must be "constitutional" morality and not public morality. Popular morality, as distinct from a constitutional morality derived from constitutional values.

The Court upheld the "fundamental right to privacy" over the "enforcement of morality". As it is a settled point of law that "what is illegal, not immoral and what is immoral is not illegal". As it is a settled point of Law that "what is illegal, not immoral and what is immoral is not illegal". The Court observed that "morality cannot be a ground for imposing restrictions on fundamental rights". Further, the Court expounded on the concept of popular morality which has no legal sanctity nor legal recognition. The Court observed that "morality cannot be a ground for imposing restrictions on fundamental rights".

In view of this, the Supreme Court rejected the notion that "public morality of homosexual conduct might open floodgates of delinquent behavior is not founded upon any substantive material." The Court also referred to the Wolfenden Report of 1957, of England and Wales, that moral indignation unnatural, sinful or disgusting., however strong, is not a valid basis for overriding individuals' fundamental rights of dignity and privacy.

Thus, the Supreme Court of India in *Suresh Kumar Koushal & Anr.,* sought to correct the age-old or draconian "Victorian notion of sexual morality" which included only procreative sex is unreasonable as condemnation of non-procreative sex is no longer a legitimate state object. The Supreme Court reiterated the ratio held in these judgments as held in *Gobind* v *State of Madhya Pradesh* and another (1975) 2 SCC 148, *Lawre* v. *Texas* 539 U.S. 558 (2003), *Dudgeon* v. *UK, European Court of Human Rights Application No.7525/1976, Norris* v. *Republic of Ireland, European Court of Human Rights Application No. 10581/19.3, The National Coalition for Gay and Lesbian Equality* v. *The Minister of Justice, South African Constitutional Court 1999* (1) SA 6.

The 172nd report of Law Commission of India documents heightened realization about "urgent need to follow global trends on the issue of sexual offences". In this case, the Court expounded on the right to privacy, right to personal liberty and expression and referred to a series of significant national, international cases. Accordingly, the Supreme Court of India upheld the "constitutional morality safeguarding equal fundamental rights of all homosexuals, same-sex partners without any discrimination".

7.2   Homosexuality – Same-Sex Relationships under Section 377 of the Indian Penal Code (IPC)

Navtej Singh Johar v. Union of India Ministry of Law, 2018 (Navtej Singh Johar v. Union of India Ministry of Law, 2018)

The colonial vestiges of the Macaulay's legacy are manifest in Law, even after hundred and fifty-eight years ago, a colonial legislature Section 377 of the Indian Penal Code, 1860. This section is used as an instrument of repression. This provision denied truly equal citizenship seven decades after Independence. In *Navtej Singh's* case, it is found that Section 377 "IPC" has made 'carnal intercourse against the order of nature' an offence prohibiting non-peno vaginal intercourse, reflecting the imposition of a particular set of morals as "morality of anachronism". "Anachronism" is imposed only on Gays and lesbians, transgenders and bisexuals as the "antithesis of constitutional morality". They were denied equal citizenship seven decades after Independence.

Whereas in UK, the Wolfenden Report of 1957 of England and Wales, supported by the Church of England, proposed that there 'must remain a realm of "private morality" as former and "immorality" as latter, the former is not the Law's business' and recommended that homosexual acts between two consenting adults should no longer be a criminal offence. The England Sexual Offences Act of 1967 decriminalized private homosexual sex between two men over twenty-one. Britain amended laws governing same-sex intercourse to make them more equal, including lowering the age of consent for gay/bisexual men to sixteen in 2001. In 2007, United Nations (UN) Human Rights Council, the United Kingdom (UK), which imposed criminal prohibitions against same-sex intercourse in its former colonies across the world, committed itself to the cause of worldwide decriminalization of homosexuality.

Though, India is one of the British colonies that continues to enforce this archaic Law. It is contended in the petition that "Indian citizens belonging to sexual minorities have waited and watched as their fellow citizens were freed from the British yoke while their fundamental freedoms remained restrained under an antiquated and anachronistic colonial-era law – forcing them to live in hiding, in fear, and as second-class citizens". Perusing the petition, the Supreme Court of India held that certain sections of our society, including the gay, lesbians, and homosexuals are denied these rights, this section of society are still living in the bondage of dogmatic social norms, prejudiced notions, rigid stereotypes, parochial mindset, and bigoted perceptions. "The Supreme Court of India upheld the ideals of individual autonomy and liberty, equality for all sans discrimination of any kind, recognition of identity with dignity and privacy of human beings constitute the cardinal four corners of our monumental Constitution forming the concrete substratum of our fundamental rights". Thus, *Navtej Singh*'s case is about an aspiration to realize constitutional rights. It is about a right that every human being has, to live with dignity. It is about enabling these citizens to realize the worth of equal citizenship.

7.3 Sedition under Section 124 A, Indian Penal Code, 1860 (IPC)

Roopesh v. State of Kerala, 2022, (Roopesh v. State of Kerala, 2022), S.G. *Vombatkere v. Union of India, 2022* (S.G. Vombatkere v. Union of India, 2022), *Vinod Dua v. Union of India & Ors* (Vinod Dua v. Union of India & Ors. 2020), 2020

The Prime Minister Jawaharlal Nehru, Indian Parliament on May 29, 1951: "Section 124 A of the Indian Penal Code, it *should have no place both for practical and historical reasons, if you like, in any body of laws that we might pass. The sooner we get rid of it the better."* (*Parliamentary Debates*; Volume XII, Part II, Col. 9621.)

The offence of sedition as Section 124A of the Indian Penal Code, 1860 (IPC), was absent in the early draft of the Indian Penal Code, 1860 (IPC) formulated by Thomas Babington Macaulay (1800–59) and passed in 1860 by the Legislative Council. Subsequently, the offence of Sedition, criminalizing 'disaffection towards the Government established by law' was introduced following revision of IPC in the year 1870 by British politician and lawyer James Fitz James Stephen through the IPC (Amendment Act), 1898 (IPC (Amendment Act, 1898), for political and administrative reasons to penalize criticism or condemnation of the British Government's policy.

The sedition law owes its origin to the British colonial regime, which caused legitimate limits to political liberties. Section 124A IPC as Sedition states that "Whoever by words, either spoken or written, or by signs, or by visible representation, or otherwise, brings or attempts to bring into hatred or contempt, or excites or attempts to excite disaffection towards, the Government established by law in India shall be punished with imprisonment for life, to which fine may be added, or with imprisonment which may extend to three years, to which fine may be added, or with fine". The term "disaffection" includes disloyalty and all feelings of enmity.

In *Queen Empress v. Jogendra Chunder Bose, 1891* (Queen Empress v. Jogendra Chunder Bose, 1891), the editor of a Bengali magazine was tried for sedition for publishing and criticizing the British Government's policy regarding age of consent for sexual intercourse. In Q*ueen-Empress* v. *Bal Gangadhar Tilak & Keshav Mahadev Bal*, (Queen-Empress v. Bal Gangadhar Tilak & Keshav Mahadev Bal, 1897) Bal Gangadhar Tilak, a leading freedom fighter was tried for sedition for alleged incitement through speech that led to the killing of two British Officials.

Post-Independence, in *Tara Singh Gopi Chand* v. *The State, 1951* (Tara Singh Gopi Chand v. The State, 1951) was one of the first reported cases before the then-Punjab High Court, in independent India deliberating on the constitutional validity of section 124A of the IPC. Section 124A was held as a restraint on freedom of speech and expression under Article 19 of the Indian Constitution. Following this, independent India's first Constitution (First Amendment) Act, 1951 was enacted by the Parliament, introducing new grounds of "reasonable restrictions" such as "public order", "relations with foreign states", and "incitement to an offence", for restricting the freedom of speech and expression.

In the year 1971, 42nd report of Law Commission of India proposed amendments in section 124A IPC.

In tandem with the same, in *M/s Aamoda Broadcasting Company Pvt. Ltd. & Anr.* v. *The State of Andhra Pradesh & Ors,2021* (M/s Aamoda Broadcasting Company Pvt. Ltd. & Anr. v. The State of Andhra Pradesh & Ors., 2021), that "sedition is an assault on the freedom of speech and expression under Article 19(1)(a) of the Constitution of India." In *Vinod Dua v. Union of India & Ors.,2020* (Vinod Dua v. Union of India & Ors., 2020), the misuse of sedition law was deliberated, and its adverse impact prevented every journalist from their right to enjoy the freedom of speech. It was held that "the decisive ingredient for establishing the offence of sedition under Section 124A IPC is the doing of certain acts which would bring to the Government established by Law in India hatred or contempt etc. which would incite violence or create public disorder, incite violence or create public disorder".

In *S.G. Vombatkere v. Union of India*, 2022 (S.G. Vombatkere v. Union of India, 2022), the Supreme Court suspended the application of Section 124A of the Indian Penal Code (IPC). The Supreme Court directed the "State and Central Governments to restrain from registering any FIR, restrain from any investigation or taking any coercive measures by invoking Section 124A of IPC." In case of any new case being registered under Section 124A of IPC, "the affected parties are entitled to appropriate relief from the court". The Supreme Court directed that "all pending trials, appeals and proceedings under Section 124A of IPC be kept in abeyance" so that no prejudice would be caused to the accused. The Court directs the "Union of India, the State Governments/Union Territories to prevent any misuse of Section 124A of IPC" (S.G. Vombatkere v. Union of India, P.9, 2022).

In *Roopesh v. State of Kerala, 2022* (Roopesh v. State of Kerala, 2022), the Kerala High Court held that "amidst the raging controversy as to the retention of offence of sedition in the IPC"; which the naysayers categorize as "a relic of the colonial past"; "a symbol of British hegemony", "to suppress dissent, critic, anti-national feelings"! The Court adduced that Section 124A of IPC represents the colonial mindset as this is not in consonance with "current social milieu" infused with "civil liberties and human rights", "maintaining and protect the sovereignty and integrity of the nation," hence, there is need to re-consider the provision of section 124A of IPC as this provision criminalized sedition to suppress democratic dissent.

The law of sedition per se stands inconsistent with the freedom of speech, and expression of the citizens of a country. There is an increase of arrests but very less convictions. The sedition law is in effect in India, with "around 326 sedition cases being filed in the period of five years from 2014–19 year, out of these 326 sedition cases, only six were convicted. Hence, it is evident this law has been used exploitatively". This is misused, generally leading to arbitrary arrest and denying dissent.

Whereas in the United Kingdom (UK), The sedition law Act stands abolished in the UK, as sedition, libel is considered "arcane" and antithesis to the legal objectives of " right to freedom of thought and expression" under the UK Human Rights Act of 1998.

7.4 Adultery under Section 497 of Indian Penal Code (IPC)

Joseph Shine v. Union of India, 2018 (Joseph Shine v. Union of India, 2018)

This case adjudicated upon the decriminalization of adultery tracing its origin from the colonial notions of "moral corruption" as being mainly "sexist and archaic" and from the "common law doctrine of coverture". The common law doctrine of coverture merged the identity of the wife in the husband itself, as the wife has no separate legal existence other than her husband. The wife was considered as the shadow of the husband. This implied that the wife's agency or autonomy or right to self-determination was subject to her husband's consent. The wife can't take a decision on her own without the approval of her husband. Upon marriage the consent of the wife for all-purpose, decision making was vested solely in her husband.

In 1650, England enacted the infamous Act for Suppressing the Detestable Sins of Incest, Adultery and Fornication, which introduced the death penalty for sex with a married woman. In the United States, Puritans living in the American colonies carried Cromwell's criminal Law with them, thereby making adultery a capital offence. This case brings forth the issue of "moral corruption" prevalent in the colonial mindset in England, America, being archaic, and sexist.

The concept of Adultery as written under Section 497 of Indian Penal Code (IPC) is taken after the English based on this same common law doctrine of common law doctrine of coverture.

Section 497 of Indian Penal Code (IPC) reads thus: "Whoever has sexual intercourse with a person who is and whom he knows or has reason to believe to be the wife of another man, without the consent or connivance of that man, such sexual intercourse not amounting to the offence of rape, is guilty of the offence of adultery, and shall be punished with imprisonment of either description for a term which may extend to five years, or with fine, or with both. In such a case, the wife shall not be punishable as an abettor." The existing laws for the punishment of adultery were considered to be altogether inefficacious for preventing the injured husband from taking matters into his own hands. However, the Supreme court rejected the strict morality of the early English colonists reflected in the "moral corruption" as being mainly "sexist and archaic" and from the "common law doctrine of coverture".

The Supreme Court (SC) determined whether adultery should be a criminal offence in India; accordingly, the SC observed that "Adultery under section 497 IPC is a 158-year-old law is unconstitutional being inconsistent with Article 21 (Right to life and personal liberty) and Article 14 (Right to equality) of Indian Constitution". The Supreme Court (SC) held that it is not for the state to regulate "sexual morality" in such cases of infidelity or cheating between two parties. It is a matter of privacy between the couples if they wish to separate or reconcile or divorce. The State should not regulate sexual morality by imposing criminal sanctions as this is a subject matter of the private sphere or the privacy of couples alone. Further, the Court held that "Section 497 is based on the Doctrine of Coverture which is not recognized by the Constitution of India, holds that a woman loses her identity and legal right with marriage, is violative of her fundamental rights, including Article 21 (Right to life and personal liberty) and Article 14 (Right to equality) of Indian Constitution". The Court elaborated that "marriage does not mean ceding autonomy of one to the other, the ability to make sexual choices is essential to human liberty. Even within private zones, an individual should be allowed her choice".

8   The Way Forward

8.1   Indianization of Legal System Propounded by Jurists

The judges from the Supreme Court of India have espoused "Indianization of Indian Legal System". The reason being the colonial legal system of adversarial litigation is neither suitable for the Indian legal system nor for the Indian population. The present adversarial system, taken after the English Common Law system, seeks to increase the pendency of cases, and arrears in cases leading to delayed justice. The adversarial system presupposes legal awareness and knowledge of Law in a society whereas in India, there are issues of literacy and ignorance of Law.

Under an adversarial system, respective advocates will represent both parties in the Court of Law. The onus of the burden of proof lies in the advocates to present evidence, and testimony, so as to establish the guilt or otherwise. The judge is a neutral party and the judge has to deliver the verdict based on the representation by both the advocates. Considering the social and economic issues as poverty, inequality in income, and status, the right to access and avail lawyers or advocates is not equally available for all.

For the same reasons, the Chief Justice of India N.V. Ramana had called for the "Indianization" of "legal system to provide greater access to justice to the poor" as the "need of the hour" (Rajagopal K., 2021). There is a need for better and Indianized justice delivery systems. Hence, "the need of the hour is the Indianization of the legal system".

The former Chief Justice of India, Justice Sharad Arvind Bobde expressed "the need to "Indianize" the system to provide access to justice to the poor"; the justice delivery system should be litigant-centric and justice centric". There is a need to replace the technicalities of the court process and trials of the westernized legal system (Nigam S., 2022).

One of the leading judges of the Supreme Court of India, Justice Nazeer voiced for the Indianization of the legal system. He elaborates that the Indianization of the legal system is traced from the indigenous treatise, epics, monographs, and other authoritative secondary sources. Under Kautilya's Arthashashtra (322–298 BC), the indigenous legal system identified in India was the "Inquisitorial Legal System" not the "Adversarial legal system" (Akhil Bharitiya Adhivakta Parishad, 2021). As it was the duty of the King to do justice. As per *Brishaspati Smiritis*, there was much emphasis on the functioning of Law courts which were established at the meeting places of districts as Sangrahanas. There was a practice of alternative means of dispute resolution as well, there was a system of Family Courts, and Family Arbitrator.

8.2 *Decolonization of Criminal Justice System*

Another reason for an emphasis on the Indianization of the legal system, is a more authoritative regime granting harsh "power to the police" under the colonial-era Criminal Procedure Code (Shahrukh Alam, 2021). The Police Act of India, 1861 was enacted during the colonial era for the control and suppression of civil society with stringent use of force. The Supreme Court in *Prakash Singh* v. *Union of India, 2006* (Prakash Singh v. Union of India, 2006) dealt with three aspects of police organization – autonomy, accountability and efficiency. (Desai M., 2009) The Supreme Court gave detailed directions which are to be followed by the Centre and State Governments until legislations in this regard are enacted (Commonwealth Human Rights Initiative 2010).

According to the Press Information Bureau, Government of India, Ministry of Home Affairs notification dated 22-July-2015, so far 15 States viz. Assam, Bihar, Chhattisgarh, Haryana, Himachal Pradesh, Kerala, Maharashtra, Meghalaya, Mizoram, Punjab, Rajasthan, Sikkim, Tamil Nadu, Tripura and Uttarakhand have formulated their State Police Act and 2 States, viz. Gujarat and Karnataka have amended their existing Police Act. Thus, total 17 State Governments have either formulated their State Police Acts or amended the existing one (Model Police Act 2015).

Also, major changes have been made in the criminal justice delivery system through the Criminal Procedure Code (Amendment) Act, 2008 which came into force on 31 December, 2009. Among other changes, the Amendment Act provides that:

With the permission of the court, a rape victim can engage an advocate to help the prosecution. Any victim's statement will have to be recorded at the victim's home or in a safe place or a place of her choice. As far as practicable, the statement should be recorded by a women police officer in the presence of the victim's parents or guardian or near relatives or social worker of the locality (Amendment of Sections 157 and 161).

Statements can be recorded through audio/video or other electronic means. Investigation of rape/child sex abuse must be completed in three months from the date when information was recorded by the officer in charge of the police station (Amendment of Section 173).

For the possibility of having in camera trials and protection of the victims' identity, maintaining the confidentiality of the name and address of the parties and conduct of trials by a woman magistrate. It will enable the victim to go on appeal against any order passed by the court acquitting the accused or convicted him of a lesser offence or awarding inadequate compenzation. Such appeal shall be made in the court where an appeal is ordinarily made against the order of conviction (CrPC Amendment Sec, 327, 2008).

Similarly, the Criminal Law (Amendment) Act, 2013 introduced several reforms relating to sexual offences and the Criminal Law (Amendment) Act, 2018 amended the Indian Penal Code, Indian Evidence Act, 1872, the Code of Criminal Procedure, 1973 and the Protection of Children from Sexual Offences Act, 2012.

8.3   *Transformative Constitutionalism through Judiciary*

The judiciary spearheaded by the Supreme Court of India in the catena of cases afore mentioned invoked the "transformative constitutionalism" by upholding "constitutional morality over popular morality" in "constitutional morality upholds and respects protection and preservation of fundamental rights, constitutionally ordained rights" as in *Suresh Kumar Koushal & Anr., v. Naz Foundation & Ors., 2013* (Suresh Kumar Koushal & Anr., v. Naz Foundation & Ors., 2013).

The "enumeration of four cardinal corners of our monumental Constitution" including "a.ideals of individual autonomy and liberty, b. equality for all sans discrimination of any kind, c.recognition of identity with dignity d. privacy of human beings these constitute the concrete substratum of our fundamental rights" in *Navtej Singh Johar v. Union of India Ministry of Law, 2018* (Navtej Singh Johar v. Union of India Ministry of Law, 2018).

In *Joseph Shine v. Union of India, 2018* (Joseph Shine v. Union of India, 2018), the Supreme Court (SC) deliberated upon the legality of criminal offence of Adultery under Section 497 of IPC. The SC reinforced the transformative constitutionalism by upholding "the fundamental rights including Article 21 (Right to life and personal liberty) and Article 14 (Right to equality) of Indian Constitution" as overriding the colonial notion of sexual morality and rejected the Doctrine of Coverture which is not recognized by the Constitution of India, holds that a woman loses her identity and legal right with marriage is violative of constitutional, statutory right.

In *S.G. Vombatkere v. Union of India, 2022* (S.G. Vombatkere v. Union of India, 2022), the Supreme Court suspended "the application of Section 124A of the Indian Penal Code (IPC) as a relic of the colonial past"; "a symbol of British hegemony", "to suppress dissent, criticism, anti-national feelings". The Court invoked transformative constitutionalism by upholding the "civil liberties and human rights", "current social milieu" in a modern democratic state over and above the colonial era law under section 124A IPC.

8.4 *Academic Deliberations towards Revision of Colonial Laws*

The National University of Singapore during an International Conference on: A Model Indian Penal Code Adhering to the Philosophy of Macaulay 2010. This was a part of "the project on Model Indian Penal Code", which caused rethinking and reform of Indian Penal Code, 1860 for "a modern set of penal Law which could be incorporated into an up- dated version of the Indian Penal Code". It was also reiterated that IPC was intended by Macaulay and the framers of the Indian Penal Code to be regularly revised whenever gaps and ambiguities were found. However, this has to be undertaken gradually in keeping with the post-colonial constitutional ethos. It is suggested that "every Indian University must include Indian jurisprudence as a compulsory subject in Law degree courses" (Jain M., 2021).

Some of the leading National Law universities and Central Universities in India, are organizing conferences and conclaves on the Indianization of Legal System. Such academic conclave is done in collaboration with National Legal Services Authority (NALSA) Supreme Court of India, Faculty of Law at Central University.

8.5 *State Obligation under Post-colonial Welfare Constitution*

Finally, it is the State Duty to balance needs – aspirations of individuals & society. It is proposed that the State is under a positive obligation not only to update the existing law, but also to enact new laws as per the needs and aspirations of society. That State has an obligation to assume moral leadership roles in matters of criminalization and decriminalization of conduct constantly. That new criminalization must go side by side with the task of classification and categorization on the basis of interests protected and their significance for the society (B.B. Pande, 2010).

Given the above, these are certain measures towards the holistic decolonization of India legal framework with the active support and involvement of all government mechanisms including legislature, executive and judiciary. The judiciary, through transformative constitutionalism and constitutional morality is pervading the way for the same.

Bibliography

Abul Hassan And National Legal v. Delhi Vidyut Board & Ors., AIR 1999 Delhi 88.

Akhil Bharatiya Adhivakta Parishad. (2021, December 26). Speech on decolonization of Indian legal system. 16th National Council Meetings. *Live Law*. Hyderabad. https://www.livelaw.in/pdf_upload/lectureofjusticesabdulnazeer-406739.pdf.

Alam, S. (2021, October 14). CJI Ramana wants 'Indianization' of the justice system. What does that entail? *The Wire*. Retrieved from https://thewire.in/law/indianisation-justice-system-nv-ramana-democracy-nation-state.

Amalgamated Coalfields Limited and Ors. v. Janapada Sabha Chhindwara, AIR 1961 SC 964.

Anil JS v. State of Kerala & Ors. (2010). WP(C) NO. 32519 OF 2010.

Anil Kumar Bhatt v. State of Uttarakhand, 2022. Criminal Jail Appeal No. 47 of 2013.

Arasanayagam, J. (1987). A colonial inheritance. *Journal of South Asian Literature, 22*(2), 209–212. http://www.jstor.org/stable/40872982.

Arms Act. (1959). Act No. 54 of 1959.

B.B. Pande. (2010, December). Philosophy and history of the Indian Penal Code and criminal law reforms in India. International Seminar on Relevance of Indian Penal Code in Controlling and Combating Crime in Modern Age, Dr. Ram Manohar Lohiya National Law University, Lucknow.

B.K. Pavitra v. Union of India, (2017) 4 SCC 620.

Bar Council of India. (2010). Bar Council of India Rules, Chapter-IIIA3, Added vide Res. No. 58/2006. Retrieved from http://www.barcouncilofindia.org/wp-content/uploads/2010/05/BCIRulesPartVonwards.pdf.

Baskar, B. (2023). Conundrums of the colonial mindset. *The Hindu Business Line*. https://www.thehindubusinessline.com/opinion/columns/from-the-viewsroom/conundrums-of-the-colonial-mindset/article66447737.ece.

Baxi, U. (2018, August 15). Independence Day: The lingering effects of the British colonial rule on the Indian legal system. *Bar and Bench*. Retrieved from https://www.barandbench.com/columns/datar-and-dieter-the-origins-of-basic-structure.

Black's Law Dictionary. (2004). (8th ed.). https://opil.ouplaw.com/display/10.1093/law:epil/9780199231690/law-9780199231690-e924.

Campbell, H. (1991). *A dictionary of law* (8th ed.). The Lawbook Exchange, Ltd.

Centre's clean-up act: Modi government terminates 1,500 archaic laws. (2018, July 28). *India Today*. Retrieved from https://www.indiatoday.in/mail-today/story/centre-s-clean-up-ct-modi-government-terminates-1-500-archaic-laws-1299212-2018-07-28/.

Choudhry, S., et al. (Eds.). (2016). Tribunals. In *The Oxford handbook of the Indian Constitution*. Oxford University Press.

Commonwealth Human Rights Initiative. (2010). Report: Seven steps to police reform. Retrieved from http://www.humanrightsinitiative.org/programs/aj/police/india/initiatives/seven_steps_to_police_reform.pdf.

Corbett Haselgrove-Spurin. (2004). Constitutional conventions. Chapter Five. Retrieved from https://www.nadr.co.uk/articles/published/ConstitutionalLaw/Chapter005Conventions.pdf.

Corporation Pvt. Ltd. v. Secretary, Board of Revenue, Trivandrum and Anr. (1964). AIR 1964 SC 207.

Criminal Procedure Code (Amendment) Act. (2008). Retrieved from https://evaw-global-database.unwomen.org/en/countries/asia/india/2008/criminal-procedure-code-amendment-act-2008.

Dasgupta, S. (2022, October 26). From beating drums to kite-flying, the bizarre British colonial-era laws India wants to scrap. *Independent, UK*. Retrieved from https://www.independent.co.uk/asia/india/kiren-rijiju-colonial-laws-abolition-b2210914.html.

Desai, M. (2009). Red Herring in Police Reforms. *Economic and Political Weekly*, 44(10), 9.

Devy, G. N. (2007). Human rights status of de notified tribes and nomadic communities – Delhi, Gujarat, Maharashtra, 2007. National Human Rights Commission (NHRC). Retrieved from https://nhrc.nic.in/sites/default/files/CRS_HR_Status_denotified_Nomadic_Communities_Delhi_Gujarat_Maharashtra_20042018.pdf.

Elias, T. O. (1954). Form and content of colonial law. *The International and Comparative Law Quarterly*, 3(4), 645–651. https://www.jstor.org/stable/755592.

Government of India, Ministry of Culture. Azadi Ka Amrit Mahotsav. Retrieved from https://amritmahotsav.nic.in/.

Hukum Chand v. State of U.P. (2012). MISC. SINGLE No. – 1019 of 2001.

IPC (Amendment Act). (1898). Ins. by Act 27 of 1870, s. 5 and subs. by Act 4 of 1898, s. 4, for s. 124A.

Iyer, P. (2022, October 21). India must get rid of redundant colonial statutes. *Hindustan Times*. Retrieved from https://www.hindustantimes.com/opinion/india-must-get-rid-of-redundant-colonial-statutes-101666361242490.html.

Jain, M. (2021, December). Neglect of ancient Indian legal giants like Manu, Kautilya & adherence to colonial legal system detrimental to constitutional goals: Justice

Abdul Nazeer. *Live Law*. Retrieved from https://www.livelaw.in/top-stories/just ice-abdul-nazeer-ancient-indian-jurisprudence-manu-kautilya-colonial-legal-sys tem-188437.

Jaswal, C. (2022, July 29). India at 75: Colonized & decolonized. *The Museum of British Colonialism*. Retrieved from https://www.museumofbritishcolonialism.org/ourb log/2022/7/29/india-at-75-colonised-decolonised.

Jayaswal Shipping Company v. The Owners And Parties. (1954). AIR 1954 Cal 415, 58 CWN 468.

Joseph Shine v. Union of India. (2018). SC 1676.

Joseph Shine v. Union of India. (2018). WRIT PETITION (CRIMINAL) NO. 194 OF 2017.

Kumbhar, K. (2022, March 21). Health, Epidemic Diseases Act, India's 123-year-old law to help fight the pandemic. *The Wire*. Retrieved from https://thewire.in/hea lth/epidemic-diseases-act-india-pandemic.

Letters. (2021, October 1). The colonial mindset is deeply embedded and persists today. *The Guardian*. Retrieved from https://www.theguardian.com/world/2021/oct/01 /the-colonial-mindset-is-deeply-embedded-and-persists-today.

Lok Sabha Debates. (2015, December). Further discussion on the motion for consideration of Indian Trusts. *Indian Kanoon*. Retrieved from https://indiankanoon.org /doc/133419108/.

M.V. Elisabeth And Ors. v. Harwan Investment And Trading, 1993 AIR 1014, 1992 SCR (1) 1003.

M/s Aamoda Broadcasting Company Pvt. Ltd. & Anr. v. The State of Andhra Pradesh & Ors., (2021). W.P. (Cr.) No. 217/2021.

Maharashtra Land Revenue Record of Rights and Registers (Preparation and Maintenance) Rules. (1971). § 30. Retrieved from https://www.landsofmaharash tra.com/rules1971.html.

McLeod v. St. Aubyn, (1899) AC 549 (PC).

Model Police Act. (2015, July). *Press Information Bureau, Government of India, Ministry of Home Affairs*. Retrieved from https://pib.gov.in/newsite/PrintRelease.aspx?relid= 123494.

Mudane, H. (2020, December). The colonial inheritance. *ResearchGate*. Retrieved from https://www.researchgate.net/publication/346568101.

N.V. Sankaran alias Gnani v. The State of Tamil Nadu, [2013] 1 CTC 686.

Nair, H. (2018, June 21). Goodbye, old laws: Modi government scraps 1,200 redundant Acts, 1,824 more identified for repeal. *India Today*. Retrieved from https://www.ind iatoday.in/mail-today/story/narendra-modi-law-ministry-ravi-shankar-prasad-984 025-2017-06-21.

NALSA v. Union of India, (2015). WRIT PETITION (CIVIL) NO. 400 OF 2012.

National Council Meetings Akhil Bharitiya Adhivakta Parishad. (2021, December 26). Speech on decolonization of Indian legal system, 16th National Council Meetings

Akhil Bharitiya Adhivakta Parishad, Hyderabad. Retrieved from https://www.livelaw.in/pdf_upload/lectureofjusticesabdulnazeer-406739.pdf.

Navtej Singh Johar v. Union of India, (2018). WRIT PETITION (CRIMINAL) NO. 76 OF 2016.

Navtej Singh Johar v. Union of India, AIR 2018 SC 4321.

NHRC, 2020, Report on atrocities on SCs & STs, Section – I, Violence: The social edifice, Human rights social stigmatization de-notified tribes (DNTs). Retrieved from https://nhrc.nic.in/press-release/central-and-state-authorities-urged-prevent-atrocities-against-scs-report-prevention.

Nigam, S. (2022, January 31). People-centric legal system not decolonization or Indianization is the need of the hour. *Counter Currents*. Retrieved from https://countercurrents.org/2022/01/people-centric-legal-system-not-decolonization-or-indianization-is-the-need-of-the-hour/.

Nimeshbhai Bharatbhai Desai v. State of Gujarat. (2018). R/CRIMINAL MISC.APPLICATION NO. 26957 of 2017, R/CRIMINAL MISC.APPLICATION NO. 24342 of 2017.

Nimeshbhai Bharatbhai Desai v. State of Gujarat. (2018). R/SPECIAL CRIMINAL APPLICATION NO. 7083 of 2017.

Nimeshbhai Bharatbhai Desai v. State of Gujarat. (2018). SCC Online Guj 732.

Prakash Singh v. Union of India. (2006). 8 SCC 1.

Prime Minister's Office. (2014, August). PM sets up Committee to identify obsolete laws within three months. *Press Information Bureau, Government of India*. Retrieved from https://pib.gov.in/newsite/PrintRelease.aspx?relid=109106.

Priyanka Wd/O. Yogesh Rathod v. The State of Maharashtra. Cri. W.P.No. 548/2019.

PRS India. (2017). Annual Policy Review, April 2016 – March 2017. Retrieved from https://prsindia.org/files/policy/policy_annual_policy_review/APR%202016-17.pdf.

PTI. (2022, October 10). Govt scrapped 2,000 obsolete laws. *Indian Express*. Retrieved from https://indianexpress.com/article/cities/ahmedabad/my-govt-scrapped-2000-obsolete-laws-helped-india-reach-from-142-to-63rd-in-ease-of-business-pm-8201156/.

Queen Empress v. Jogendra Chunder Bose. (1892). ILR 19 Cal 35.

Queen-Empress v. Bal Gangadhar Tilak & Keshav Mahadev Bal. (1897). ILR 22 Bom 112.

R. v. Almon. (1965). Wilm 243.

R. v. Blackburn. (1968). 1 ALL ER 763.

Rajagopal, K. (2021, December 29). Indianization of the Legal System. *The Hindu*. Retrieved from https://www.thehindu.com/news/national/supreme-courts-views-on-indianisation-of-the-legal-system-have-varied/article38057819.ece.

Rajasthan High Court. (2019, July 15). Notice no. 788.

Rajesh Upadhyay v. The State of Bihar. (2023). Miscellaneous Appeal No.354 of 2016.

Rapatsa, M. (2015, December). South Africa's transformative Constitution: from civil and political rights doctrines to socio-economic rights promises. *Juridical Tribune, 5*(2). Retrieved from http://www.tribunajuridica.eu/arhiva/An5v2/14%20Rapatsa.pdf.

Re: Prashant Bhushan and Anr. SUO MOTU CONTEMPT PETITION (CRL.) NO.1 OF 2020.

Rojer Mathew v. South Indian Bank Ltd And Ors Chief. (2019). Civil Appeal No. 8588 of 2019. [Arising out of Special Leave Petition (Civil) No.15804 of 2017].

Roopesh v. State of Kerala. (2022). Crl. R. P Nos.732, 733, 734 of 2019.

S.G. Vombatkere v. Union of India, Para. No. 9, (Crl.) No.217/2021, W.P.(Crl.) No. 216/2021.

S.G. Vombatkere v. Union of India. (2022). WRIT PETITION(C) No.682 OF 2021.

Sarkar, S. (2001). Indian democracy: The Historical Inheritance in the Success of India's Democracy. Princeton University. Retrieved from https://assets.cambridge.org/97805218/01447/sample/9780521801447ws.pdf.

Schmidhauser, J. R. (1997). The European origins of legal imperialism and its legacy in legal education in former colonial regions. *International Political Science Review / Revue Internationale de Science Politique, 18*(3), 337–351. Retrieved from http://www.jstor.org/stable/1601347.

Second Appeal No. 388 of 2016. (2019, January 4). Retrieved from https://indiankanoon.org/doc/51827725/.

Section 2, 8 of The Indian Treasure-Trove Act. (1878).

Shri Ishwar Singh v. Land and Building Department and Anr. (2018). W.P.(C) 8178/2018.

Shri Salek Chand Jain v. Ministry of Social Justice. (2022). W.P.(C) 1542/2020.

Shrimati Sarala v. State of Chhattisgarh. (2021). WPCR No. 508 of 2021.

Sunil Kisanrao Bagul, Nashik, v. Assistant Commissioner of Income Tax. (2022). ITA No.704/PUN/2022.

Suresh Kumar Koushal & Anr. v. Naz Foundation & Ors. CIVIL APPEAL NO.10972 OF 2013, (Arising out of SLP (C) No.15436 of 2009).

Tara Singh Gopi Chand v. The State. (1951). CriLJ 449.

The Contempt of Courts Act. (1971). No. 70.

The Dramatic Performances (Delhi Repeal) Act. (1963). Act NO. 35 OF 1963, [26th September 1963].

The Dramatic Performances Act. (1876). (No. 19 of 1876), [16th December 1876].

The Dramatic Performances Act. (1876). (Repealed by Act No.04 of 2018).

The Epidemic Diseases Act. (1897). Act No. 3 OF 1897, [4th February 1897].

The Foreign Recruiting Act. (1874). Act 4 of 1874.

The Foreigners Act. (1946). (Act 31 of 1946).

The Indian Treasure-Trove Act. (1878). Act No. 6 OF 1878, [13th February 1878].

The Legal Practitioners Act. (1879). Act No. 18 of 1879, [29th October, 1879].

The Official Secrets Act. (1923). (Act 19 of 1923).

The Transgender Persons (Protection of Rights) Bill. (2016). (2018, December). Lok Sabha Debates, Ministry: Social Justice and Welfare. Retrieved from https://prsindia.org/billtrack/the-transgender-persons-protection-of-rights-bill-2016.

Transgender Persons (Protection of Rights) Act. (2019). Act No. 40 of 2019.

University of Delhi. (2022). Indianization of legal system. Retrieved from https://districts.ecourts.gov.in/sites/default/files/Conclave%2029_30%20Sept.pdf.

Vinod Dua v. Union of India & Ors. Writ Petition (Criminal) No.154 of 2020.

CHAPTER 6

Criminalization of Undertrial Prisoners in the Context of Specific Offences: Social Work Responses to Marginalization

Sharli Mudaliyar

1 Case Study (Prayas, 2023): Journey of Two Young Undertrial Prisoners towards Release[1]

Rita and Meena (name changed)[2] are two sisters, aged 20 and 21, respectively. Their biological father was an alcoholic, hence their mother left him and remarried. Both the girls were unhappy with the mother's second marriage and did not share a happy relationship with their stepfather.

Broken family and strained relations impacted their schooling as well. They studied up to class 9 and dropped out. They avoided going home and would spend more time outside. They started working as domestic helps during the day. They wandered out alone in the nights during which they were influenced to commit crimes. The girls were eventually arrested for theft under sections 380 and 34 of the Indian Penal Code and sent to the Byculla District Prison.

The Prayas social work fellow first met the sisters in the first week of December 2018 in the prison and spoke to them as they looked relatively younger than the other inmates. From the converzation, it was known that bail was granted in November 2018 in their case. However, bail compliance (conditions for release) was not met, hence they were still in prison. In order to meet the bail conditions, it was important to meet their family. Based on the details provided by them, the social work fellow attempted to call the stepfather, but he did not respond. Then, she attempted several home visits to contact the mother. However, as the address was incomplete the house could not be traced. Incidentally, the girls had a court date, so the social work fellow visited the court, found the correct address and attempted the home visit again.

---

1 The first draft of case was written by Prayas social worker Devayani Tumma. I have further developed the case, based on my interaction with Prayas social work fellow Rama Kale and legal fellow Bhujang More.
2 Names in all the case studies are not disclosed to maintain confidentiality.

Eventually, she met the mother, however, the mother showed a lot of reluctance to speak to the social work fellow and did not let her inside the house. The mother feared that the social work fellow was from law enforcement representing either the police or prison authorities and if she spoke, they would land in further trouble. After repeated visits, finally, the social work fellow won the trust of the mother and convinced her to meet on the nearby highway, as she did not want her neighbours to be suspicious. Despite persuasion, the mother was adamant that she did not want to be associated with her daughters in any way, and she did not want to support them. The social work fellow then met the girls in prison and informed them about the home visit. The girls were upset knowing the response of the mother. Few counselling sessions were done with the girls to bridge the gap between the mother and help them accept the circumstances. The girls opened up their bottled feelings and shared that they were upset about the mother's remarriage, hence they had a strained relationship. Further, the social work fellow also tried to make the girls understand the mother's perspective, especially the biological father's alcoholism and abuse that led her to remarry.

While the social work fellow was engaging in re-building family ties and mediating between the mother and daughters, the Prayas legal fellow met the Investigating Officer to get more information on the case and also facilitated a bail modification[3] application through the panel advocate.[4] The bail was granted with a condition that a person will stand a surety[5] of INR 15,000 each. Due to a lack of family support to arrange for surety, a modification application was filed to convert the surety to cash bail[6] and the same was granted. Despite granting of bail, the girls still were languishing in prison as it became difficult to meet the conditions set by the court. The poverty of the undertrials and discord between the sisters and the family made it challenging to arrange cash bail amounts. Hence, to facilitate the cash bail of INR 15,000 per person, an NGO supporting financial assistance, especially for cash bail matters was contacted, which agreed to pay the bail money for both girls.

However, despite the above successes, a final hurdle remained – another condition for the bail order was to provide identity documents and the girls

---

3 Set aside or modify any condition – reduction of bail, converting surety bail to cash bail or release on personal bond imposed by a Magistrate when releasing any person on bail.
4 Panel advocate is a legal aid lawyer appointed on the legal aid panel.
5 Bail bond – It is an undertaking/ guarantee given by person to the court for appearance of accused in his bail bond. If accused does not appear in court, then surety guarantee's to pay a sum of money.
6 Bail amount to be paid in cash.

did not have any. Hence, the social worker contacted the corporator of the area. After explaining the situation to him, the corporator issued a letter, with his stamp and signature on the letterhead, certifying that the girls and their mother had been living in that district for the last five years. The social work fellow went to the court and submitted the letter as a valid ID document to the Judge. Despite securing release papers, an unexpected issue came up. Rita did not want to leave the prison because she did not want to live with her mother while Meena was ready to be released. Respecting the decision of Rita, the social worker convinced her to leave the prison and gave her the option of staying in a shelter home and pursuing vocational skills for employment. Finally, both the girls came out of prison and the social worker ensured that the mother was also present. When they saw each other, all their resentment and anger was forgotten. Through the intervention of the Prayas' social worker and legal fellow, not only was legal assistance given but the girls were also reunited with their mother.

The above is an illustration of a positive case story of two young undertrial prisoners who were provided timely socio-legal support and released on bail. The case demonstrates a partnership between the social worker and the lawyer. It depicts the crucial role of a social worker in releasing the two young undertrial prisoners, facilitating their bail compliance conditions, and rebuilding family ties. The social worker worked holistically in this case keeping the vulnerability of the young girls in mind. As the mother and daughters did not share cordial relations, and one of the girls did not want to go back to the mother, the social worker sketched an aftercare plan of a temporary safe shelter and employment opportunities for a smooth transition from prison to society, and ensuring the girl does not re-enter into crime or contact old circle of friends. Despite granting of bail, it took nearly two months for a qualified and professional social worker to run from pillar to post to get the two young undertrial girls released. One can only imagine the plight and ordeal of an uneducated person from a poor vulnerable background with no resources. Although this case is a success, such stories are rare as many undertrials languish in prisons due to a lack of legal awareness and timely socio–legal support.

2   Prison Situations: Exceeding Official Capacity of Prisons

Prison and its administration are state subjects enlisted in list II – Schedule VII of the Indian Constitution. Prison population comprises convicts, undertrial and detenues. An undertrial prisoner is a person who is arrested for committing

TABLE 6.1 Occupancy and percentage of undertrial population

Year	Actual capacity of prisons	No. of prisoners at the end of the year	Occupancy rate[a]	No. of undertrial prisoners	Percentage of undertrial population to total prison population
2019	4,00,934	4,81,387	120.1%	3,32,916	69.15%
2020	4,14,033	4,88,511	118.0%	3,71,848	76.11%
2021	4,25,609	5,54,034	130.2%	4,27,165	77.1%

a Occupancy rate is calculated based upon the number of inmate population to total capacity in prisons. If the number of prisoners is more than the sanctioned official capacity, then it amounts to overcrowding.
SOURCE PRISON STATISTIC REPORT OF INDIA, 2021

a crime and kept in prison custody while the trial is pending / ongoing in court. He/she is not yet proven guilty of the crime committed.

A large proportion of the prison population, nearly three million, is represented by pre-trial detainees across the world; and an overcrowded prison system is found across two-thirds of the world's prisons. Sixty per cent of the countries are affected by overcrowding. India tops the list with 68 per cent undertrials of the total prison population across ten countries[7] in five continents (Herald & Fair, 2019).

Undertrial prisoners especially in petty offences constitute a large proportion of the prison population in India. According to the Prison Statistics Report of India, 2021 (Prison Statistics India, 2021), Indian prisons had an average occupancy rate of 130 per cent (Males 134 per cent, Females 78 per cent, Transgender 211.6 per cent) and undertrials comprised 77.1 per cent of the total inmate population. The share of undertrial prisoners puts India in the fifth position in the world, and first in Asia (World Prison Brief).

Undertrial prisoners are a floating population and data in prisons varies with each day. Based on data collected by the National Crime Records Bureau, the occupancy rate[8] in 2019 was 120 per cent, which decreased marginally by 2 per cent in 2020 to 118.1 per cent, however, the percentage of undertrials

---

7 Kenya, South Africa in Africa, Brazil and the United States in the Americas, India and Thailand in Asia, England and Wales, Hungary and the Netherlands in Europe and Australia in Oceania.
8 As on 31st December of each year.

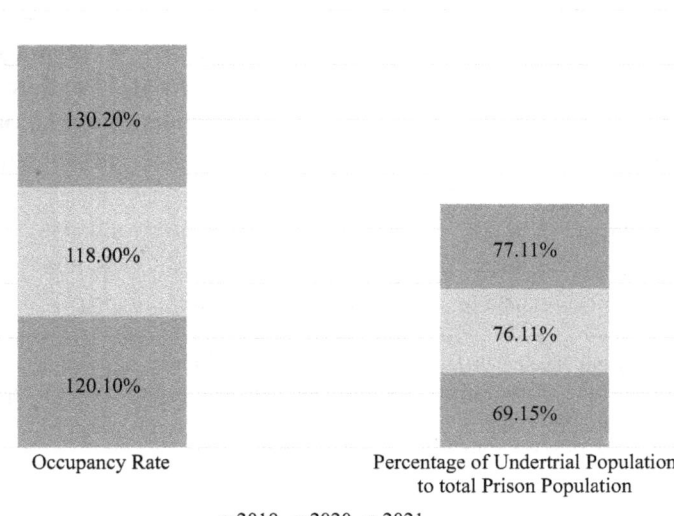

FIGURE 6.1   Occupancy

jumped by 7 per cent in the same period. In 2021, the occupancy rate further increased by 12 per cent to 130 per cent (Figure 6.1).

The number of undertrials has increased by 11.7 per cent from 2019 to 2020 and 14.87 per cent from 2020 to 2021 (Figure 6.2).With the increasing number of undertrials, those awaiting trial are spending a longer time in prison. 29.1 per cent of all undertrials had been in prison for more than a year, at the end of 2021 ((Table 6.2)

Overcrowding impacts the prison administration and affects the basic rights of prisoner's i.e. inadequate living conditions, endangering physical and mental health, which in turn affects penal reformation and rehabilitation programmes. Thus, despite India being a signatory to United Nations Standard Minimum Rules (reformation and rehabilitation) for the treatment of offenders, prisoners are kept under unacceptable conditions (Government Advisory No.17011/2/2010-PR).

2.1   *Free Legal Aid to the Poor: Access to Justice*

The State (The Indian, Constitution, 42nd amend, Legal Services Authorities Act 1987, & Code of Criminal Procedure, 1973) provides free legal aid services to the underprivileged section of society, especially to those who are unable to afford legal fees and do not have access to adequate legal representation. Legal services under the Legal Services Authorities Act, of 1987, is mandated

CRIMINALIZATION OF UNDERTRIAL PRISONERS

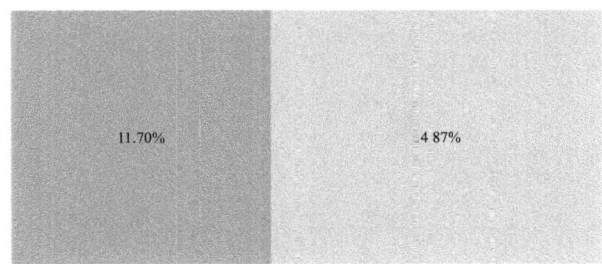

FIGURE 6.2 Share of undertrials

TABLE 6.2 Duration of confinement

Duration of confinement	Percentage of undertrial prisoners		
	2019	2020	2021
Up to 3 months	37	35	34
3–6 months	21	19	20
6–12 months	17	17	16
1–2 years	13	15	13
2–3 years	7	8	8
3–5 years	4	4	6
Above 5 years	1	2	3

SOURCE PRISON STATISTIC REPORT OF INDIA 2019, 2020, 2021

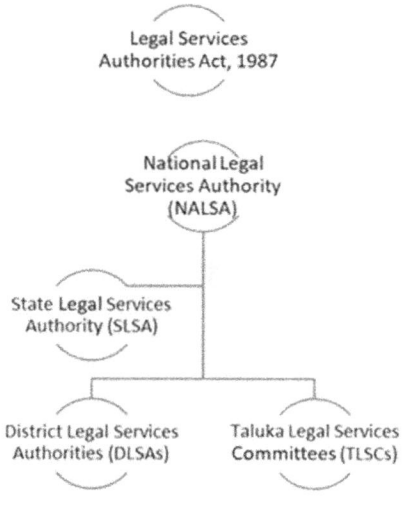

FIGURE 6.3   Legal services for the poor-state mandate

through a statutory body called the National Legal Services Authority (NALSA) to provide free legal services to those who need these services. The legal rights of the undertrial include free legal aid, a legal practitioner of their choice, bail etc. Legal assistance is accessible at police stations and production hearings in magistrate courts (remand hearing) (NALSA Framework, 2019) and legal aid clinics in prison (NALSA, Regulations 2011 and NALSA SOP 2016) .Under the regulations and supervision of NALSA, in each state, the State Legal Services Authority (SLSA) is constituted, and at district and taluka levels, the District Legal Services Authorities (DLSAs) and the Taluka Legal Services Committees (TLSCs) have been constituted. The role of SLSA, DLSA and TLSC is to ensure marginalized sections get legal guidance and aid and thus get access to justice.

2.2   *Prayas's Experience: Legal Aid and Bail Project across Six Prisons in Maharashtra*[9]

Social work education in the country has evolved as a response to the changing needs in post-colonial India. The social development of the country stems from welfare schemes and protection measures for vulnerable sections.

---

9   Prayas, TISS is one of the implementing partners of the model programme instituted by Azim Premji Foundation in collaboration with Government of Maharashtra (GoM).

Eventually, these developments led to the creation of 'trained personnel' in the social welfare department and the first social work education facility Tata Institute of Social Sciences (TISS), was set up in 1936 in the country. Social work education provides an interface between classroom teachings and actual practice. Field reality helps the student to understand the social realities in the complex socio-politico-economic structures and devise policies for the marginalised. Field action projects (FAP) were one such innovative method of demonstrating social work interventions and validating practice – theory continuum (Dave, Raghavan, Solanki & 2012).

Prayas, is one such FAP of the Centre for Criminology and Justice, School of Social Work, TISS. It is a social work demonstration project working with custodial populations (undertrials), offering legal aid and rehabilitation services to persons from resource-poor communities, who get processed within the criminal justice system (CJS), or those at the margins of crime, victimization, or destitution, since more than three decades in select prisons in Maharashtra and Gujarat. Trained social workers of Prayas are placed at police stations, courts, legal aid systems, prisons, and women's and children's institutions to understand the impact of their placements both on citizens processed by CJS and the system (Dave, Raghavan, Solanki & 2012).

A cadre of trained, specialist Social Workers helps create spaces that help them reconstruct their lives and distance them in a sustained way, from crime, exploitation, violence and vulnerabilities. On the one hand, Prayas works to *enhance knowledge, and influence policy and processes of criminal justice (and allied) systems* in India, while on the other it ensures *access to information, education, training, health, opportunities for livelihood and a safe environment* for those affected by the system (Prayas, Concept Note).

Prayas's presence within prisons and courts is in a way, targeted to mitigate disruptive life trajectories accompanied with imprisonment. Individuals who come in contact with the criminal justice system are mostly found to be deprived socially, economically and culturally with strained family ties. Systemic marginalization makes them 'invisible' to welfare agencies, thus devoid them of any support system, thus denying basic rights (Dave, Raghavan, Solanki & 2012). The deprivation of basic fundamental rights leads to marginalization which in turn creates circumstances that compel and force an individual to interact with the criminal justice system either as an offender or victim. Such interactions expose them to layers of additional deprivation, marginalization, isolation, and stigma. These processes negatively influence life trajectories, furthering marginalization and social exclusion resulting in social and economic hardship. Such hardships act as a hindrance in smooth re-integration and finding alternate employment services for them (Menezes

& Raghavan 2019). In this context, Prayas's initiatives can be viewed within the framework of the social work intervention in the criminal justice system, also known as criminal justice social work, with a focus on the protection of legal rights and rehabilitation of marginalised groups coming in contact with the CJS (Menezes & Raghavan 2019).

This chapter explores the experiences of Prayas working towards facilitating legal aid and bail for undertrial prisoners (2018–2021) through a collaborative approach of trained social workers and lawyers working together to facilitate access to free legal aid and bail, and counter criminalization and marginalization of vulnerable undertrial prisoners across six prisons in Maharashtra namely Mumbai Central, Byculla District (Male and Female), Taloja Central, Thane Central (Male and Female), Kalyan District (Male and Female) and Latur District Prisons:

a) To identify undertrial prisoners who need legal aid or are unable to get released on bail despite bail being granted.
b) To facilitate access to legal aid and release on bail, with the help of lawyers appointed through the DLSA/TLSC.

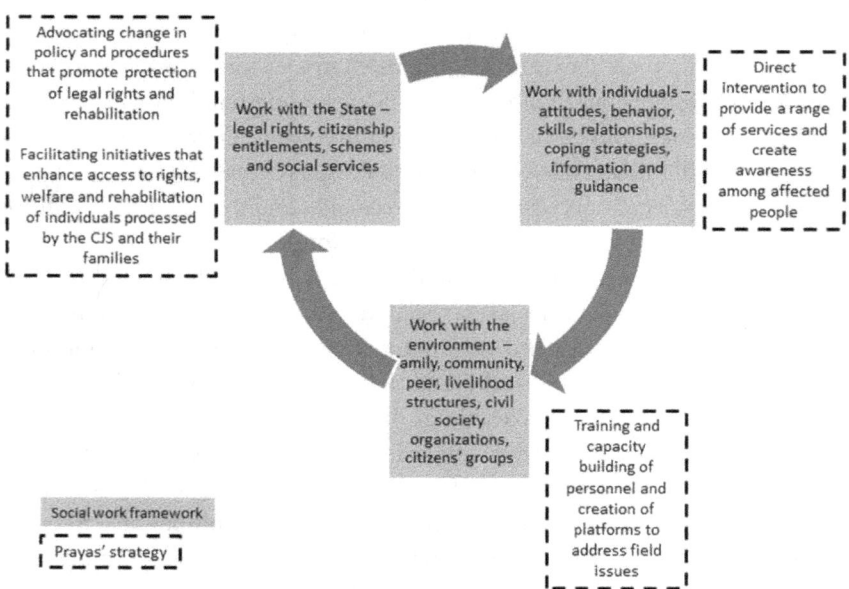

FIGURE 6.4 Prayas strategy within framework of social work as stated in the proposal submitted
STARTUP, 2020

c) To work in collaboration with prison authorities and DLSA/TLSC to strengthen legal aid services and provide psycho-social support to reconstruct the lives of undertrials.

As per the PSI 2021 report, the state of Maharashtra reported the third highest in terms of undertrial population 7.4 per cent (31,752) in the country. As on December 31, 2021, Maharashtra had a total prison population of 36,828 prisoners with an average occupancy rate of 149 per cent (Male 151.4 per cent, female 102.8 per cent and transgender 150 per cent) and an average undertrial population of 86 per cent as stated by the Maharashtra Prison Department in 2021.

2.3 Cyclical Nature of Overcrowding: Lack of Access to Legal Aid and Non-release of Poor Undertrials

Tables 6.3 and 6.4 above indicate the rate of crowding in the prisons supported by Prayas. The official statistic indicates, nearly 95 per cent of the official prison capacity is occupied solely by undertrial prisoners across the prisons. More than 40 per cent of undertrials had been in the prisons of Maharashtra for more than a year. Poor Judge – population ratio, lack of prompt and quality legal aid services for undertrials, the financial system of bail and the lengthy trial process, and non-production of undertrials on court dates are some reasons for the high proportion of undertrials (Raghavan 2020; 2016).

2.4 Inability Due to Poverty to Comply with Bail Conditions: 'Victim' of the Criminal Justice System

Over a period of 4 years, between 2016 and 2019, 7.91 per cent of the undertrials admitted into prisons utilized legal aid services (Surendranath & Andrew, 2022). Imprisonment of undertrials from especially marginalised backgrounds, despite the due process of law and lack of legal representation, make them 'victims' of the criminal justice system (Kumar, 2022). Class, caste and gendered inequities limit the opportunity to raise their voice and explore resources (Menezes & Raghavan, 2019). Poor and destitute undertrials from disadvantaged backgrounds arrested in minor offences are more susceptible to arrest and pre-trial detention, and due to a lack of financial resources they cannot afford good legal representation, languish for longer periods in cases wherein bail amount is high, are unable to pay bail or comply with other conditions (guarantors nor assets to furnish as bonds) (Herald & Fair, 2020) in the court and their inability to arrange surety as mentioned in the 2013 advisory .

The Supreme Court directed the setting up of an UnderTrial Review Committee (UTRC) in each district to review the cases of undertrials to be

TABLE 6.3 Occupancy and percentage of undertrial population, Maharashtra Prison

No.	Prison name	Prison capacity	Actual population	Occupancy rate	Undertrial prisoner population	Percentage of undertrials[a]
1	Mumbai Central	804	3347	425.00	3340	97.75
2	Byculla District Male	200	353	176.50	269	76.20
3	Mumbai Women section (Byculla)	262	294	112.2	287	97.62
4	Thane Central Male	1080	4315	399.54	4141	95.97
5	Thane Central Female	25	156	624	154	98.72
6	Taloja Central	2124	2819	132.72	2733	96.95
7	Kalyan District Male	505	1821	360.6	1760	96.65
8	Kalyan District Female	35	128	365.7	121	94.53
9	Latur District Male	480	404	84.2	401	99.26

a Ratio of number of Undertrials to the total prison population
SOURCE MAHARASHTRA PRISON DEPARTMENT, DECEMBER 2021

TABLE 6.4   Duration of confinement, Maharashtra Prison 2021

Duration of confinement	Percentage of undertrial prisoners (Maharashtra) 2021
Up to 3 months	25
3–6 months	19
6–12 months	15
1–2 years	13
2–3 years	11
3–5 years	11
Above 5 years	6

SOURCE PRISON STATISTIC REPORT OF INDIA

released; to ensure effective implementation of Section 436[10], and 436A [11] of the Cr.P.C. so that undertrial prisoners are released at the earliest, and they should not be incarcerated due to their inability to furnish bail bonds due to their poverty. The India Justice Report 2020 highlights factors contributing to overcrowding i.e., downsizing prisons, and closing down of sub –jails thus admitting prisoners to the nearest District and Central prisons. Further, the report looks at *'unnecessary arrests, conservative approaches to granting bail, uncertain access to legal aid, delays at trial, as well as the inefficacy of monitoring mechanisms such as UnderTrial Review Committees'* (India Justice Report, 2020). During the pandemic, overcrowded prisons within Maharashtra like Solapur, Nanded, Parbani, and Beed transferred their prisoners to Latur District Prison as it had the official capacity to admit prisoners. However, these undertrials could not be produced on court dates due to geographical distance and less manpower, thus eventually adding to longer stay in prison.

10   Undertrial arrested in a minor bailable offence can be detained in prison for a maximum period of 7 days and also a person who is unable to furnish bail within 7 days could be released on personal bond without surety.

11   Applicable to seek bail for those undertrials who have completed one half of the maximum possible sentence inside the prison. No one can be detained in prison for a period exceeding the maximum possible sentence (not applicable for offences punishable with death sentence).

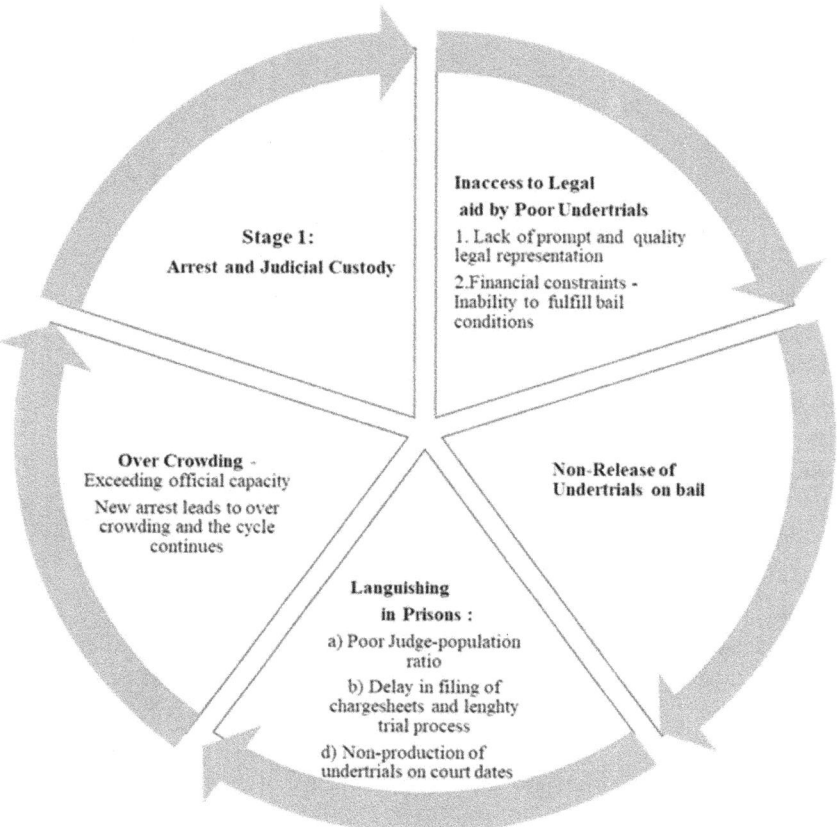

FIGURE 6.5 Cyclic representation of arrest to non-release to overcrowding

2.5   *Prolonged Detention: Unconstitutional and Violative of Rights*

Prolonged detention violates the right to liberty and fair trial. An undertrial prisoner had completed nine and half years of incarceration, the Supreme Court observed in Asim Kumar Haranath v. National Investigation Agency, 2021 (Asim Kumar Haranath v. National Investigation Agency, 2021). 'Deprivation of personal liberty without ensuring speedy trial is not consistent with Article 21 of the Constitution of India. Court has consistently observed in its numerous judgments that the liberty guaranteed in Part III of the Constitution would cover within its protective ambit not only due procedure and fairness but also access to justice and a speedy trial is imperative and the undertrials cannot indefinitely be detained pending trial. Once it is obvious that a timely trial would not be possible and the accused has suffered incarceration for a significant period of time, the Courts would ordinarily be obligated to enlarge him on bail'.

Allahabad High Court in Rajnish v. State, 2022 (Rajnish v. State, 2022) granted bail to a man languishing for 11 years with no access to legal aid, citing it as a systemic failure. The court remarked *'The applicant belongs to the bottom heap of humanity and unfortunately forgotten class of citizen'.* As a corrective measure, it ordered DSLA, Uttar Pradesh to draw up a list of prisoners who are incarcerated for long period and to examine reasons for not moving bail applications.

Overcrowding persists, despite landmark judgments and several directions from the Apex court and various High Courts. The Supreme Court took *suo motu* cognizance regarding the rights of the prisoners in Re: *Inhuman Conditions in 1382 v. State of Assam*. Four issues were highlighted namely overcrowding in prisons; unnatural deaths of prisoners; gross inadequacy of staff; and the available staff being untrained or inadequately trained. It pointed out the high percentage (67 per cent) of the undertrials population and observed overcrowding as a violation of human rights (SLIC (n.d.)). In another Public Interest Litigation, the landmark case of *Hussainara Khatoon v. Home Secretary, State of Bihar, 1980* (Hussainara Khatoon v. Home Secretary, State of Bihar, 1980), Supreme Court declared the detention of undertrials as unconstitutional. It observed that those undertrials are unaware of their rights and due to poverty, they cannot afford legal representation. Hence free legal counsel and services be compulsorily provided to every accused and they should be treated in a fair and just manner. It highlighted the need for a comprehensive legal services programme, due to the non-release of undertrial prisoners on bail. The judgment said a speedy trial is a fundamental right of every accused person (Pillay, 2020).

3 Reaching out to Undertrials: Facilitate and Ensure End-to-End Support, Release on Bail and Rehabilitation of Undertrial Prisoners

Prayas reached out to 6800 undertrials across 6 prisons in Maharashtra from 2018–2021 under the legal aid and bail project. Prayas social workers and fellows regularly interacted with the undertrials, as per their fixed weekly schedule to visit the barracks. More than 90 per cent of case referrals were received directly from the prison. The outreach was 86.83 per cent in the pre-pandemic period[12] and 13.16 per cent post-pandemic[13] period. The total number of

---

12   Period between May 1, 2018 to March 31, 2020.
13   Period between April 1, 2020 to October 31, 2021.

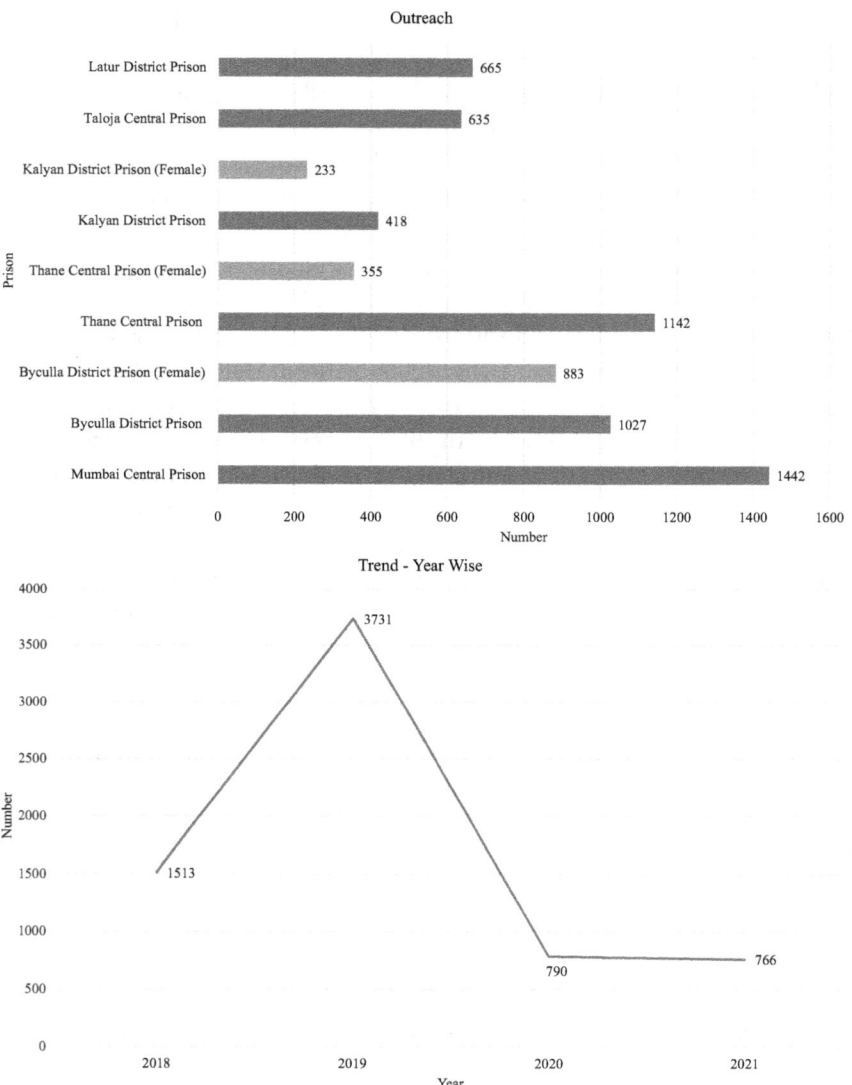

FIGURE 6.6 Total outreach and year wise trend

outreaches increased by 148 per cent in 2019. Due to prison entry restrictions, the outreach decreased by 78.82 per cent during the first wave of the pandemic (COVID-19) in 2020 and further dropped slightly in 2021 by 3.03 per cent.

CRIMINALIZATION OF UNDERTRIAL PRISONERS

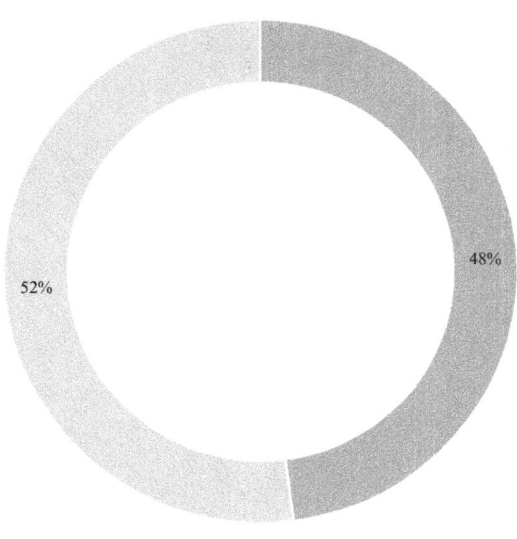

FIGURE 6.7   Services provided

3.1   *Service Provided by Prayas*

Need-based services are provided to the undertrials. 52 per cent requested detailed intervention i.e., legal aid representation to appoint a panel advocate and file bail applications, whereas 48 per cent requested only one-time assistance, which includes a request for phone call support to family or his/ her lawyer, requesting to read out the legal document like a charge sheet, FIR, writing any application, giving guidance or legal advice etc.

3.2   *Demography: Socio-economic Vulnerability*

The demographic profiles of the undertrials reflect their socio-economic vulnerabilities in terms of gender, age, education, livelihood, and income. According to the Government prison data for 2021, 25 per cent were illiterate and 39 per cent studied below class 10, more than 65 per cent of undertrial prisoners belong to the Schedule Caste, Scheduled Tribe and Other Backward Classes categories; 47 per cent of them were in the age group of 18–30 years. Poverty, marginalization, discrimination, and lack of access to legal and social services characterised the situation of Muslim undertrials (Raghavan, 2020).

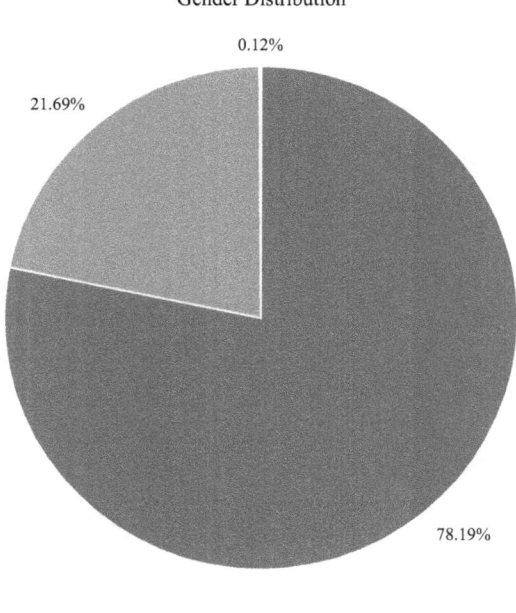

FIGURE 6.8 Gender

Thus, an undertrial prisoner largely belongs to a younger age, is unlettered and socio-economically backward.

Out of the total outreach (6800), *males* constituted *78 per cent, and* females constituted *22* per cent. Of the 4 per cent female prison population (as per Prison Statistics 2021), Prayas reached out to 22 per cent females. Prayas represented 8 clients from the third gender.

The age of the undertrials ranged from 16 to 80 years. The highest number of undertrials 45 per cent belonged to the age group of 21–30. Amongst the total, 48 per cent of males belonged to the age group of 21–30 whereas 37 per cent of females were between 31–40. Male youths below the age of 20 accounted for 19 per cent.

More than 70 per cent of males and females had not completed matriculation (Class 10th).

Literacy rates among males were higher than females indicating minimum access to education. 38 per cent of females were non-literate as compared to 16 per cent of males.

Out of 8 third-gendered undertrials, 2 were illiterate, 2 studied below Class 10th.

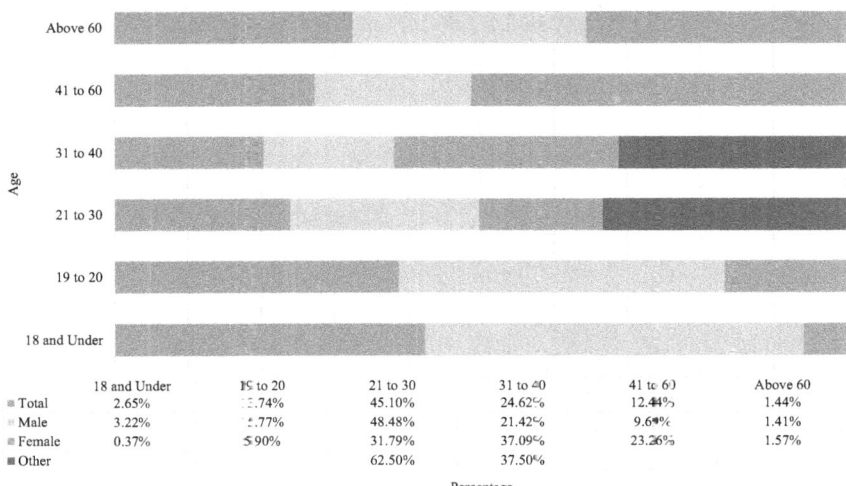

FIGURE 6.9 Age

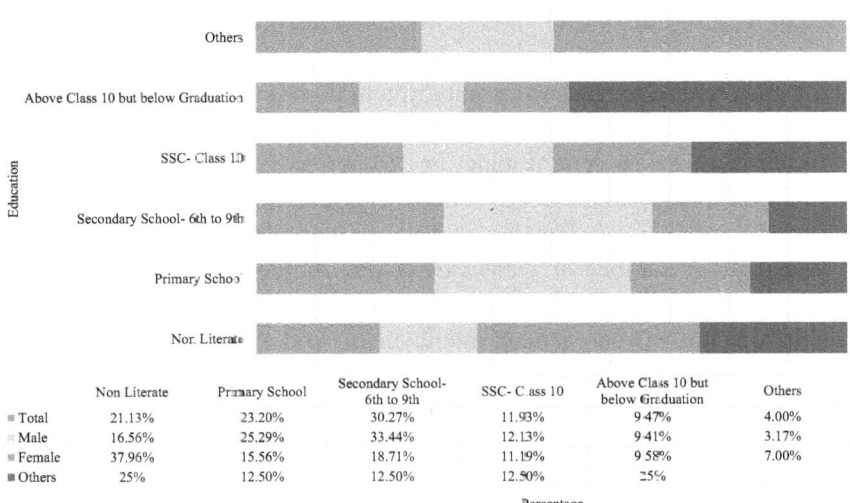

FIGURE 6.10 Education

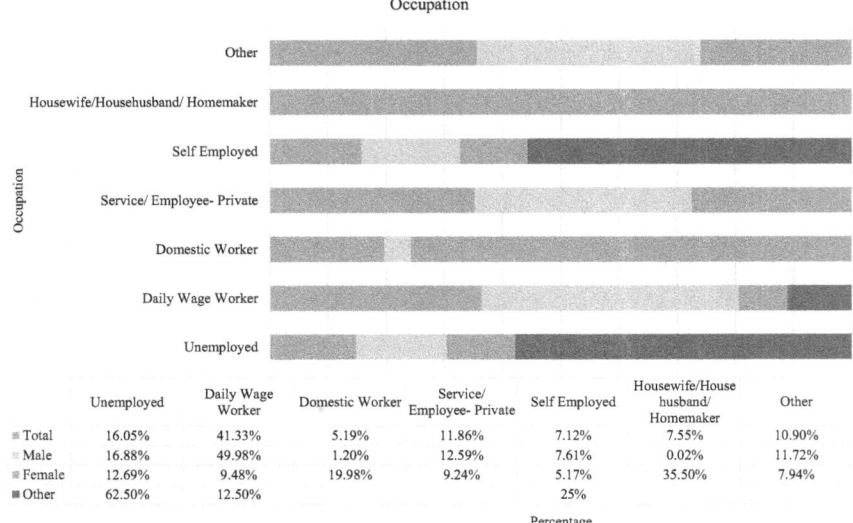

FIGURE 6.11 Occupation

At the time of the arrest:

16 per cent were unemployed (17 per cent of males and 13 per cent of females, 5 out of 8 third gender were unemployed). The top occupations for both genders varied, almost 50 per cent of males were employed as daily wage workers and 20 per cent of females were employed in domestic work and 35 per cent were homemakers.

28 per cent (20 per cent of males and 67 per cent of females and 2 clients from third gender) had no source of income. A total of 69 per cent (76 per cent males and 30.59 per cent females) earned less than INR 1, 20,000 per annum.

The highest number of male clients was in the age group 21–30 and females between 31–40. Hence, we did a cross-tabulation to understand the co-relationship between gender, employment, and education. Illiteracy and unemployment were the highest at 41 per cent in both males and females in the age group of 21–30. In the age group of 31–40, female illiteracy was highest at 36 per cent and unemployment at 27 per cent. Among the third gender, 62.50 per cent (age group 21–30) were unemployed.

Male illiteracy was highest at 50 per cent in the age group of 21–30 and unemployment at 44 per cent in the age group between 18–20. It is also found that nearly 2 per cent of the total population (male and female) were studying at the time of the arrest. It can indicate that 44 per cent were not studying or working at the time of the arrest which makes them even more vulnerable. Thus, a correlation indicates between age, gender, education, and employment.

CRIMINALIZATION OF UNDERTRIAL PRISONERS 121

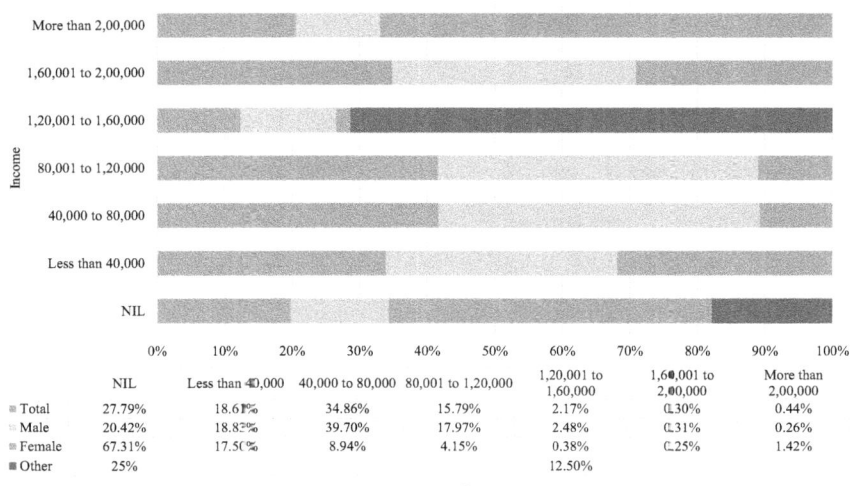

FIGURE 6.12 Income

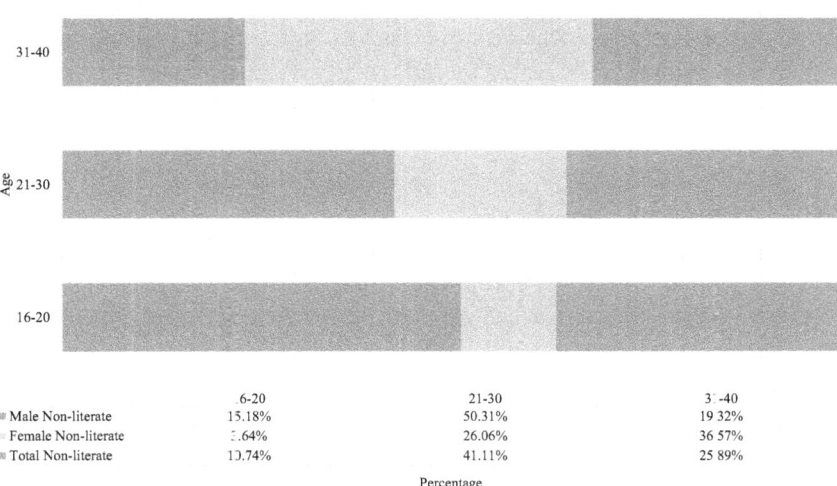

FIGURE 6.13 Age, gender, illiteracy

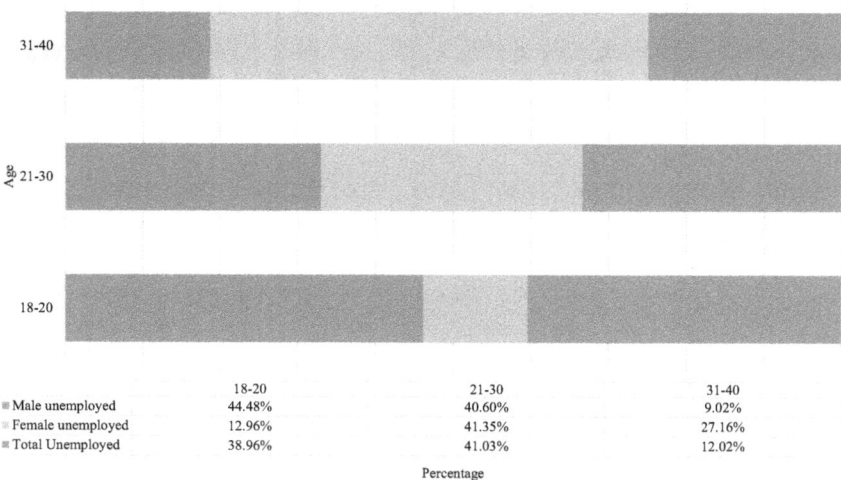

FIGURE 6.14 Age, gender, unemployment

The findings indicate that the majority of the undertrials were from low socio-economic strata resonating with the marginalized profile reflected in the prison statistics of India. The lack of access to basic education, employment, and no source of income, makes an individual even more marginalized, thus confirming minimal support for pursuing their rights of access to bail and inability to afford bail fees.

3.3 Offences and Punishment

3.3.1 Type of Offences

Theft constituted the highest proportion (19.91 per cent) of cases handled by Prayas. The highest proportion of males was charged with theft, whereas females were charged with trafficking and ITPA [The Immoral Traffic (Prevention) Act, 1956]. Inside the prison, undertrials arrested for petty offences or first-time offender with poor family support undergo a secondary level of discrimination. They struggle to find 'space' in the system, which implies only serious offenders with financial backing have rights (Raghavan, 2020). The data indicates they are young and arrested under petty offences, hence, there is a need to widen the scope of probation services[14] to rehabilitate them and prevent

---

14 Referrals by Magistrate to provide the benefit of probation to young offenders, refer a sufficient number of cases to them for pre-sentence enquiry and for supervision of cases, which would be helpful in their future rehabilitation.

CRIMINALIZATION OF UNDERTRIAL PRISONERS

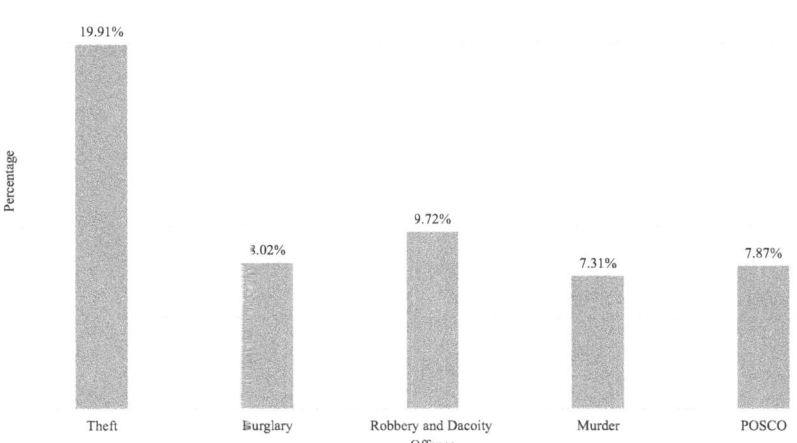

FIGURE 6.15 Offence-wise case categorization

pleading guilty case (many inmates feel pleading guilty is a simple way to get out of prison than languishing inside).

The largest category of cases was punishable beyond 7 years 36.43 per cent, whereas cases punishable with less than 3 years as punishment were the next largest category- 28.04 per cent cases. Serious offences were the highest both amongst males (35 per cent) and females (42.6 per cent). Females constituted the highest category in serious offences and lowest for petty crime offences (12.4 per cent).

86.87 per cent of cases were for non-bailable offences and 61.12 per cent of cases were for offences triable by magistrates while 38.88 per cent of cases were triable by the Court of Sessions judge. Females constituted the highest for non-bailable offences, as compared to males.

3.4 *Advocate Status at Case Intake*
At the time of case intake, nearly 39.58 per cent did not have a panel advocate, while only 9.51 per cent had a panel advocate and 50.91 per cent had private advocates. Females had more legal representation, as compared to males. The needs of undertrials at the intake stage indicated a requirement for legal aid representation.

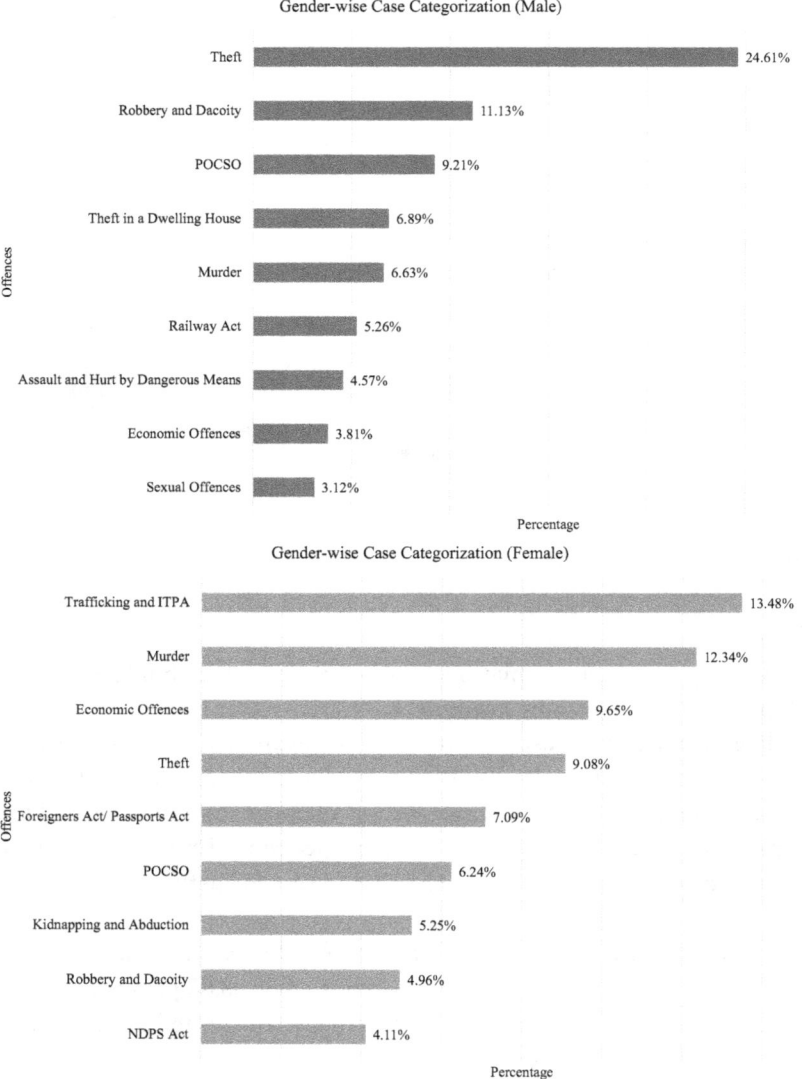

FIGURE 6.16 Gender wise categorization of cases

3.5 *DLSA (Free Legal Aid) Status at Case Intake and Prayas Interventions*

The free legal aid process was not initiated in more than 80 per cent of cases. Only in 10 per cent of the case, applications were submitted for appointing a panel advocate and 6.36 per cent of undertrials already had a panel advocate at the time of intake.

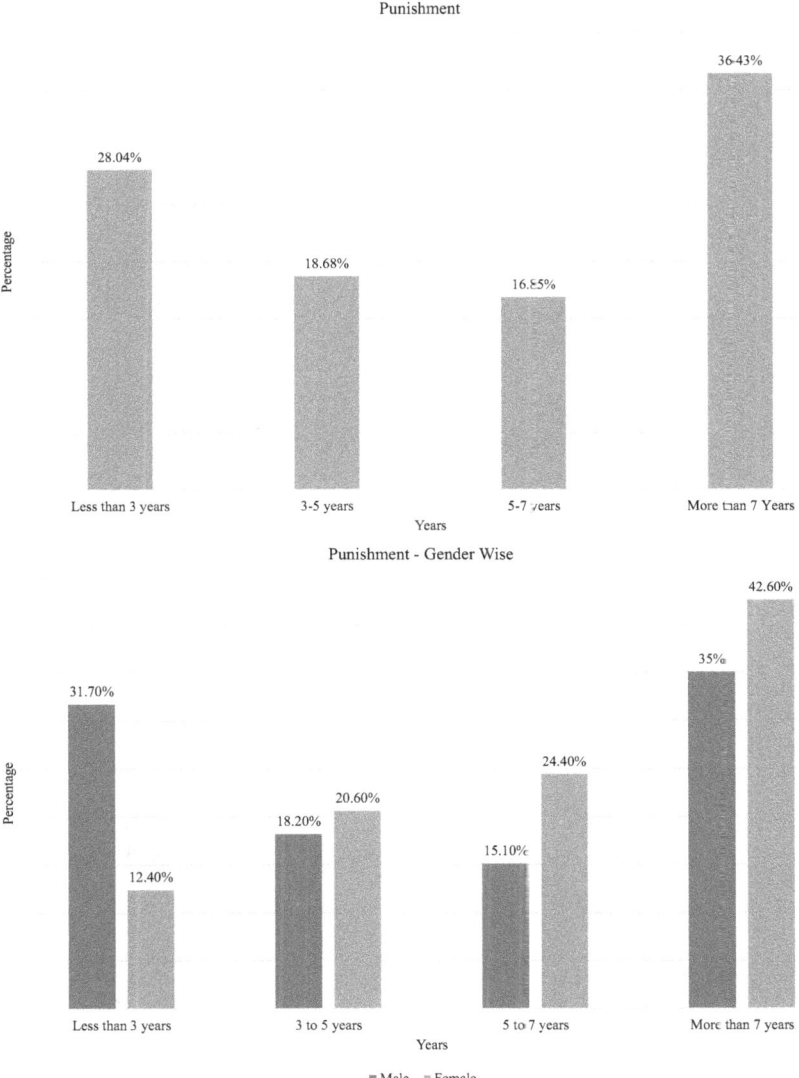

FIGURE 6.17 Punishment

Those who did not have advocates approached Prayas for legal assistance. Around 2560 applications were submitted to DLSAs on behalf of undertrials asking for panel advocates, out of which nearly 1866 panel advocates were appointed which is approximately 72.89 per cent. Out of which, 6.80 per cent were appointed during the post-pandemic COVID period from April 2020 to October 2021.

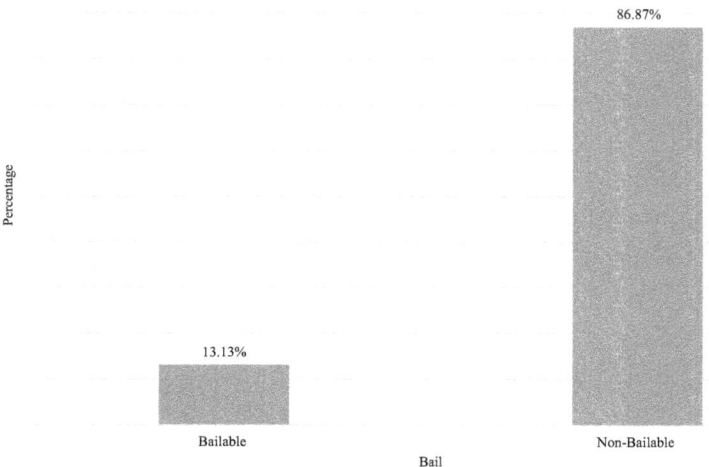
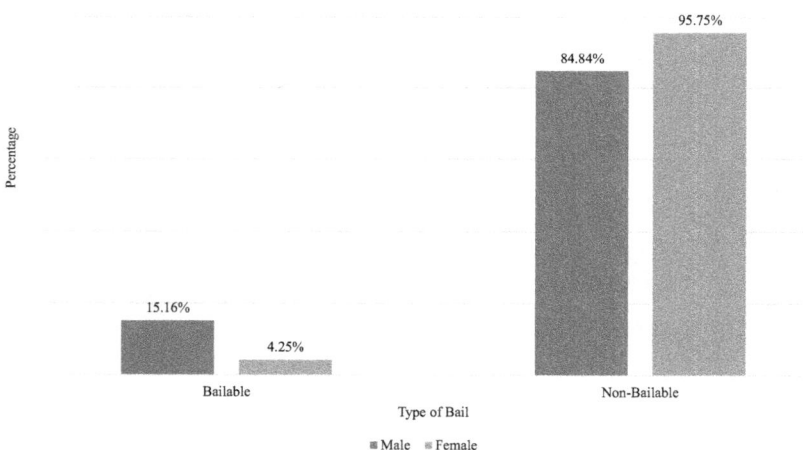

FIGURE 6.18 Case categorization bail

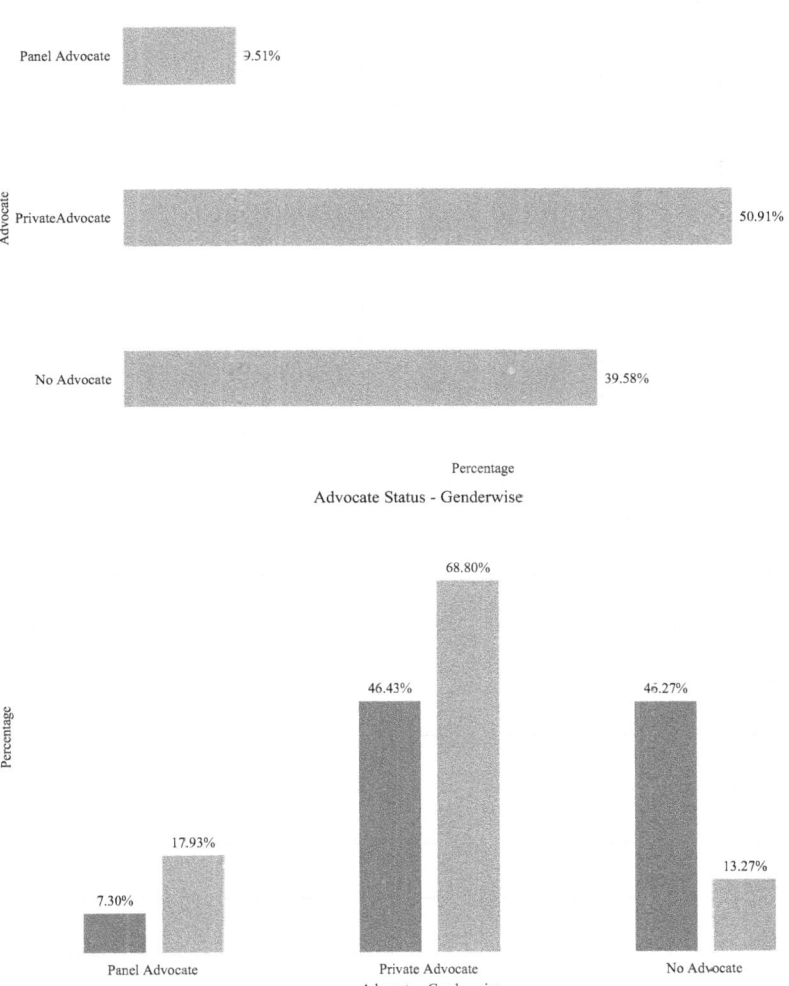

FIGURE 6.19 Advocate status at case intake

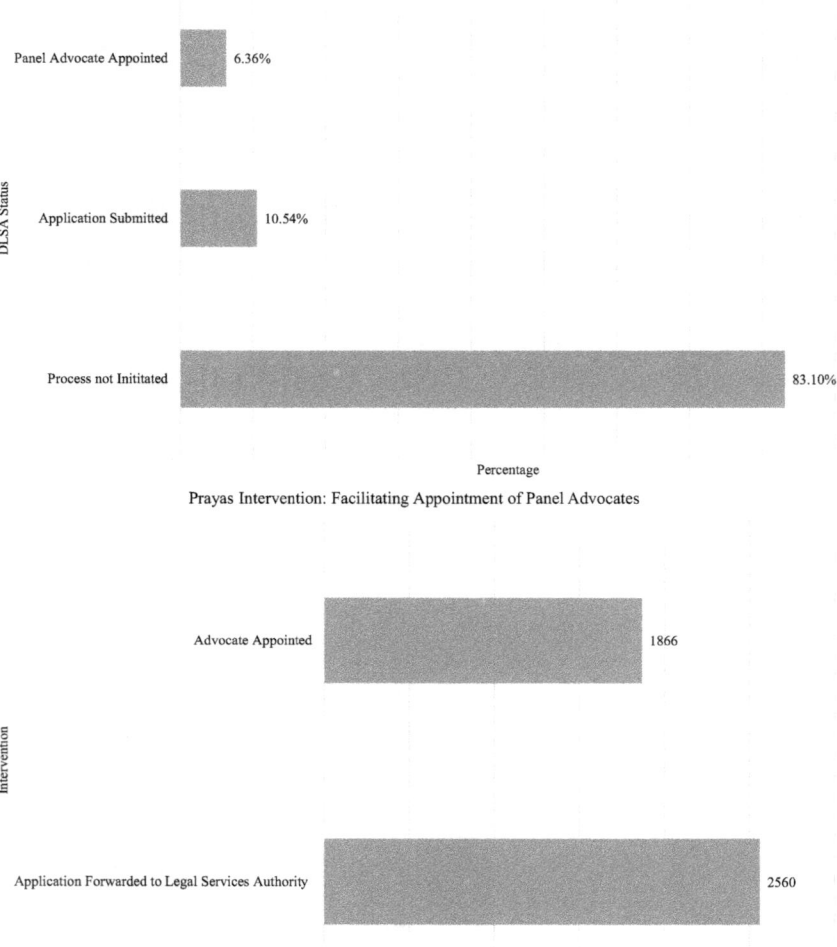

FIGURE 6.20 DSLA status at Prayas intervention

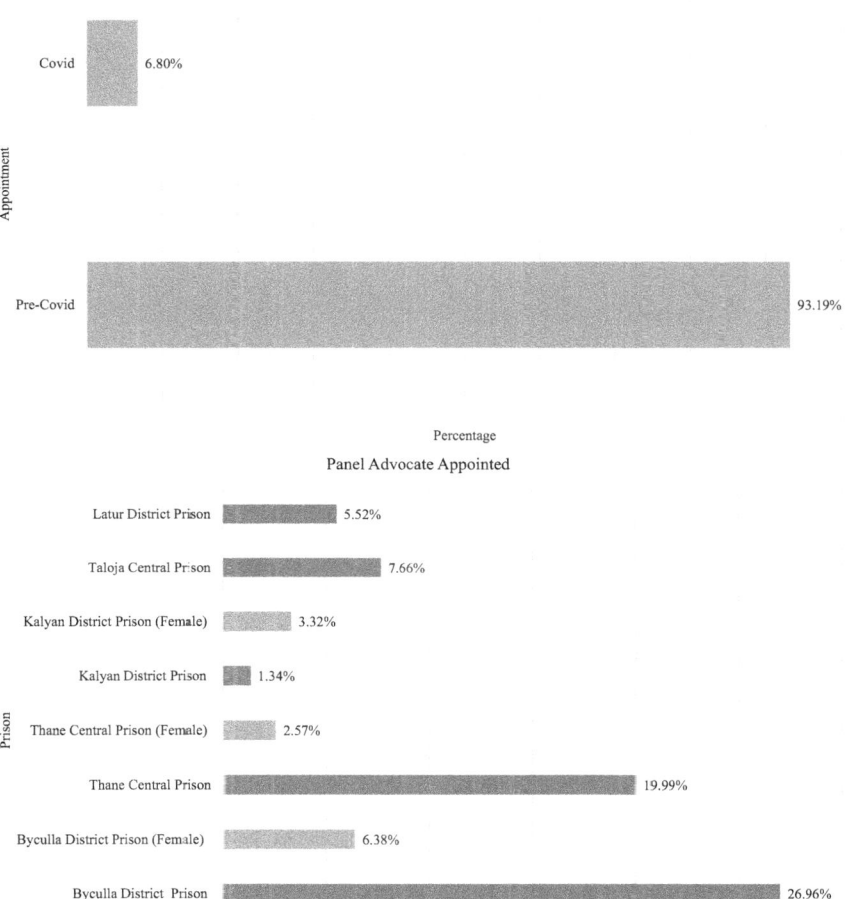

FIGURE 6.21 Panel advocates

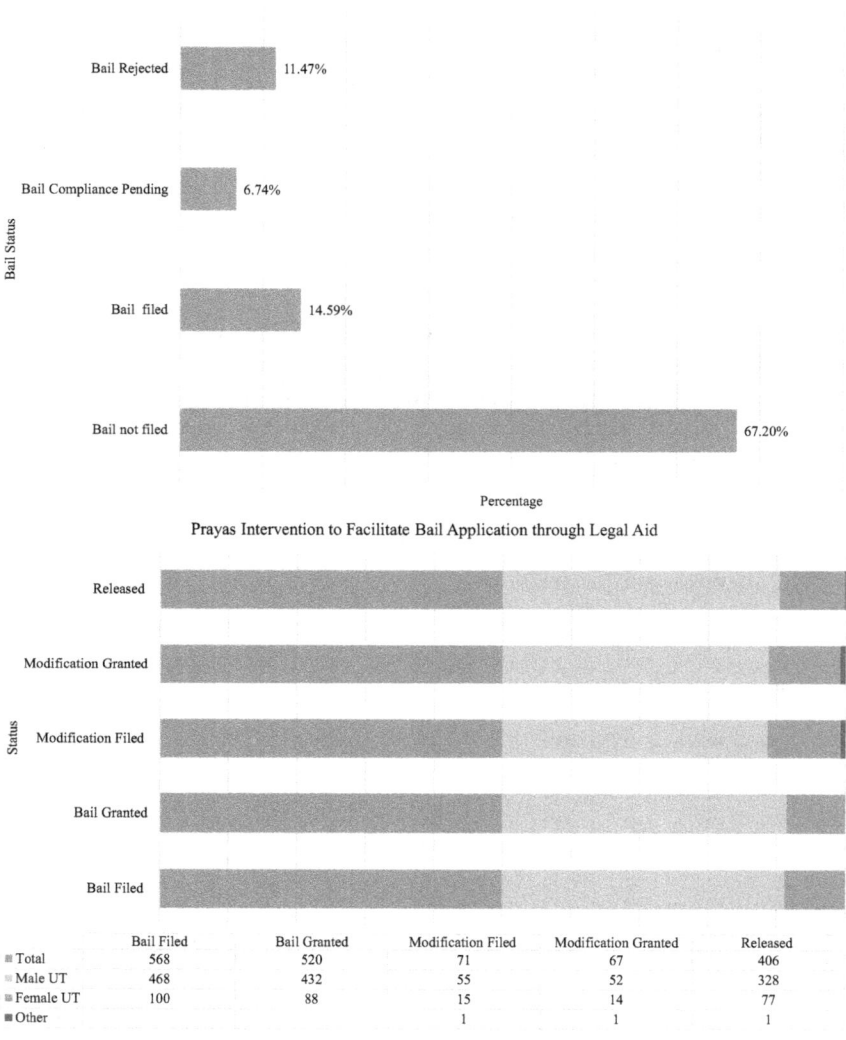

FIGURE 6.22 Bail status at intake and Prayas intervention to facilitate bail application through legal aid

87.67 per cent of panel advocates were appointed for male undertrials, 12.27 per cent for females and 0.5 per cent for the third gender.

3.6 Bail Status at Case Intake and Prayas Interventions to Facilitate Bail and Release through Legal Aid

Although panel advocates were appointed in 9 per cent and private advocates in 51 per cent of cases, bail was not filed in more than 65 per cent of the cases, which shows advocates were inactive. Bail orders were sought in 6.74 per cent of cases, however, bail compliance was pending. It indicates undertrials' inability to comply with bail conditions, hence were still in prison. Many undertrials arrested for petty offences (like Sec.379 IPC – theft) end up pleading guilty in such circumstances. Thus, at the beginning of the chapter, we discussed the efforts taken in the case of two young undertrial prisoners to meet the bail compliance conditions, to avoid undertrials falling prey to plead guilty.

Prayas worked in coordination with the panel advocates and facilitated 568 bail applications, out of which 92 per cent (520) of the bail applications were granted. 13.65 per cent (72) of the granted bail applications (520) were applied for modification (reduction of bail, converting surety bail to cash bail or release on personal bond, etc.), out of which 94.37 per cent (67) were granted; and a total of 406 undertrials were released on bail and modification orders. The highest number of bails were granted in theft 25.58 per cent.

Prayas facilitated a release of 4128 undertrials (76.2 per cent males, 23.6 per cent females, and 6 undertrials belonged to the third gender) which is nearly 60 per cent of the undertrials reached.

406 (10 per cent) were released through panel advocates. Apart from working with panel advocates, Prayas facilitated release through private advocates resulting in the release of 740 undertrials. Bail compliance (other than cases where bail was filed by Prayas) was done in 1,827 undertrials and 344 undertrials were released through Personal Recognisance (PR) Bond[15] (including HPC releases),[16] especially in some of the cases, there was no appointment of advocates and the undertrials were in prison for 7 days, homeless undertrials without documents belonging to Pardhi community (a nomadic tribe) and for those languishing in prison as they were not able to furnish surety or cash bail. Apart from bail releases, the released category includes acquittal, plead guilty, and others.[17]

---

15 PR bond is granted by the Judge. The person need not pay any bail amount, and has to attend court dates and not tamper with evidence.
16 High Powered Committee set up by the Supreme Court to reduce overcrowding of prisons to prevent the spread of Corona Virus.
17 Case Compounded / Withdrawn by Complainant, Convicted and Transferred to Juvenile Justice Board (child in conflict with law).

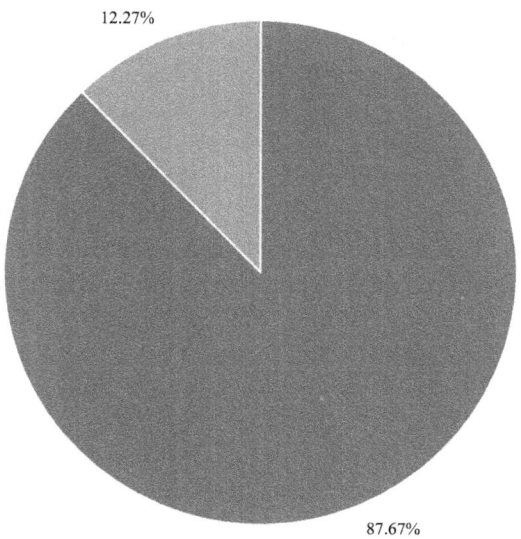

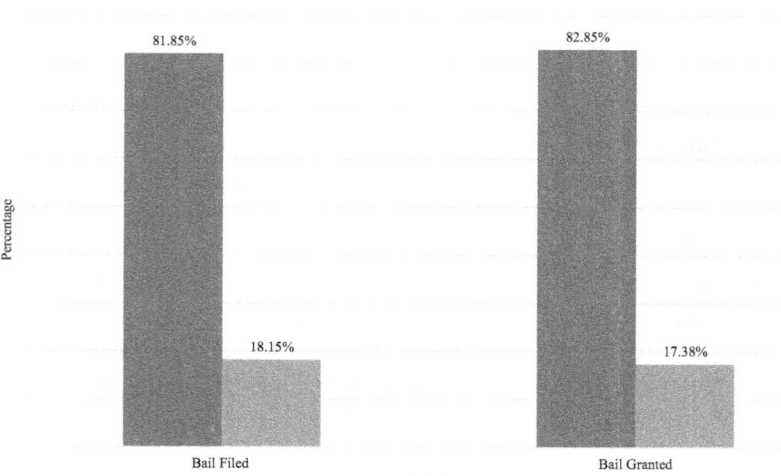

Released through Panel Advocate

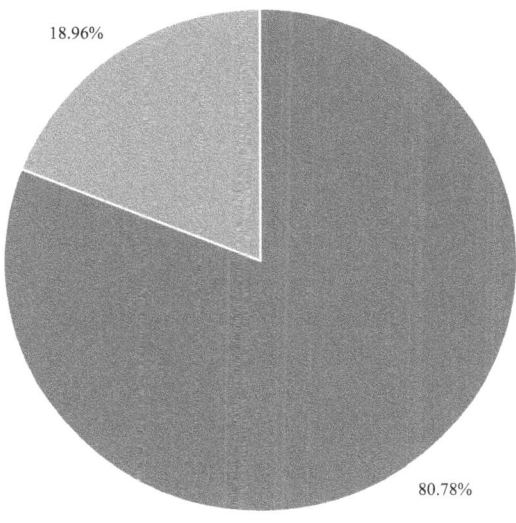

FIGURE 6.23 Panel advocate, bail and release through legal aid

4   Innovative Partnership of Social Worker and Lawyer in Facilitating the Release

4.1   *Contact with Family*

Around 56.5 per cent of the undertrials were not in touch with their family. The lack of communication with the family members acts as a major hurdle in accessing legal aid, arranging surety, and furnishing cash bail support. There is always an ambiguity if the family has already appointed an advocate in the case, also the undertrial is unaware of the case's progress. In cases of pending bail compliance, the undertrial is thus, unable to arrange any documents or fulfil bail conditions.

The appointment of trained social workers is important for the social integration of the prisoners and for providing socio-legal counselling services (Krishna Iyer Committee Report) (Raghavan 2013). The socio-legal approach highlights *weaving the social with the legal*. While practising a socio-legal approach, it is important to understand the socio-political realities and interventions that legally protect the rights of the marginalised and vulnerable sections (Dave, Raghavan & Solanki 2012).

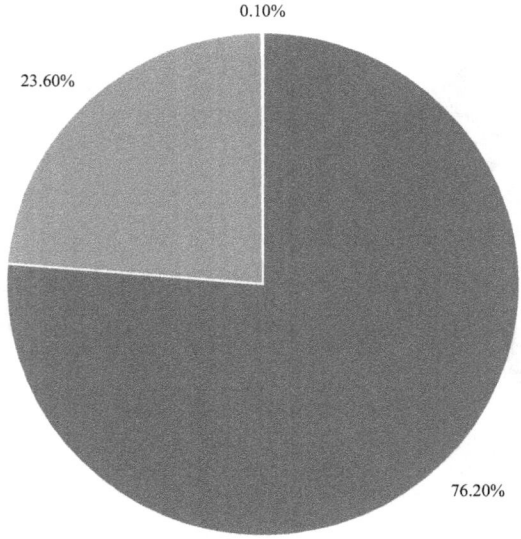
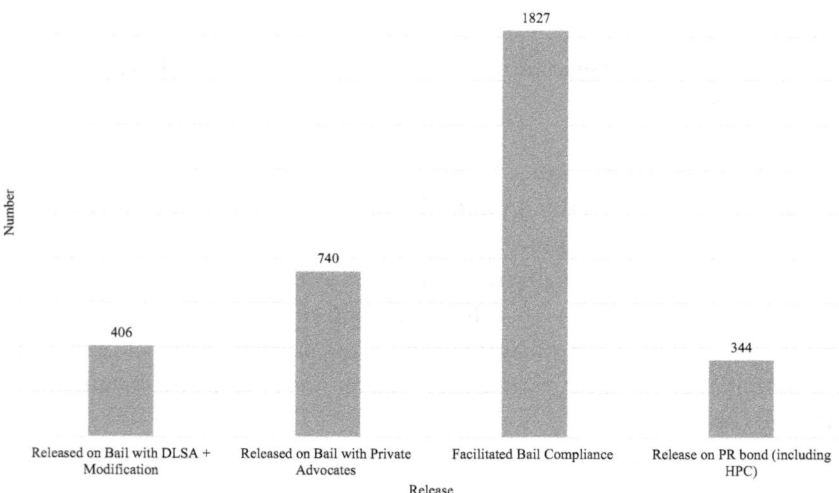

FIGURE 6.24 Release

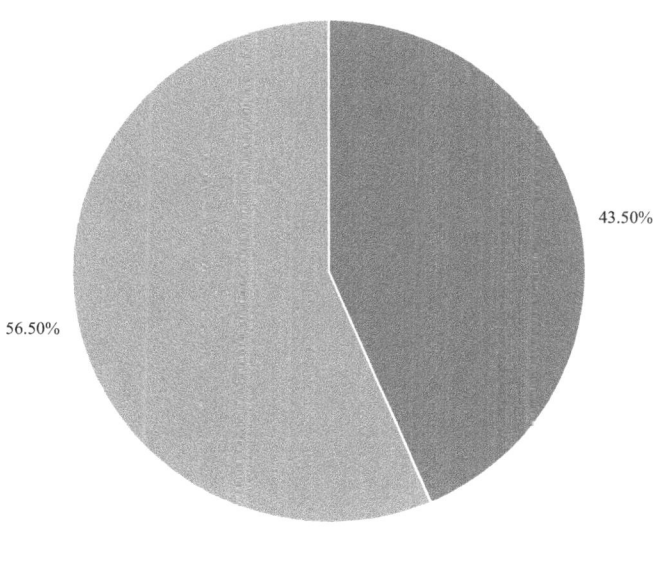

FIGURE 6.25 Contact with family

The importance of providing quality services to the incarcerated population is recognised by NASW's *Social Work Speaks* (2012) in its policy statement related to social work in the criminal justice system. Given the rise in the imprisoned population, there is a desperate need for social-work services in all areas of criminal justice practice (Matejkowski, Johnson & Severson, 2014).

The role of social worker and lawyer complete one another and are fluid However, if one has to look at the roles in facilitating bail compliance within and outside the ambit of court and social settings, then legal fellows have a slightly larger role in coordinating with advocates (legal aspect) and social workers with families and NGOs. It is this innovative partnership and sociolegal skills that work towards a successful outcome of the release of undertrials on bail. Legal fellows followed up with the advocates in 34 per cent of cases wherein bail compliance was pending. Fellows have regularly maintained a follow-up in 29 per cent with private advocates to facilitate bail compliance.

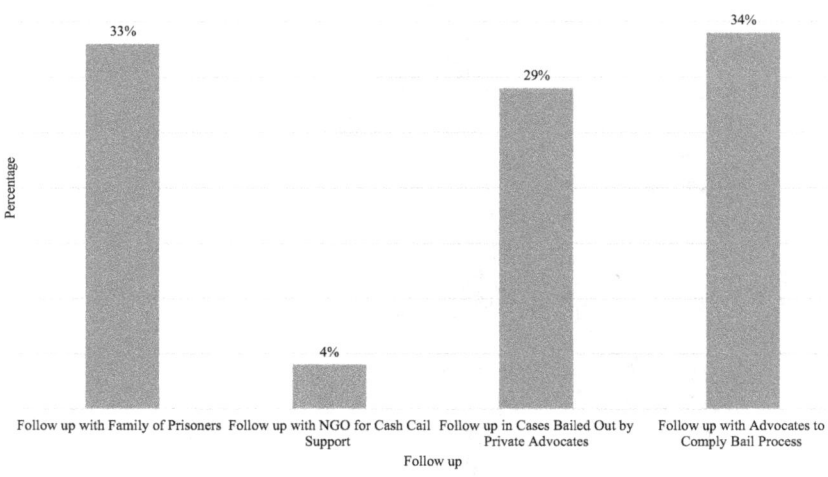

FIGURE 6.26 Facilitated bail compliance

4.2 Facilitated Bail Compliance: Home Visits, Phone Calls, and Visits to Offices

Rehabilitation entails building a proactive relationship with the undertrial, strengthening the relationship between the undertrial and the family and ensuring the family is in a position to provide shelter and basic subsistence to the released undertrial (Raghavan & Menezes 2017).

Social workers largely played a role in facilitating bail compliance by following up with the family of prisoners conducting home visits, phone calls, meeting NGOs for cash bail support, visiting the workplace and other visits as required etc. Overall, 62 per cent of the total release was released by facilitating bail compliance. Nearly 33 per cent were released through follow-up with the family of prisoners and around 4 per cent of the release account to cash bail support provided by NGOs.

4.2.1 Home Visits

Home visit is one of the key interventions, as it plays an important role in relationship building with undertrials in prison. Many times, the family is not aware of the whereabouts of the undertrial. The role of a social worker is crucial in facilitating the support required by the undertrial and bridging a gap by communicating their needs (*material, emotional or otherwise*) either through letters, phone calls or home visits as mentioned in the Handbook Series by

Prayas, 2012. Home visits helped the undertrials to get the basic requirements from the family, to understand the socio-economic background (marginalised and homeless population), get the undertrials documents to furnish bail and understand the case background (additional details related to the case), to verify the information provided by the undertrial; understand the relationship with the family members, any addiction history of the undertrial as well. Home visits helped to inform the family members about the undertrial and encourage them to come for *mulakat* (meeting). In one case, it helped trace the daughter of an undertrial which had a positive impact on his behaviour inside the prison.

4.2.2 Phone Calls

The largest number of migrant undertrials were from Uttar Pradesh, West Bengal, Bihar and Karnataka. It became challenging to conduct home visits. Hence, phone calls were made. Through phone calls and home visits, it was observed that the family's acceptance had increased towards the undertrials, and their family members started coming for *mulakat*s. This facilitation helped in providing the undertrials with regular updates about their families, which in turn helped in overcoming their stress. Apart from phone calls to family, phone calls were made to advocates and police stations to facilitate the bail compliance process. Phone calls helped Prayas to act as a channel between the undertrial and the family and between the undertrial and advocates.

4.2.3 Police Station Visits

At the time of the arrest, the original documents of the undertrials (personal identification like pan card, and Aadhar card) and belonging (mobile phones) are kept in police custody. Multiple visits are made to police stations (sometimes for a single case) to procure those documents to furnish bail. Also, to request the Investigating Officer to file his say in the matter, as the delay affects the bail process. Police station visits also help to acquire the chargesheets, seek information regarding the C.R. Nos. of the undertrials and undertrials' home addresses, especially in those cases wherein details are not available, and in some cases, to resolve problems faced by the released undertrials and their families.

4.2.4 Visits to Work Site

Based on the request of the undertrial, work site visits are done to seek information about the undertrials (especially in those cases of migrant undertrial and also when the home address was not available). Such visits helped to procure documents and trace the address of the family.

4.2.5 Visits to Offices (Civic Bodies)

If houses were not traced, the visit helped to get the proper address of the undertrials. In some cases, the local corporator issued a document certifying that a particular undertrial resides in the area. The document was submitted as a valid identity document proof which helped to furnish bail. Similarly, a visit was also made to the Aadhar Center to get the Aadhar Card status of the undertrials family, which was also helpful in furnishing bail.

5 Double Marginalization of Women Undertrials and Children of Prisoners

Although 34 per cent of women prisoners were in touch with family and had high legal representation, it also indicated a lack of support to produce identity documents and fulfil bail compliance conditions. Parental and marital families do not provide them support rendering them 'socially isolated'. In such cases, the social workers have to put almost double the effort to meet and convince both marital and natal families to bridge the gap and facilitate the conditions required for bail. Of all the women in prison (4 per cent of the total prison population), more than 1,400 women undertrial prisoners were accompanied by 1,600 one or more children below the age of 6 (PSI, 2021). Women prisoners have to take responsibility for their children (both inside prison up to the age of six and outside placed under the care and supervision of family and institutional care). Children living with imprisoned mothers do not get a conducive age-appropriate environment for growth. *Although Supreme Court guidelines (issued in the PIL R.D. Upadhyaya Vs. State of Andhra Pradesh and Others) clearly mention the provision of crèche and nursery facilities outside prison premises to ensure their "proper biological, psychological, and social growth"*

Most important, they are distanced from their children living outside. They do not have any information about their children, which causes mental stress and agony. Prayas' study found that the children living outside live in an unhealthy environment, inadequate in terms of food, housing, care, health, and schooling. They are forced to take care of younger siblings. Unsupervised children are separated from siblings and Institutionalized. Imprisoned mother first contacts the social worker to assess the whereabouts and well-being of her children (Raghavan, 2020). In one case, the mother went to the police station and she was arrested for enquiry. The baby was left unattended till the neighbor telephoned her husband. Women from other states are unable to communicate with their families as the home address is not complete or too far away, hence untraceable. In such situations, *mulakats* (meetings) with the family and children become a challenge (Tata Trust and Prayas, 2017). Social isolation (especially distancing from children) impacts the mental health of the women prisoners, which often leads to internal fights amongst inmates. Sometimes due to the language barrier, the women are unable to express their thoughts and are compelled to keep to themselves, which makes them more anxious.

Lack of communication regarding their legal case adds to their emotional breakdowns, which hinders their rehabilitation. Low emotional support and limited access to education (38 per cent non-literate) and employment opportunities (20 per cent were employed in domestic work and 35 per cent were homemakers) add to their existing vulnerability. Post-release, often vulnerable women prisoners are compelled into re-offending or trafficking to meet the basic needs of the house and children (Prayas, 2023). Data too confirms that the highest number of females were charged with trafficking and ITPA (Figure 6.16: Gender wise Categorization of Cases).

5.1 Case Study (Prayas, 2023): Female Prisoner with No Support System Languished in Prison from 2017 until Bailed Out in 2021[18]

Rani (name changed), aged 55 years old, was in Thane Central Prison for four years, before she got bail in 2021. Before the arrest, she used to work as an agricultural labourer in her village in Akola district, Maharashtra. The whereabouts of her husband are not known. Apart from her husband, there are no details available of her family, as, throughout the four years in prison, she didn't get any help from her family or her husband.

Prayas attempted to trace Rani's husband based on the address provided by her. As the village was in the interiors, the social worker wrote a letter at the address, but the letter came back as there was no one there to receive it. Next the social worker connected telephonically with the local police station to connect with Rani's husband, but there was no breakthrough. With no social support, Rani was mentally traumatized. Whenever the family of other inmates would come to meet them, she would feel lonely, become emotional and often break down during counselling sessions. She would often question the length of her stay in prison. The social worker found it extremely difficult to handle such emotional situations, as there was no answer to the social worker (her family was non-traceable).

In Rani's case, there were four other accused, who were already bailed out. So, often her court dates would be taken after 3–4 months, as the other

---

18 I have drafted the case based on my interaction with Prayas social worker Priyanka Kamble.

co-accused had to travel from interior villages. Before 2018, during one of her court hearings, Rani requested the judge to appoint an advocate in her case. Based upon her request, the judge had appointed an advocate to file bail for her, but the bail got rejected by the Sessions court. Also, the advocate was not very supportive. The social worker also faced a coordination challenge in this regard. Hence, Prayas facilitated her bail in the Session court through another advocate. However, the second bail was also rejected. Due to a lack of personal identification documents, her bail used to get rejected.

The social worker regularly communicated with Rani regarding the interventions done in her case. This brought, Rani mental relief as she was aware of the next steps to be taken in her case. Prayas then approached a High Court advocate. The social worker collected the charge sheet, rejected bail papers from the Session's court and approached the High Court advocate. The advocate knew about the socio-legal services provided by Prayas and was helpful in the matter. Once the advocate got to know her vulnerable background of Rani, he did not charge any honorarium fee and filed the bail free of cost. After one and half months, bail was passed with a condition to arrange two sureties of 15,000 thousand each. As she did not have any social support system, she could not arrange surety, and hence languished in prison for two more years and COVID too delayed her stay further.

In the meanwhile, an ex-inmate of the prison who was with Rani inside the prison (she was released two years back) contacted the social worker. The ex-inmate arranged for an advocate. Due to the pandemic, the social worker could not physically meet the advocate, hence emailed all the documents to the advocate who then filed for modification of bail, and hence the surety amount was reduced. The ex-inmate took Rani's surety of 15,000, and thus, she was released from prison. In her case, follow-ups were difficult, too, since there were no family members to interact with or to gain information to carry on the case process smoothly. With perseverance and constant follow-ups, the social worker facilitated her release from prison. Presently, Rani is working as a domestic help and earns her living.

5.2   Case Study (Prayas, 2023)

Another case depicted below is a success story based on a partnership between a lawyer and a social worker. While the female prisoner was in prison since 2014, the Legal fellow helped in the appointment of a panel advocate and followed up on the case regularly to finally lead to her acquittal in the case – leading to her mother uniting with her children post-8 years before she was released. While she was in prison, the social worker provided support to her two children and admitted them to the shelter home. Post her release, the social worker arranged a physical *mulakat* between her and her children.

5.2.1 Lessons on Partnership between Lawyer and Social Worker: *Mulakat* between Released Women Prisoner and Children[19]

Sushma (name changed), aged 30 years, a single parent (widow), is originally from Kolkata. She had two sons, staying in a shelter home in Mumbai. She was arrested in 2014 and since then was imprisoned in Kalyan District Prison, until her acquittal in August 2021. Her elder son was studying in class 9th, and her younger son was in class 3rd.

As her legal case was not progressing, she would often get frustrated and inflict her anger on her younger child. So, keeping in mind the child's best interests, he was moved to a shelter home. The social worker facilitated a *mulakat* between the mother and children once in a couple of months (pre-lockdown). Post-lockdown, physical *mulakat*s were suspended; they would converse through phone and video-calling. The children longed to meet their mother in person. Meanwhile, Prayas Legal Fellows helped in the appointment of a panel advocate and followed up on the case regularly to finally lead to her acquittal in case – 8 long years before she was released.

Post Sushma's release from prison, the social worker admitted her to a shelter home as she had no place to go. The children were very happy to hear the news and were keen to meet her. So, the social worker accompanied Sushma (mother) to meet her two children in their shelter home. At the shelter home, both the children and mother got extremely emotional about physically meeting each other. The children then insisted to stay with their mother for at least 2 days. As this request was sudden, the social worker telephoned a Child Welfare Committee (CWC) member, who was empathetic to the needs of the children and passed an oral order allowing the children to stay with the mother for 4 days. This physical *mulakat* between mother and children was possible as both social workers and legal fellows worked in tandem to ensure progress both in terms of the legal case and social rehabilitation. Legal fellows worked in close coordination with panel advocates and social workers closely worked with the CWC, the prison authorities, and the shelter home.

---

19   I have drafted the case based on my interaction with Prayas social worker Reena Jaiswar and Legal fellows Maitrayee Gadhave and Saugata Hazra.

6 Recidivism – Limited Access to Programs and Lack of Opportunities for Socio-economic Rehabilitation of Undertrials

Undertrials, while they spend time in prison, they do not have access to work, rehabilitation programs, education, or training. Model Prison Manual 2016 provides paid work[20] and vocational training only to volunteering undertrials subject to the availability of potential work and vocational ability. Extramural work is not allowed for undertrial prisoners. The time spent in prison is not productively utilised. The poor infrastructure inside prisons with no resource mobilization adds to mental turmoil. The duration an undertrial spends inside prison affects his health both physically and mentally; they lose out on employment outside and have a high chance of losing on rental accommodation as well (Herald & Fair, 2012). The extended duration indirectly impacts the family, and associated households, living outside both socially and economically (Muntingh & Redpath, 2012). The prison population is highly stigmatised and hence needs coping skills while they re-enter society. The lack of socio-economic rehabilitation and employability potential within the prison pushes the undertrial post-release back into the world of crime as well as indicating high chances of re-offending.

6.1 Good Practice New Initiative

Prayas facilitated a wall painting programme in Thane Central Prison:[21] 141 prisoners enrolled and 90 prisoners completed the wall painting training programme. Out of 90 prisoners, 29 are released from prison, out of which *10 released undertrial prisoners secured a job* as a painter (Prayas Newsletter, 2022). If more such programs are initiated for undertrials, it will help them stand on their feet, once they are back in society. It demonstrates a good example of skill building in prison, facilitating smooth reintegration into society.

7 Aftercare and Rehabilitation Model

Released prisoners face issues related to livelihood and survival challenges, inability to pay the rent, and possible loss of shelter, leading to anxiety, stress, fear, hopelessness, and associated psychological conditions.

---

20 Suitable wages paid as prescribed by State government.
21 Programme is initiated for a year (March 2022-April 2023) in collaboration with Akzonobel India Ltd and implemented by Global Hunt foundation.

Post-release aftercare services are essential firstly to provide emergency support related to food, travel, shelter, accommodation etc, to help the released prisoner cope mentally with trauma and stigma; facilitate reconnecting ties with family and society; facilitate the development of employable and entrepreneurship skills, provide educational and vocational training needs. These skills are important to avoid recidivism.

Prayas services are focused not only on the needs of affected persons but also their families (especially children). Social workers make provisions for safe shelter for the children and admit them into institutions and re-admit the children into schools, thus ensuring their education continues. It has designed a social re-integration programme called the NGO Placement Programme, wherein affected persons are placed in NGOs across the country, to develop employable skills in the NGO sector. It provides them access to banking facilities and citizenship documents, alternative shelter, pro-social relationships, and reconnecting family ties. As they are often treated like non-citizens without any documents and do not have access to welfare schemes or employment in the formal sector (Raghavan, 2020). While they are placed in a placement programme, they receive a stipend and are mentored into entrepreneurship activities. With a sustained source of income, the affected person achieves psychological stability for a sustained period as they do not have to struggle for basic sustenance and will stabilize relationships with their families. Thus, they can concentrate on rebuilding their lives (Dave, Raghavan & Solanki 2021). Prayas Interventions were focused on keeping in mind the need and well-being of the released undertrials (Table 6.5)

7.1 *Psycho-social Support*

Counselling helps the undertrial feel mentally relaxed. Initially, they used to be very disturbed, but after psycho-social counselling, they feel relaxed and hopeful. Through counselling, undertrials were informed about their family conditions and spoke openly about the incidents that took place, their past history, peer group and so on. Hence, the Fellows were able to understand them properly and design an aftercare plan.

7.2 *Aftercare Support*

Post-release rehabilitation work focused on referring inmates to government and private institutional care to refer undertrial and their children for shelter support, education support, and government hospitals for medical treatment. Also, meeting the bank officials regarding the money transferred to the bank accounts of undertrials.

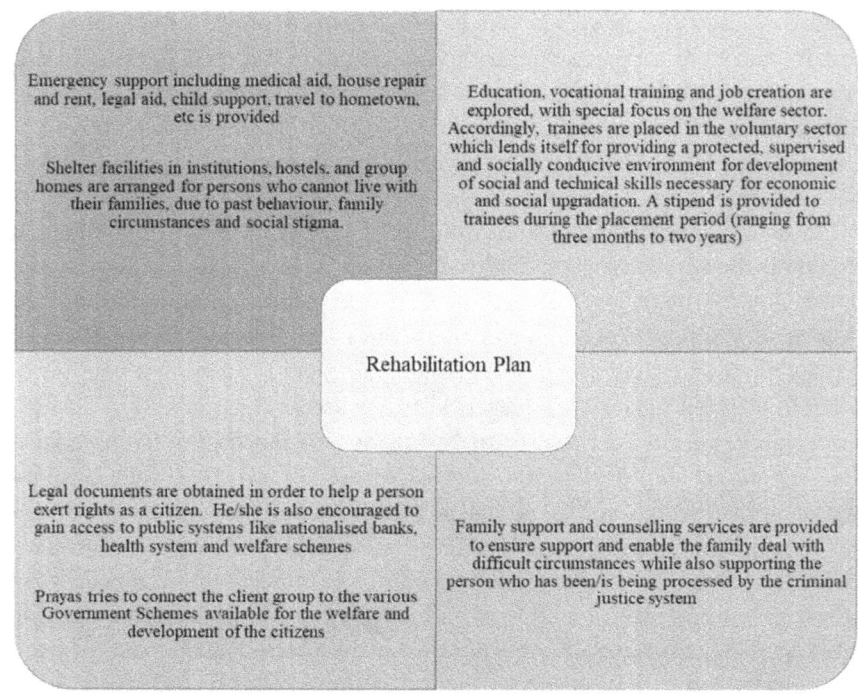

FIGURE 6.27 Rehabilitation plan
SOURCE: PRAYAS WEBSITE-HTTP://WWW.TISS.EDU/VIEW/11/PROJE
CTS/PRAYAS

276 cases were referred for rehabilitation and repatriation. In terms of support to the family, 22 schools/ colleges were visited, providing education support to 18. Emergency support was provided to more than 400 and shelter support to more than 50. To provide shelter support, more than 100 government homes/ institutions and NGOs were visited. In post-release cases, follow-ups were done in more than 350 cases.

7.3   *Case Study (Prayas Newsletter, 2021)*
a)   A woman prisoner with mental health issues was arrested in a kidnapping case. She was provided support in bail. She did not have any family support. Post her release, the social worker admitted her to a shelter home, wherein her mental health deteriorated due to the lack of treatment. She was shifted to Thane Mental Hospital for treatment. In the meanwhile, the social worker traced her house and found that her house was locked by the police. She met the police, got her house unlocked and

TABLE 6.5   Interventions for release, rehabilitation and livelihood support

Intervention for release and post-release	Number of visits
Home visit	1068
Number of phone calls to family/advocates/police stations	18147
Counselling – psycho-social support	5909
Visits to police stations	367
Visits to government homes/institutions	119
Schools/colleges	22
Visits to workplace	127
Visits to meet local corporator	7
Visits to NGOs	315
Intervention for rehabilitation and livelihood support	Undertrials supported
Follow up post-release	370
Shelter support	53
Education support	18
Emergency support	436
Cases referred for rehabilitation and repatriation	276
Vocational training (online programs)	18
Enrolled for online programs for computer, tailoring and literacy programs	04
Jute folders	08
Mask making and Shabnam bags	11
Empowering through self-help groups	4 groups

took her to her house. Prayas continues to stay in touch with her (Prayas Newsletter, 2021).

b) In the case of the woman prisoner from Jharkhand, the Prayas social worker arranged shelter support for her, post the woman's interim bail in November 2020, and facilitated her employment as a cook in the shelter home under the Prayas NGO placement program. She was also enrolled in a nursing course through the Pratham organization. The team also facilitated a home visit in her hometown in Jharkhand and provided ration support to her family (Prayas Newsletter, 2021).

7.4 Rehabilitation Support during the Pandemic (*Prayas Newsletter 2020*)

Despite constitutional safeguards and policies, and programmes, these vulnerable groups do not have access to their rights and entitlements. The absence of social support like the aid of civil society or social work intervention, entraps them further into criminalization (Prayas 2019). This was demonstrated during the pandemic, as in the absence of social support, these groups would have been highly vulnerable to being pushed into exploitative circumstances. However, the social workers were on the front line, finding innovative ways of reaching out to released prisoners and their families and providing them with alternate livelihoods and a source of income to meet basic sustenance.

7.4.1 Building Entrepreneurs' Skills and Employment Opportunities for Released Prisoners and Families at Their Doorsteps

During the lockdown, many released prisoners' families were rendered unemployed and struggled to meet basic needs. Prayas provided financial assistance in the form of cash transfers. The monetary support helped the female released prisoners to begin new small ventures like selling eggs, fish, vegetables, making masks, etc. It paved a new way to become self-sufficient economically.

7.4.1.1 Case Study: The Case Highlights the Initiative Shown by a Woman in the Face of Adversity-COVID-19[22]

Salma (name changed), is 28 years old and lives with her 3-year-old daughter at her maternal home. She had started a small-scale business of selling eggs, from the cash transfer made by Prayas of INR. 2000/- (as financial assistance during the lockdown period). Initially, she planned to sell vegetables, but due to the lockdown, she postponed the idea. However, one day, she called up Prayas's social worker, and shared that her neighbours need onions and potatoes; hence she wanted to explore the idea of selling these. To start the business, her brother planned to help her buy onions and potatoes, but due to police *bandobast*, he could not move out of the locality.

She thought since vegetables are expensive in her area, her neighbours would not buy from her. After much brainstorming, she came up with the idea of selling eggs. She approached a wholesale dealer selling eggs and initially bought 3 trays of eggs (1 tray has 30 eggs) daily. On days when the vehicle did not come, she would walk half to an hour to his shop to buy eggs from him.

---

22   I have drafted the case based on my interaction with Prayas social worker Priyanka Kamble.

She first started selling eggs in her building and then moved to selling in the market between 12.00 noon to 4.00 pm. As her sale increased, she started buying 5 trays per day (which means 150 eggs). Eventually, she sold all the eggs that she purchased and made a profit of around INR. 150 per day. She planned to sell eggs in special markets on Wednesdays, Fridays, and Sundays. She also told Prayas that post the lockdown, she would expand her business plan to sell vegetables, onions, and potatoes. She is happy that she is able to make a profit with her hard work.

7.4.2   Vocational Training (Prayas Newsletter, 2020, 2021 2022)

14 females and 4 males released prisoners were supported with vocational training, and online motivational sessions on mental health and hygiene to be maintained at home specially to prevent the coronavirus. Online training taught embroidery, bag making, laptop bags, fruit baskets, spectacle covers, etc. and enrolled some into online programs i.e. (computer, tailoring and literacy programs)

7.4.3   Income Generation – Involving Released Prisoners and Families: Mask Making and Jute Folders

Prayas Income Generation Unit upgraded its production capacity during the lockdown. Prayas trained the released prisoners through online mediums and sent the required raw material to them via courier, including sanitizers and notes explaining the precautionary measures to be adopted while opening and packing the courier boxes to maintain hygiene given the COVID-19 pandemic situation.

The group was chosen based on their tailoring skills. As the group was not exposed to a smartphone or online training, the social worker supervised them minutely and helped to accustom them to the online mode of training. Their vulnerability deprived them of smartphones or the internet, in such circumstances, home visits were conducted in the interior districts of Thane, Palgar, and Raigad districts (Maharashtra) to provide them with raw materials, demonstrate product training with sample creation and to assess their skills.

A source of livelihood was provided to 14 female released prisoners and 5 male released prisoners across Mumbai and Thane districts on a piece-rate basis. The group prepared more than 30,000 masks,[23] 1000 *Shabnam*

---

23   It includes donations worth INR 1 lakh from Srujana Charitable Trust, wherein women have produced 8000 masks which have been distributed to prisoners of Mumbai Central, Byculla, Thane, Kalyan, Latur and Solapur.

bags,[24] and 4,000 jute folders for the inmates, prison staff and shelter homes in Mumbai and Thane districts. Through these activities, the released prisoners have been able to earn a dignified wage for themselves. The social workers also visited their homes to supervise the final finished product, and the quality of the products and collect the completed orders. This was the first time that Prayas delivered large-scale orders. It exposed the group as well as Prayas to learn about business, generating local employment on a piece-rate basis, and purchasing large-scale raw materials. It built the confidence of released prisoners and prepared them to take up large-scale orders.

7.4.4 Empowering Women through the Formation of Four Women Self-Help Groups

With the help of Mahila Arthik Vikas Mahamandal (MAVIM), Prayas has been able to form 4 women's Self-Help Group (SHG) of women from similar social-economic backgrounds who save small sums of money at regular intervals. They can take a loan from the group's savings with a nominal interest rate.

7.4.5 Lending a Helping Hand

Released Male prisoners provided help and support to the needy by providing a vehicle to distribute rations, eatables to stranded migrants and health support in the midst of the pandemic.

8 Learnings from the Project

- Prayas's work has shown that in the absence of support, poor undertrials with marginalised backgrounds could get further criminalized. More than 40 per cent belonged to the age group of 21–30, 70 per cent studied up to Class 9, 16 per cent were unemployed and 28 per cent with no source of income.
- Prayas, by its constant presence in the system with its experience and training, was able to create a positive impact in terms of bridging the interests of various stakeholders of undertrial prisoners such as the family and friends, prison authorities and legal aid institutions.
- With constant follow-ups, Prayas facilitated reduced time for the appointment of panel advocates from one to two months to a week (or less than a

---

24 Shabnam bags are traditional cotton bags with single long shoulder belt used by both men and women.

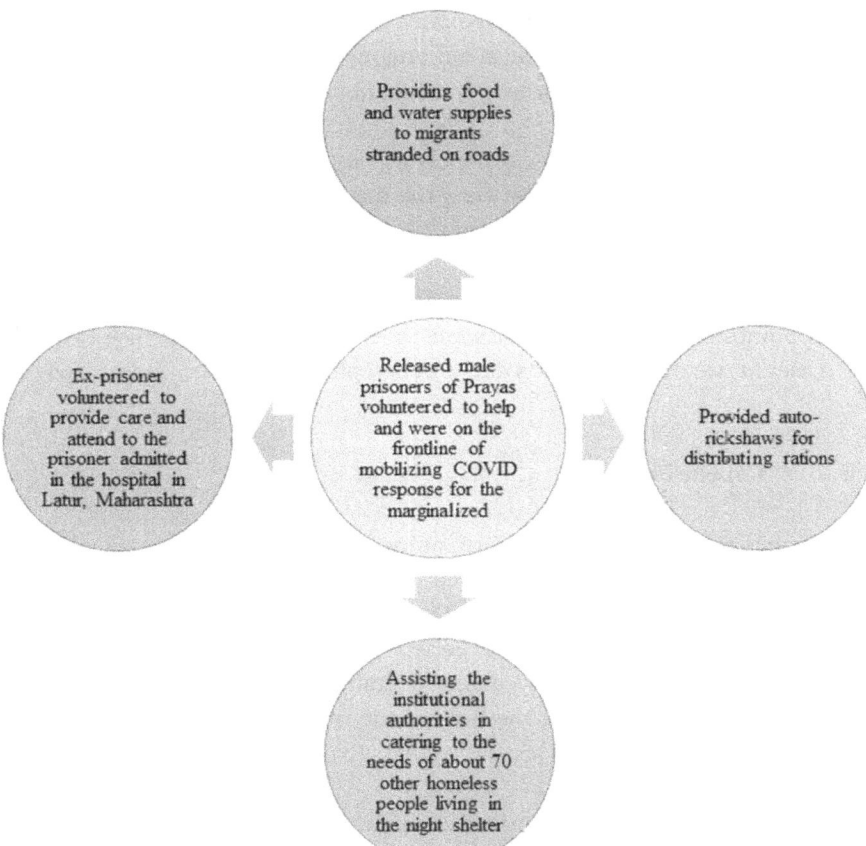

FIGURE 6.28   The above stated illustration show Released male prisoners offering support in midst of pandemic

week) to ten days. Joint efforts of social workers and lawyers culminated in appointing panel advocates in 72.89 per cent of cases.
– It is a challenging task to fulfil bail conditions. Poor and migrant undertrials do not have appropriate ID proof documents and no support from their family to furnish surety or the cash amount. There are limited agencies and NGOs to furnish cash bail support. Yet, Prayas facilitated a 10 per cent release of undertrials on bail by panel advocates and 62 per cent by facilitating bail compliance conditions.
– Delay in appointing a panel advocate and filing of bail, compels an undertrial to plead guilty. Around 6 per cent of the undertrials of Prayas have switched to private advocates, due to inactive panel advocates.

- There is a dire need for adequate staffing, better infrastructure, and resources to implement a legal aid programme, and increase the honorarium for legal aid lawyers, a speedy mechanism for claiming honorarium and reimbursements.
- A communication gap was experienced between police, court, prison and legal aid institutions and between the district and taluka legal aid offices. For example, Taloja Central Prison has a prison population across jurisdictions, and has cases, especially from multiple courts, prisons and DLSAs, leading to coordination problems, follow-up challenges and delays in the appointment of lawyers. Also, sometimes panel advocates refuse to attend cases at two different courts due to geographical distances (Prayas, 2023).

9 Conclusion

In correctional settings, social work intervention has proved beneficial. It has helped to outline the scope and need for a rehabilitation policy for released persons from custodial institutions as well as a scheme to benefit them (Prayas Handbook Series, 2012). Prayas' experience demonstrates the need for criminal justice social work i.e. placement of trained social workers in prisons to rehabilitate and reconstruct the lives of the marginalized groups coming in contact with the criminal justice system. Expert diagnoses help to assess psycho-social needs.

Undertrials languishing in prison due to non-compliance of bail conditions emerged as one of the reasons for overcrowding. The case studies in the chapter highlight the resilience, innovative and varied roles of the social worker in coordinating with the system, families of prisoners (despite resistance), advocates, employers and civil society organizations in facilitating free legal aid, compliance of bail conditions and providing timely socio-legal support, thus getting them released. The social workers have sensitized judicial officers, prison officials and legal aid authorities on the poverty of undertrials and the implications of the bail orders, thus getting bail orders modified and, on the need, to release undertrials on PR bond.

On one hand, the social worker worked with the children outside the prison to provide them with safe shelter and education. On the other, the woman undertrial prisoner could cope emotionally knowing that there is someone taking care of her children in her absence. The social worker is the main actor between the undertrials, families of prisoners, panel advocates and the Criminal Justice System. Re-building and reconnecting family ties are crucial for a smooth re-integration process and improved chances of rehabilitation.

The social worker continues to work with the released prisoner and family post-release by providing entrepreneurial and vocational training skills, to reintegrate them into society.

Bibliography

Ashim @ Asim Kumar Haranath v. National Investigation Agency. (2021). SLP(Criminal) No(s). 6858.

Dave, A., et al. (2012). Centrality of field action in social work education: A case for socio-legal work. *Social Change, 42*(4), 451–466. https://doi.org/10.1177/0049085712468133.

Duxbury, A. (2022). Guilty till proven innocent? Safeguarding the rights of pre-trial detainees across the Commonwealth. Retrieved from https://www.humanrightsinitiative.org/download/1655289166CHRI%20CHOGM%202022.pdf#page=23.

Herald, C., & Fair, H. (2019, December). Pre-trial detention and its over-use: Evidence from ten countries. Retrieved from https://www.prisonstudies.org/sites/default/files/resources/downloads/pre-trial_detention_final.pdf.

India Justice Report 2020: Ranking States on Police, Judiciary, Prisons and Legal Aid, Tata Trusts, New Delhi, India 2021, (Dec. 06,2022, 12.14 PM), https://indiajusticereport.org/files/IJR_2020_Full_Report95d33e.pdf.

Kumar, P., et al. (2022). Prisoners are too 'victims' of the criminal justice system. Can they have an idea of 'fair access to justice'? https://doi.org/10.1177/25166069221134215.

Logananthan, P. (2020). A study on undertrials in the country. *Lawyers Club India*. Retrieved from https://www.lawyersclubindia.com/articles/a-study-on-under-trial-prisoners-in-the-country-11397.asp.

Maharashtra Prison Department. (2022, December 5). Retrieved from http://mahaprisons.gov.in/Uploads/pdf_GR/3b3a6c7f-4906-4326-bd77-c22ad80ef5fa2021.pdf.

Matejkowski, J., et al. (2022). Prison social work.. https://doi.org/10.1093/acrefore/9780199975839.013.1002.

Ministry of Home Affairs (MoHA). (2011). Government advisory on prison administration – No.17011/2/2010-PR, dated 9th May 2011. Retrieved from https://www.mha.gov.in/sites/default/files/PrisonAdvisories-1011.pdf

Ministry of Home Affairs (MoHA). (2022). Advisory No. V-13013/70/2012-IS(VI), Use of Section 436A of the Cr.P.C to reduce overcrowding of prisons, dated 17th January 2013. Retrieved from https://www.mha.gov.in/sites/default/files/AdvSec436APrisons-060213_0_0.pdf

Muntingh, Lukas and Jean Redpath, The Socio-Economic Impact of Pre-Trial Detention in Kenya, Mozambique and Zambia. (Dec.7, 2022 3.51 PM) https://dullahomarinstitute.org.za/acjr/resource-centre/socio-economic-impact-web-lowres.pdf.

National Crime Records Bureau (NCRB). (2022, December 5). Prison statistics India 2021. Retrieved from https://www.ncrb.gov.in/uploads/nationalcrimerecordsbureau/post/1696317373PSI-2021.pdf.

National Crime Records Bureau (NCRB). (2022, December 5). Prison statistics India 2020. Retrieved from https://www.ncrb.gov.in/uploads/nationalcrimerecordsbureau/post/1696317249PSI-2020.pdf

National Crime Records Bureau (NCRB). (2022, December 5). Prison statistics India 2019. Retrieved from https://www.ncrb.gov.in/uploads/nationalcrimerecordsbureau/post/1696316594PSI-2019.pdf

National Legal Services Authority (NALSA). (2016). Standard operating procedure on representation of persons in custody. Retrieved from https://nalsa.gov.in/acts-rules/guidelines/standard-operating-procedure-for-representation-of-persons-in-custody.

National Legal Services Authority (NALSA). (2019). Early access to justice at pre-arrest, arrest, and remand framework 2019. Retrieved from https://nalsa.gov.in/acts-rules/guidelines/early-access-to-justice-at-pre-arrest-arrest-and-remand-stage.

Pillay, S. (2020). The Supreme Court declares detention of under-trial prisoners is unconstitutional. *Lexforti Legal News Network*. Retrieved from https://lexforti.com/legal-news/supreme-court-declares-detention-of-under-trial-prisoners-is-unconstitutional/.

Prayas & Centre for Criminology and Justice, School of Social Work (CCJSSW), Tata Institute of Social Sciences (TISS). (2019, October 25). The round table on field work placements in criminal justice. Retrieved from https://www.tiss.edu/uploads/files/Round_Table_Field_Placements_in_CJS_Final_Final_.pdf.

Prayas Newsletter. (2020–2022). March – July 2020, August – September 2020, January 2021- March 2021, April – November 2021, December 2021- August 2022. Retrieved from https://tiss.edu/view/6/projects/prayas/outcomespublications-5/

Prayas. (2012). Initiating work in prison settings: Handbook series on social work in criminal justice. Tata Institute of Social Sciences (TISS). Retrieved from http://download.tiss.edu/fap/Prayas/Prayas_Publications/Prayas_reports/Initiating_work_in_prison_settings.pdf.

Prayas. (2012). Initiating work with children of prisoners: Handbook series on social work in criminal justice. Tata Institute of Social Sciences (TISS). Retrieved from https://www.tiss.edu/uploads/files/initiating_work_with_children_of_prisoners.pdf.

Prayas. (2020). Impact on field, policy, law and procedure (1990–2020). Retrieved from https://www.tiss.edu/uploads/files/Prayas_Impact_on_Policy_-_February_1990_to_March_2020.pdf.

Prayas. (2020). Rehabilitation plan. Retrieved from https://www.tiss.edu/view/11/proje cts/prayas/.

Prayas. (2021). Annual report, April 2020 to March 2021. Retrieved from https://tiss.edu /uploads/files/Prayas_Annual_Report_for_the_Period_from_April_2020_to_March _2021.pdf.

Prayas. (2023). Legal aid to undertrials prisoners in Maharashtra: A socio-legal intervention model in the criminal justice system. Retrieved from https://tiss.edu/uplo ads/files/Prayas_Report-_Legal_Aid_to_Undertrial_Prisoners_in_Maharashtra_A _Socio-Legal_Inte_JwAfRVW.pdf.

Raghavan, V. (2020). Delays in the Criminal Justice Process: Consequences for Undertrial Prisoners and Their Families, Justice Frustrated: The Systemic Impact of Delays in Indian Courts, (Eds.) Vidyasagar, S., Naik, S. and Narsappa, H., New Delhi: Bloomsbury India

Menezes, S. and Raghavan, V. (2019). Criminal justice social work in India: Conceptualising from teaching and practice. In Indigenizing social work practice in India, (Eds.) Popli Ushvinder kaur and Singh, Ashvini Kumar, New Delhi: Bloomsbury India.

Raghavan, Vijay *Undertrial Prisoners in India – Long Wait for Justice,* Vol. 51, Issue No. 4, Economic and Political Weekly (2016).

Raghavan, V. (2013). Social work intervention in criminal justice: Field theory linkage. (2013). In: *India Reader* (Ed.) Singh, S. Lyceum Books: Chicago, pp. 265–289.

World Prison Brief, *Highest to Lowest – Prison Population Rate,* (Dec. 09,2022, 23.20 PM), Highest to Lowest - Pre-trial detainees / remand prisoners | World Prison Brief (prisonstudies.org).

Raghavan, V., & Menezes, S. (2017). Prayas: Demonstrating criminal justice social work. *Indian Journal of Social Work.* Retrieved from https://journals.tiss.edu/ijsw/index .php/ijsw/article/view/132.

Raut, A. N., Pal, G., & Tripathi, A. (2024). *Decrypting the Sanhita: An Analysis of the Newly Introduced Offences Under Bharatiya Nyaya Sanhita.* (Latest 2024 Edition) Whitesmann Publishing Co. ISBN 9788119725953.

Surendranath, A., & Andrew, G. (2022). State legal aid and undertrials: Are there no takers? *Indian Law Review.* https://doi.org/10.1080/24730580.2022.2029018.

Surendranath, A., et al. (2021). Legal representation for undertrials in Maharashtra, 2018–2021. Retrieved from https://tiss.edu/uploads/files/Legal_Representation_for _Undertrials_in_Maharashtra__2018-2021_iLWKW58.pdf

Tata Trusts & Prayas. (2020). Scoping study in Maharashtra prisons towards institutionalizing social workers in the prison system. Retrieved from https://www.tiss.edu /uploads/files/REPORT_OF_THE_SCOPING_STUDY.pdf.

CHAPTER 7

Rehabilitation and Restorative Justice in Italy: Themes, Methods and Experiences in Adult and Minors Criminal Law Systems

Chiara Scivoletto

1 The Probation Model: A Set of Tools for the Rehabilitation

Probation is a criminal justice model aimed at enhancing responsibility towards the community and also at avoiding the negative effect of imprisonment. Some international recommendations have described probation as a set of measures that keep offenders out of prison and away from its negative effects, in order to promote their responsibility-taking and rehabilitation.

Primarily, it useful to remember Recommendation CM/Rec (2010) 1 of the Committee of Ministers to Member States on the Council of Europe, Probation Rules, where "the aim of probation is to contribute to a fair criminal justice process, as well as to public safety by preventing and reducing the occurrence of offences; and considering that probation agencies are among the key agencies of justice and that their work has an impact on the reduction of the prison population." The text of the recommendation explains that the

> rules guide the establishment and proper functioning of probation agencies. These rules also apply to other organizations in their performance of the tasks covered in these rules, including other state organizations, non-governmental and commercial organizations. These rules need to be read together with Recommendation No. R (92) 16 on the European rules on community sanctions and measures. Furthermore, these rules complete the previous provisions of Recommendation No. R (97) 12 on staff concerned with the implementation of sanctions and measures, Recommendation No. R (99) 19 concerning mediation in penal matters, Recommendation Rec (2000)22 on improving the implementation of the European rules on community sanctions and measures, Recommendation Rec(2003)22 on conditional release (parole), Recommendation Rec(2003)23 on the management by prison administrations of life sentence and other long-term prisoners, Recommendation Rec(2006)2 on the European Prison Rules, Recommendation Rec(2006)8

on assistance to crime victims and Recommendation Rec(2006)13 on the use of remand in custody, the conditions in which it takes place and the provision of safeguards against abuse, and are to be read together with them.

The Recommendation gives some definitions of probation, the probation agency, community sanctions and measures, and the process called *aftercare* and explains the basic principles of probation agencies, which "shall aim to reduce reoffending by establishing positive relationships with offenders, respect the human rights of offenders", and also "the rights and needs of the victims", where the case. Furthermore, "the interventions of probation agencies shall be carried out without discrimination. In implementing sanctions or measures, the agencies shall seek the offenders' informed consent". In any case, "probation agencies, their tasks and responsibilities, as well as their relations with the public authorities and other bodies, shall be defined by national law". Consequently, "probation shall remain the responsibility of the public authorities, even in the case when services are delivered by other agencies or volunteers". The recommendation also states that "probation agencies shall work in partnership with other public or private organizations and local communities to promote the social inclusion of offenders, and also that coordinated and complementary inter-agency and inter-disciplinary work is necessary to meet the often-complex needs of offenders and to enhance community safety. All activities and interventions undertaken by probation agencies shall conform to the highest national and international ethical and professional standards".

Some years before, another Recommendation (R (92) 16) provided for "community sanctions and measures", as sanctions and measures that keep the offender in the community and involve some restriction of his or her freedom through the imposition of conditions and/or obligations, and which are implemented by bodies designated in law for that purpose. The term designates any penalty imposed by a court or a judge and any measure taken before or instead of a decision on a sanction, as well as ways of enforcing an imprisonment sentence outside a prison establishment.

So, the probation structure can be considered as a part of the wider framework of community measures, or any case can be connected to it. This set of rules, internationally established, should facilitate the exchange of experience, in particular concerning methods of work.[1]

---

[1] As this paper does not discuss juvenile justice, it is important to bear in mind also the European Rules for juvenile offenders subject to sanctions or measures, laid down in

2 "Messa alla prova" in Italy

In this international socio-legal scenario, Italy has different probation tools in force, namely probation after judgement (for convicted offenders, such as the 'affidamento 'in prova ai servizi sociali', L. n. 375/1975 and subsequent amendments) and probation before judgement (for defendants).

A typical probation measure applied in Italy is 'messa alla prova' (MAP), a kind of probation before judgement, introduced in 1988 for minors and in 2014 for adult defendants.

The Juvenile one was introduced in 1988 (Italian Presidential Decree 448/88: Art. 28–29); it's applicable to any type of crime, even particularly serious ones and those causing significant social alarm, and can have a maximum duration of three years. Trial suspension is ordered during the preliminary hearing or during the trial, and the measure provides for the minor an educational project prepared by the juvenile social services (USSM). The probation measure can consist of prescriptions to do or not to do, mainly concerning education or work, but also sports, social activities or voluntary work. Furthermore, the judge may issue prescriptions aimed at repairing the consequences of the crime and promoting the reconciliation of the minor with the victim (Italian Presidential Decree 448/88: Art. 28, para 2, Art. 29). This is the first appearance of Restorative Justice approach in the Italian legal system, even if the measure, belonging to the restorative model, is a typical rehabilitative tool. The probation's favourable outcome generates the extinction of the offence, pronounced with a non-prosecution ruling; on the contrary, a negative outcome triggers resumption of the trial from where it was interrupted.

The Probation before judgement measure for adults was introduced in Italy in 2014 with law no. 67,[2] really not for a cultural opening to a non-punitive approach, but, more empirically, to manage a difficult situation in the penitentiary sector (the overcrowding of the prisons, at first); it is used for defendants accused of crimes punished with short prison sentences.[3] Also, the adult one

---

Recommendation CM/Rec (2008)11 of the Committee of Ministers to Member States on the European Rules for juvenile offenders subject to sanctions or measures.

2   Recently, the Law no.159/2023 added the Art. 28 paragraph 5-bis, which prohibits to apply the MAP for children accused of some serious crimes: homicide, aggravated sexual violence (art. 609-ter of the Criminal Code) and aggravated robbery (art. 628, paragraph 3, n. 2, n.3 and n. 3-quinquies of the Criminal Code).

3   The Italian State was sentenced by the European Commission and should necessarily reduce the number of prison population (European Court on Human Rights,8 gennaio 2013 – Ric. nn. 43517/09, 46882/09, 55400/09, 57875/09, 61535/09, 35315/10 e 37818/10 – Torreggiani e al. contra Italia).

consists in suspending the trial and in placing the defendant under the social service supervision. Social workers prepare and define, in agreement with the defence counsel and the Court, a treatment programme. The programme provides for mandatory unpaid community service work (differently from the minors' scheme) to be done for healthcare or social charities or for public institutions.

Also, the adult measure provides for the accused to carry out restorative activities, aimed at eliminating the dangerous or harmful consequences of the crime, at compensating the damage caused and, *if possible*, activities of mediation with the victim (Cortesi, 2023).

The treatment programme is prepared by the UEPE, social work units at the Ministry of Justice, responsible for the local area, after a formal application is filed by the defendant. It is prepared on the basis of the defendant's specific characteristics. The measure may be granted, by the judge, for crimes punished with prison sentences of up to six years. The measure may be applied no more than once (or possibly twice, for offences perpetrated before the first suspension). Application to habitual, professional and trend-based offenders is ruled out; this is another important difference versus the juvenile scheme, where the measure is always permitted and is applicable several times (not once only). The juvenile measure is informed to the *favor minoris*, i.e., the justice system must do everything possible to educate (better than rehabilitate) the minor and to prevent the labelling consequences of the offence (Goffman, 1963/1983). In the adult system, the trial may not be suspended for a period of over two years, if the prosecuted crime is punished with a prison sentence of more than one year and for prosecuted crimes punished with a pecuniary penalty only. The positive outcome of the proof generates the extinction of the crime, exactly as in the juvenile field. At the same time, if the defendant (adult or minor) makes serious and repeated infringements of the treatment programme, or if the defendant refuses to perform community service work or perpetrates, during the probationary period, a new intentional crime or a crime of the same nature of the one he or she is being prosecuted for, the judge shall order the revocation of the measure and the resumption of the trial.

3 Juvenile "messa alla prova" in Italy

Italian Juvenile Courts (called Tribunali per i Minorenni) may suspend the trial and put him/her in proof in order to observe the personality of the minor defendant. This observation is oriented to grade penal liability, introduce administrative or civil penalties, and every other necessary intervention to support the minor and her/his family and to activate his or her social environment. Since last year, no limits are fixed by law as regards the kind of offenders and offences: juvenile messa alla prova was applicable to all offenders (also for repeat offenders) and all offences; the new Law no. 159/2023 introduced some limits for some serious crimes. The trial can be suspended by the judge for a variable period, ranging between one year and three years, depending on the seriousness of the offence. During the probationary period, the minor defendant agrees to comply with a programme consisting of various activities (education, work, voluntary work and also restorative practices, if the judges decide these activities are an opportunity for the minor and the social work refers to the availability of the victims).

As regards restorative practices, the law allows the judge to supplement the proof programme with some activities aimed at remedying the consequences of the offence and at promoting reconciliation between the defendant and the victim.

This is a very big topic of analysis, and we have a lot of literature dedicated to the relationships between messa alla prova and restorative justice. The Italian scientific debate has recently intensified when messa alla prova was extended to adult defendants, and it became clearer that the implementation of restorative justice is one of the main opportunities but, at the same time, one of the biggest problems that we have (Scivoletto, 2017).

When the probationary period ends, the same judge that admitted the minor to the measure will evaluate the proof in order to decide whether to rule for the extinction of the crime, depending on the evolution in the offender's personality. In any case, we must keep in mind that the main objective of juvenile criminal trial is not to punish but educate young defendants. The law also envisages a negative outcome when no change has occurred in the young offender's personality and behavior: in this case, the trial will restart from where it was suspended (Italian Presidential Decree 448/88: Art. 29).

The purpose of messa alla prova is to promote educational and supporting strategies for minors, with the help – if possible – of their families and their networks of relationships and background; the aim is to strengthen and enhance the defendants' personal skills and resources in order for them to re-engage in society. As socio-legal studies show, being found guilty in trial often reinforces a negative image of him/herself (the "deviant label") (Goffman, 1963/1983; Moyersoen, 2018); on the contrary, the pursued ideological purpose is to prevent any conditions that would make the juvenile defendant perceive him/herself as a criminal (De Leo, 1981). Messa alla prova has two other objectives: to contribute to keeping the juvenile criminal justice system focused on its key concept, i.e., the "child's best interest" and to help the minor to take responsibility for past actions and to use the experience to move forward (Vezzadini, 2017).

Data resulting from socio-legal research programmes over the thirty years the measure has been applied, give evidence that this tool has a lot of pros, but also some cons. As concerns pros, we can easily notice that the measure allows the minor and his/her family and life context to be involved. We can say that messa alla prova is able to combine education and punishment, the main objectives of juvenile criminal justice (Pavarini, 1991). Messa alla prova does certainly have a lot of pros: first of all, it ensures that the young offender is made more accountable, in order to increase his/her responsibility-taking, but, at the same time, it also has some limits. The quantitative data resulting from several socio-legal research works conducted over the 30 years of its application give evidence that the outcomes of juvenile probation in Italy are mainly positive: approximately 98% of the trials suspended to admit the defendants to this kind of probation had a positive outcome and ended with the extinction of the crime; we know how important this goal is in order to prevent any labelling effect (Becker, 1963/1987; Palomba, 1989; Ministry of Justice, 2022).

At the same time, we have to analyse the contents of the proofs and, even before that, we must take a look at the selection criteria used by the Courts to decide the defendants to be admitted to and those to be denied this measure. Statistical data give evidence that a large part of suspended trials ends with the extinction of the crime, but not that many trials are suspended. In Italy, the minors admitted to the messa alla prova in 2006 accounted for 10% of the total defendant minors and, in 2017, for 18%. Almost all the minors admitted to messa alla prova are Italian (Ministry of Justice, Juvenile and Community Justice Department, 2022).

In this, we find a big research question. What are the reasons that Juvenile Judges consider when they decide to suspend trial? The Law allows all trials to be suspended (in theory), but we know that only 20% is suspended. As clearly emerged from the monitoring of national data, it is obvious that, since the first Italian studies on this topic (Scivoletto, 1999; Santagata, 2005), the choice to suspend trial has always been reserved to highly selected cases, not only quantitatively but also qualitatively.

Juvenile courts decide to grant "probation" in a small number of cases, although the measure offers the big goal of criminal liability extinction. Albeit effective, it does not seem to be quite as efficient: in fact, its application requires the use of considerable resources in terms of human and social capital. The success of the measure, as the goal to be achieved, depends – in the internal legal culture of Judges and Social workers – on the correct involvement of the minor's whole network: the family, the school, and the other relevant agencies in the minor's life (Nelken, 2006), as per the well-known "Italian style" in juvenile justice (Lemert, 1981; Scalia, 2005).

In considering these data, we also know that no follow-up national data are yet available, although it should be an important research variable. So, research programmes are needed to introduce some indicators about the definition of success/failure of the messa alla prova programmes; they will be useful to investigate the criteria used by the courts for example to select the measure, to make the final decision (if positive, the crime is extinguished; if negative, the trial is resumed).

After thirty years of application, empirical data report that few foreign minor defendants are admitted to messa alla prova. This evidence is evaluated and explained in the literature not as a signal of opposition, but as a signal of lack of power: Juvenile Courts prefer to grant the measure only to young people that have a good family and social network. A strong network is a useful tool to make the programme strong and its outcome successful. Social workers (USSM) need to consider whether the social and family background can help and support the young defendant in changing his/her way of life. So, the family and the social environment are considered – also by judges, not only by social workers – as a necessary tool to create good messa alla prova programmes.

At the same time, although the measure has been applied for so long, we know that messa alla prova programmes do not yet comprise mediation or restorative practices as well. The reason is strictly related not only to the difficulties in spreading the culture of restorative justice as such, but also to the kind of crimes and, first of all, to the victims' will (this is especially true for mediation, which is in no case compulsory).[4]

Once again, the usefulness of the legal cultural perspective in our research is clear; it is a perfect key of investigation about the topic of probation, both if we analyse judiciary dossiers and interview judges, social workers, lawyers or other professionals involved in this socio-legal field.

---

4 Statistical data on application are available on the Ministry of Justice website, cited above.

4 Some Results from a Research Programme about "messa alla prova" for Adults

4.1 *Note on Methodology*

This paragraph reports some results obtained by a quali-quantitative research programme, focusing on messa alla prova for adults,[5] conducted in the Emilia Romagna Region between 2016 and 2021, in collaboration with the Justice Ministry Social Work Units (Italian acronym: UEPE) of Bologna and Reggio Emilia and the Voluntary Services Centers (Italian acronym: CSV Emilia), i.e., the centres that coordinate local volunteer organizations.

The first part of the research programme was dedicated to collecting quantitative data about the application of the messa alla prova measure in the Emilia-Romagna Region (Northern Italy), shortly after the introduction of Law 67/2014 (2016–2018). The collected quantitative data were: the number of offenders, types of offences, duration and content of the proof programmes and were based on UEPE records (192 records of the Bologna and Reggio Emilia UEPE).

On the other hand qualitative data were collected between 2018 and 2021 and were obtained by interviewing (a) 13 social workers about managing probation for adults (UEPE Officers on staff at the Reggio Emilia UEPE Office), but also interviewing (b) 16 defendants, on their experience after the end of the probationary period, managed by the same UEPE professionals, and (c) also collecting the opinion of 7 defence counsels[6] about the messa alla prova tool and the possibilities of introducing restorative justice practices in the messa alla prova programmes for adults (see Scivoletto et al., 2020). In addition (d), the opinion of all social workers on staff at the UEPE Offices of the Emilia Romagna region was collected by administering an online survey. The aim of the dual approach of the research, as is easy to understand, was to compare the first application and the current application in terms of implementation of law (bureaucracy, communication between institutions, work practices) and in terms of the spread of the legal culture (Nelken, 2004) in the same territory. We refer here only to the results from the survey, that was addressed to all (58) the social workers on staff at the UEPE of Region.[7]

---

5 This paper is on a quali-quantitative research programme, divided into two phases (2016–2018 and 2019–2021).
6 All the counsels who sit on the executive board of the criminal chamber of the Bar of Parma, a city in Northern Italy.
7 The complete set of data are available in C. Scivoletto, 2020 and 2022.

4.2 The Social Workers Experience – The Regional Survey Results

The professionals who replied were 37.64% of the total; 22 of them (i.e., 59%) had over twenty years of experience in the service. It means the sample had in-depth knowledge of the matter and of its changes over time. It is also a group with good experience of messa alla prova: 18 of them had managed more than 50 cases; 13 of them had managed between 30 and 49 cases.

The answers about the messa alla provameasure were, in general, positive (although not enthusiastic). It should be noted that the Italian outcome of the proof is almost always positive, but our interviews highlighted some doubts about its application in terms of the capability of messa alla prova to perform all its – ideal and many – functions.

The opinion about the main goal of the measure was investigated: whether it aims at meeting rehabilitation needs (18 out of 32 professionals, i.e., 56%, answered very much so/quite), or needs for reduction of procedures (2 out of 32, i.e., 69%, answered quite/very much so), or restorative needs (the quite/very much so answers were 24 out of 32, i.e., 75%).

Regarding their satisfaction with the collaboration with the other professionals involved in the messa alla prova application, very different results emerged. Satisfaction is high as regards the relationships with local social services (31 out of 32 respondents, 97% are very or quite satisfied) and defence counsels (30 out of 32, 94%). Indeed, quite lower satisfaction was surveyed about communication and collaboration with judges: here, the quite or very satisfied social workers dropped to 20 out of 32 (62%). This result was therefore the subject of in-depth analysis during the interviews conducted in the qualitative part of the study.

As concerns Community Service (Italian acronym: LPU), laid down as essential by Law no. 67/2014, 33% of interviewees (11 out of 33) believe that it, although legitimate, is insufficient; for 58% (19) it is sufficient and 9% only (3) gave a good opinion of it. Therefore, Community Service does not characterise the experience, it is not enough to support messa alla prova: according to the interviewees, the messa alla prova programme should also contain restorative justice activities (30 out of 33, 92%). Someone also stressed the need for more resources in terms of voluntary activities (3 out of 33, 9%).

The general experience of the social workers is however positive: 88% of the social workers taking the survey (28 out of 32). Asked about the effectiveness of messa alla prova, the most important element in their answer was: to avoid recidivism (19 out of 32 interviewees, 59%). Asked about the "effectiveness" of the measure, they answered that it lies in the experience of the proof (6 out of 32 interviewees, 19%), the usefulness of introducing restorative programmes or activities (4, 12%) and the extinction of the crime (3, the 9%).

The questionnaire also included one open-ended question, introduced to allow the interviewees to express themselves freely (or their opinions more freely). So, some interesting considerations emerged in terms of legal culture. The interviewed professionals reported great difficulty in the interaction between judges and social workers. Finally, the interviewees believe that a good relationship with defence counsels is essential: they reported that the support of defence counsels to the messa alla prova programmes would increase the chances of success. Furthermore, in their opinion the measure seems to be useful for the prevention of crimes.

5 Conclusion: Is Probation a Set for Restorative Justice?

The different situations in which the measure of probation is adopted in the Italian law system really gives us – in a general sense – a meaningful light on the quote of criminalization the State is available to spend. In other words, the use of Italian probation shows the ambivalence of the public response to the crimes and the orientation of the penalty culture. Even if it is aimed by the intention to reduce the penal reaction, it is considered that the repressive use of the legal tool, in terms of reduction of freedom, is not automatically facing the question of public security. Otherwise, the legal system needs to deal with the faith in the public response to the crimes if it perceives unjust criminalising conduct, while it is clear that no universal normative theory of criminalization exists. So, the Italian probation system could be seen as an example of a penal response-oriented to reduce the risk of over-criminalization; at the same time, this widened use of probation tools – spread in juvenile and in adult fields – shows us the opportunity to examine a specifically tailored suggestion to deal with the big problems of criminality and of criminalization. In any case, as this ambiguity is yet to be answered all over the world by the amount of governmental intervention, the Italian experience shows us an interesting nuance of criminalization where the inmate is 'forced' (as condemned) to put more responsibility toward the community where the crime was committed. The legal system encourages this kind of intervention as it considers it better than a traditional passive penalty spent in prison, and besides paid with public money.

So, the messa alla prova measure – both for adults and for juvenile defendants – is a very valuable opportunity to reflect on the orientations of the culture of a penalty and on the efficiency and effectiveness of criminal law provisions (Foucault, 1975/1976; Gallo and Ruggiero, 1989; Garland, 2001/2004; Mosconi, 2010). Indeed, the recent extension of messa alla prova to adult defendants has highlighted the attention to the central matter of criminal policies in Italy: not only does it require that offenders be assisted and rehabilitated, but also that safety and affordability be ensured. Furthermore, messa alla prova for adults gives a new and significant opportunity to rethink the most typical contents of the rehabilitation model that, for minors, has been pursued for over thirty years. The analysis of its application also permits us to rethink more in general on the probation model effectiveness, which has considerable unanswered questions, not only in social construction and legal culture but also in terms of implementation of public policies. Messa alla prova for adults requires the UEPE staff to work with users that are different from those on whom the social service has gained over thirty years' experience (Salvadori and Arata, 2014). At the same time, it requires courts to decide on the merits to rule on treatment, which is the very scope of the supervision judicial structure (in Italian: *magistratura di sorveglianza*). Furthermore, messa alla prova of adults requires several judiciary institutions to be involved, first of all, the trial courts, besides the use of coordinated resources from the civil service and private social players. Therefore, the measure requires practical organizational solutions to be deployed, aimed at limiting the unevenness of its application, ideally at a national level (an ambitious goal), or at least a regional level (Mattevi, 2023; Miraglia, 2023).

Among the main points of attention for both measures, some risks are to be pointed out: a. unequal application and benefit between defendants; b. standardization of projects; c. instrumental uses (especially as regards the measure for adults, the risk of standardised application results from the excessive workload of UEPE). Moreover, for adults, attention must be given to community service, which is a binding requirement and a mandatory part of the messa alla prova project; conversely, for minors, it is to be pointed out that, after 30 years of implementation, there is still no national follow-up monitoring of outcomes. Lastly, for both scopes (juvenile and adult offenders), there is the Restorative Justice challenge, and CM/REC 2018(8) reads that: "Restorative justice" refers to any process which enables those harmed by crime, and those responsible for that harm, if they freely consent, to participate actively in the resolution of matters arising from the offence, through the help of a trained and impartial third party (hereinafter the "facilitator").

The messa alla prova arrangement – which, from a systematic perspective, belongs to the rehabilitation model – does not seem instrumental to spreading a restorative justice culture in Italy. Rather, we could say that both legislative acts implementing the MAP (1988 for minors and 2014 for adult defendants) introduced the use of restorative justice in order to reduce the prison population without giving it the status of a true and independent legal paradigm, fit to resolve social conflicts by involving the community or, even more specifically, the victims. Mediation has proved again the most interesting and tight knot: the data we surveyed on the measure for adults shows the light and shadow already found in previous studies (Scivoletto, 1999, 2017) and the danger of assuming the equivalence of symbolic/widespread compenzation (when not a financial one only) and moral compenzation to the victim.

Therefore, scientific research will have to continue to monitor its outcomes, both in-trial ones (application methods and judicial outcome of messa alla prova), and especially out-of-trial ones (legal follow-up on reoffenders and psychological-social follow-up on personal development). In any case, and first of all, Italy now needs to introduce new public services implementing restorative justice practices (Eusebi, 2023). The recent legislative reform (Law n. 134/2021 and D. Lgs. n. 150/2022) requires to ensure at all an organic reform of restorative justice in the adults sector giving only a few months for its implementation: i.e., opening almost a couple of restorative public centres in every district; signing collaboration protocols with municipalities and courts; earning the training schools of restorative justice and the experience of the educated facilitators Scivoletto, C. (2022). That's a big challenge for the legal system in a more and more complex social and cultural environment.

Bibliography

Becker, H. S. (1963). *Outsiders: Studies in the sociology of deviance.* New York, NY: Simon and Schuster. (Originally published in 1963).

Cortesi, M. F. (2023). Le nuove disposizioni sulla "vittima" del reato. *Diritto penale e processo*, (1), 215–218.

De Leo, G. (1981). *La giustizia dei minori: la delinquenza minorile e le sue istituzioni.* Turin: Einaudi.

Eusebi, L. (2023). Giustizia riparativa e riforma del sistema sanzionatorio penale *Diritto penale e processo*, (1), 79–86.

Foucault, M. (1976). *Sorvegliare e punire.* Turin: Einaudi. (Originally published in 1975).

Gallo, E., & Ruggiero, V. (1989). *Il carcere immateriale: La detenzione come fabbrica di hándicap.* Turin: Sonda.

Garland, D. (2004). *La cultura del controllo.* Milan: Il Saggiatore. (Originally published in 2001).

Ghezzi M. *et al.*, eds., *Processo penale, cultura giuridica e ricerca empirica.* Rimini: Maggioli 251–280.

Goffman, E. (1983). *Stigma: L'identità negata.* Milan: Giuffrè. (Originally published in 1963).

Lemert, E. M. (1981). *Devianza, problemi sociali e forme di controllo*. Milan: Giuffrè.
Mannozzi, G., & Lodigiani, A. (2015). *Giustizia riparativa: Ricostruire legami, ricostruire persone*. Bologna: Il Mulino.
Mattevi, E. (2023). La sospensione del procedimento con messa alla prova dopo la riforma Cartabia – Profili sostanziali. *Diritto penale e processo*, (1), 45–49.
Ministry of Justice. (2021). La sospensione del processo e messa alla prova (art. 28 D.P.R. 448/88) Dati statistici Anno 2020. Retrieved March 1, 2023, from https://www.giustizia.it/cmsresources/cms/documents/MAP_2020_31marzo2021.pdf.
Ministry of Justice. (2022). Adulti in area penale esterna: Analisi statistica dei dati [Data as of April 15, 2022]. Retrieved March 1, 2023, from https://www.giustizia.it/cmsresources/cms/documents/Adulti_in_area_penale_esterna_15.04.2022.pdf.
Miraglia, M. (2023). La sospensione del procedimento con messa alla prova dopo la riforma Cartabia – Profili processuali. *Diritto penale e processo*, (1), 50–53.
Mosconi, G. (2010). La sicurezza dell'insicurezza: Retoriche e torsioni della legislazione italiana. *Studi sulla questione criminale*, (2), 75–99.
Moyersoen, J. (Ed.). (2018). *La messa alla prova minorile e reati associativi: Buone pratiche ed esperienze innovative*. Milan: Franco Angeli.
Nelken, D. (2004). Using the concept of legal culture. *Australian Journal of Legal Philosophy*, (29), 1–26. Retrieved March 1, 2023, from http://www.austlii.edu.au/au/journals/AUJlLegPhil/2004/11.pdf.
Nelken, D. (2006). Italy: A lesson in tolerance? In J. Muncie & B. Goldson (Eds.), *Comparative Youth Justice: Critical Issues* (pp. 159–176). London: Sage, 159–176.
Palomba, F. (1989). *Il sistema del nuovo processo penale minorile*. Milan: Giuffrè.
Pavarini, M. (1991). Il rito pedagogico. Politica criminale e nuovo processo penale a carico di imputati minorenni, *Dei delitti e delle pene*, no. 2, 107–39.
Salvadori, A., and Arata, R., (2014). La scommessa "culturale" della sospensione con messa alla prova alla verifica delle aule di tribunale. *Questione giustizia* [online], 17 October. Retrieved from https://www.questionegiustizia.it/articolo/la-scommessa-culturale-della-sospensione-con-messa-alla-prova-alla-verifica-delle-aule-di-tribunale_16-10-2014.php.
Santagata, B., ed., (2005). *Ragazzi alla prova*. Udine: Forum.
Scalia, V., (2005). A lesson in tolerance: Juvenile Justice in Italy? *Youth Justice*, no. 5(1) 33–43.
Scivoletto, C., (1999). *C'è tempo per punire: Percorsi di probation minorile*. Milan: Franco Angeli.
Scivoletto, C., (2017). La messa alla prova dell'imputato maggiorenne: Vecchi strumenti, nuove virtù? In: M. Ghezzi *et al.*, eds., *Processo penale, cultura giuridica e ricerca empirica*. Rimini: Maggioli 227–250.

Scivoletto, C., (2022). "Probation in Italy: Legal culture and justice models", Oñati Socio-Legal Series, 12(6) 1442–1462. Available at: https://www.opo.iisj.net/index.php/osls/article/view/1433.

Scivoletto, C., Mantovani, F., and Manella, G., (2020). La messa alla prova per l'imputato maggiorenne: Una ricerca in Emilia Romagna. *Studi di Sociologia*, (2) 143–158.

Vezzadini, S., (2017). Vittime, giustizia riparativa e reati sessuali. Processi decisionali e scelte operative del Tribunale per i minorenni dell'Emilia Romagna nei progetti di messa alla prova.

CHAPTER 8

Criminal Acts of Lynching and Overcriminalization: Empirical Analysis of People's Perspectives regarding Punitive Sanctions

Garima Pal and Tusha Singh

1   Introduction

Lynching is a criminal act in India but is not recognized as a separate crime. This means to say that lynching could be a means to a crime, but lynching in itself does not aggregate to a crime under the Indian Penal Code. This has varying effects and reactions when such a concept settles into the minds of people. When asked by the general public of our nation, there are mostly mixed feelings when it comes to the penal consequences of this act. This is what this research chapter is highlighting: the opinions of those people on whom criminalization of any criminal act would ultimately have an effect. The concept of overcriminalization or the arbitrary rise of punitive justice does not only need to be understood from an expert point of view; the voice of random masses of people is also something that is expertly deciphered in this chapter. In the scenario where the criminal act of lynching is centrally recognized, the trend of punitive sanctions could be predicted by the responses studied herewith.

2   Statement of Problem

Overcriminalization is a nationwide legal issue that does not gather much focus. The general perspective remains that the stricter the punishment, the more effective the steps to prevent a crime. However, the question remains – how can one measure effectiveness as a whole? Proportionality varies according to crime and the trend of society. Currently, the ever-so-rising tilt is towards high punitive incarcerations as a consequence of melting justice. Overcriminalization is used as a sword for sharpening the edge of justice, but the resultant chain of events that follow is seldom reformation, but eye-for-an-eye and tooth-for-a-tooth. How this position of our legal machinery affects the state of mind of the general public is an issue worth discussing. Apart from this, when it comes to awareness of the criminal act of lynching– the universal perspective is indicative of an unimaginative approach towards the same and is again supplemented with punitive justice. These are some of the issues that will be highlighted in the present research.

3 Hypothesis

There is a positive relation between the general perspective of the pro-deterrence position and the preferred criminalization trend for the criminal act of lynching among people in India.

4 Research Methodology

This is an empirical research study delving into an exploratory research area because of its novelty and complexity. The reason it is novel is that lynching is still an untapped research universe and is gradually picking up the importance that it should get. It is called out to be complex because when such a criminal act is being discussed that is not legally recognized in a society, it becomes difficult to pinpoint its legal boundaries and scope. Empirically understanding this subject matter is the most efficient way to scratch the surface of this vast discourse.

5 Sampling Universe

The universe of study is the general population of India. The Vastness of the universe has proved advantageous in understanding the general viewpoint of the society that we live in. This was essential so as to deliberately remove classification on the basis of any kind of affiliation. The only differentiable factors taken into account were the filters – State/Union Territory and the Age of the respondents. Since the subject matter is lynching in India, the universe was limited to India only and did not cross geographical boundaries.

6 Sampling Technique, Sample Size, and Data Collection

The technique followed was simple random sampling, wherein participants were randomly selected without prejudice or classification of any kind from different walks of life or profession, varying states/union territories, and any age. Snowballing was also effectively used as participants were urged to transfer the research project to people known to them as well. This led to expansive and varied data collection.

This was a time-based sample collection where, for a particular period of 2 months, interview schedules were circulated among the universe. In that timeline, a total of 215 respondents participated in this research by answering the online questions to the best of their knowledge. The profile of which is discussed below.

Data that is to be used in this research is collected by way of interview schedules and questionnaires. The questions put under this interview were open-ended questions with easy multiple-choice options and understandable language. The personal details of the respondents were not collected and were kept anonymous since this was a sensitive issue to deliberate.

7 Analysis

Data collected was analysed through Microsoft Excel by using data analysis techniques. Deductive reasoning was used in order to understand the response given by the respondents. Correlation analysis was used to study the hypothesis.

8 Background

In light of the lynching incidents rising in the past decade, concrete discourse had to be formulated. This study became imperative amidst the research into the punitive trend for the criminal act of lynching. The incidents started long before Indians became aware of the term lynching. However, since the year 2016, with the rise in lynching incidents, awareness of the same has also naturally risen. One of the most significant headlines that started it all was the Jharkhand Mob Lynching case in 2016, where 2 Muslim cattle traders were lynched by hanging them from a tree and the other 58 mob lynching cases that have been reported by the Jharkhand government have taken place between 2016 and 2021 (The New Indian Express, 2022). There is also the famous Pehlu Khan incident or the Alwar Mob Lynching case that happened in Haryana in 2017, wherein the man was killed on suspicion of transporting cows (Live Law, 2021). The development, in this case, has only reached the position that a Rajasthan court has issued a bailable warrant against the 6 accused (Live Law, 2021). In 2019, another Jharkhand case of Tabrez Ansari shook the nation where the man was beaten mercilessly and accused of stealing a motorcycle and succumbed to his death while treated, the video was him being forced to chant Jai Shree Ram also went viral (The Hindu, 2023-182). The very recent development that happened in the case was that the local court of Jharkhand sentenced the 10 accused in the lynching incident to 10 years imprisonment under the charge of culpable homicide not amounting to murder (Live Law, 2023). Another infamous incident was the Palghar Lynching Case of 2020, where 2 Hindu Sadhus were lynched by a mob of 400 people on the allegation of theft in Maharashtra (Hindustan Times, 2022). Another case was the Rakbar Khan Lynching incident of 2018 based on the pretext of cow slaughter in Rajasthan, where the Alwar court has recently found four guilty under the charge of wrongful restraint and culpable homicide not amounting to murder (Live Law, 2023 47). In a case named Madhu Lynching case of Kerala, where a mentally challenged tribal youth of a lower caste was lynched for stealing rice from a grocery shop, a Special Court convicted 14 accused to a rigorous imprisonment of 7 years for culpable homicide not amounting to murder (Live Law, 2023 47).

Observing these incidents, one apparent fact that was highlighted was that lynching is a grave and serious menace gripping our society. Lynching is closely analogous to hate crimes. They have shared elements of prejudice, discrimination, and violence targeting marginalized groups. In both cases, individuals or groups are targeted based on factors such as religion, ethnicity, caste, or other identities. (Bajpai et al., 2023). Though the chapter deals with lynching, the Indian judicial system can be seen to take developing steps towards a proper mechanism to deal with the same. Taking these formative events in the background, this research study dives more into the understanding of punitive measures that people of our society carry.

9 Profile

Respondents that were involved in the data collection were from various states/union territories and age groups. In further discussions, clear distinctions have been made for the variables – State/Union Territory and Age Group.

In the above Table 8.1, profile of the respondents has been showcased, differentiated on the basis of the states/union territories they belong to in India. It could be clearly observed that among the 215 respondents, the highest percentage is from the state of Uttar Pradesh, with 29.08% of the total respondents, and the second highest is Delhi, with 23.47%. The reason for this trend must also be that the field researcher is from Delhi and so the snowballing originated from the Union Territory of Delhi. However, researchers plan to expand

TABLE 8.1 Respondent profile for state/union territory

State/UT	%
AP	1.02%
Assam	0.51%
Bihar	2.55%
Bihar	0.51%
Chandigarh	0.51%
Chhattisgarh	0.51%
Delhi	23.47%
Gujarat	1.53%
Haryana	5.10%
Haryana	1.02%
HP	0.51%
J&K	1.02%
Jharkhand	1.02%
Karnataka	3.57%
Karnataka	1.02%
Kerala	1.02%
Maharashtra	6.12%
Maharashtra	1.02%
Manipur	0.51%
MP	2.55%
Nagaland	0.51%
Odisha	1.02%
Punjab	2.04%
Rajasthan	2.04%
Telangana	1.53%
TN	2.55%
UK	2.55%
UP	29.08%
WB	1.02%
Total	100.00%

their research and make this study more expansive. The lowest amount of respondent data was collected from the states of – Himachal Pradesh, Assam and Chhattisgarh, and the union territory of Chandigarh was only 0.51%.

TABLE 8.2 Respondent profile for age group

Age group	%
20–30	73.58%
30–40	16.04%
Above 40	4.72%
Below 20	5.66%
Total	100.00%

In the above Table 8.2, profile of the respondents has been showcased, differentiated on the basis of age groups. The age groups that could be seen in the present study are Below 20 years old, 20–30 years old, 30–40 years and Above 40 years. It could be easily seen that most respondent data was collected from the age group of 20–30 years old – 73.58% of the total respondents and the least was from Above 40 years old i.e., 4.72%. This would mean that the present newer generation whose opinions are still formulating – are the perspectives that we will be studying now. It could also be indicative of the future trends that our society will follow through our upcoming generation. Even though responses of people – 30 years and above were less in number, it still highlighted the perspective that can rampantly be seen.

10   The Perspective of People

From the empirical data collected from various respondents situated in varying geographical locations across India, certain data has been collated. This data is indicative of the perception formulated by the people of Indian society regarding the meeting of justice. Three invigorating questions were put up to the respondents, namely:
1. How much awareness do you think you have regarding lynching?
2. Do you think strict law-making and punishment make people commit fewer crimes?
3. What do you think is a more effective method to curb lynching?

These questions were close-ended queries with multiple-choice answers to choose from. In the first question, the answers were limited to good awareness, good awareness and medium awareness. The second question had the option a simple affirmation or negation – this input was recorded as 'strict law and

TABLE 8.3 Strict punishments in general to punishment type for lynching

Strict law and punishment in general	Lynching: lenient punishment	Strict punishment	Total
No	2.40%	27.40%	29.81%
Yes	3.85%	66.35%	70.19%
Total	6.25%	93.75%	100.00%

punishment in general' in the data given. And, in the third question, people had the option of choosing between strict punishment and lenient punishment – this input was recorded as 'punishment type: lenient punishment or strict punishment' in the data given. Based on the responses collected from 215 respondents, herewith detailed perceptions were recorded.

From Table 8.3, it can be observed that approximately only 29% of the respondents answered in negation to the question that whether strict law-making could potentially lessen crimes whereas 70% believed that strict punitive measures is the key to justice. Among the people who selected that strict law-making would not lessen the crime rate, approximately 2% believed lenient punishment would suffice but 27% still believed strict punishment for lynching should be practiced. Among the people who selected that strict law-making would definitely lessen crimes in India, approximately 3% suggested a lenient punishment for the criminal act of lynching but 66% selected strict punishment for lynching to be incorporated. Also, among the respondents, approximately only 6% chose lenient punishment as an option for the crime of lynching however more than 93% of the respondents believed that strict punishment is the way to go for such criminal activities.

It can be clearly deduced that the percentage of people opting for strict law-making and punishment procedures is more. Along with that, the trend for stricter punishment for lynching is also the most perceived response.

From Table 8.4, it can be observed that respondents have chosen their awareness quotient regarding the criminal act of lynching. Approximately 7% have responded with having bad or insufficient awareness when it comes to lynching, approximately 34% have chosen to having medium or balanced awareness with respect to lynching, and more than 57% of respondents chose the option of having good or sufficient knowledge about the criminal act. Among the respondents having bad awareness of lynching, approximately 7% people believed that there should be strict punishment for same, however, no

TABLE 8.4 Awareness of lynching to punishment type for lynching

Awareness of lynching	Lynching lenient punishment	Strict punishment	Total
Bad awareness	0.00%	7.69%	7.69%
Good awareness	3.37%	54.33%	57.69%
Medium awareness	2.88%	31.73%	34.62%
Total	6.25%	93.75%	100.00%

individual equated lenient punishment for lynching. Among the respondents having medium awareness, approximately 2% believed lenient punishment to be the answer for solving lynching but more than 31% gave strict punishment for the same as their response. Among the respondents having good awareness of the criminal act of lynching, approximately only 3% believed that lenient punishment would suffice for the said act but more than 54% of respondents believed that strict punishment should be incorporated. Also, among the respondents, approximately only 6% chose lenient punishment as an option for the crime of lynching however, more than 93% of the respondents believed that strict punishment was the way to go for such criminal activities.

It can be apparently deduced that most people have sufficient awareness about the criminal act of lynching, influenced by the boom in the crime rate of lynching. Along with that, the trend for stricter punishment for lynching is also the most perceived response.

11   Findings and Analysis

With all the data collated and studied, significant findings were documented and presented to the readers. These findings are visually depicted by the use of figures and graphs in a concise way, to make it easily understandable and accessible to all types of readers, no matter the background of the same.

From the presented research, it is deduced that out of all the respondents, more percentage of people believed in strict punitive measures and laws in

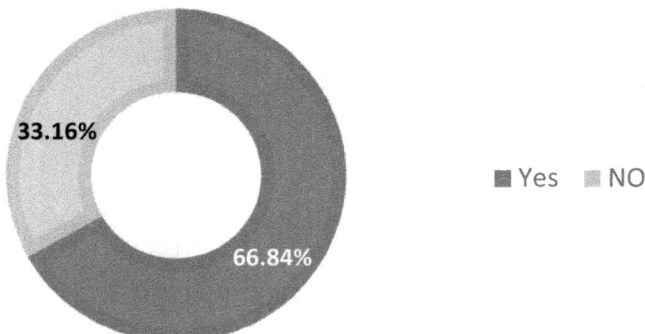

FIGURE 8.1 Percentage of people strict laws and punishment for justice

general. The public, for the most part, i.e., more than 66.84%, chose that in order to lessen the crime rate in India, stricter laws and punishments are required for the legislature to bring about. On the contrary, approximately only 33.16 % of people believed that strict punishment would not lessen crimes among people (Figure 8.1).

It was observed that when the distribution of respondents based on lynching punishment type was studied, there was a stark indication in the results. Approximately 93% of people chose stricter punishment for lynching to be the solution for this menace, whereas only 6% went for lenient punishments.

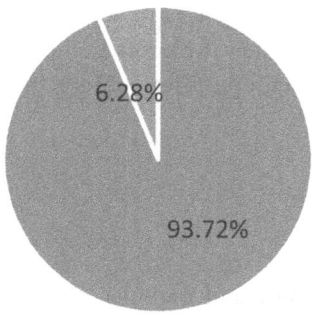

FIGURE 8.2 Percentage distribution of punitive perception for lynching

FIGURE 8.3 State/UT-wise trend for lenient punishment for lynching

This highlights the fact that more people perceived lynching to be catered by a strict punitive regime (Figure 8.2).

Responses collected from various States and Union Territories were recorded and studied. When it comes to approximately 6% of the respondents choosing lenient punishment for lynching, respondents from Delhi, which is a Union Territory and the National Capital of India, chose this response the most. That would mean that among all the respondents for lenient punishments, a trend can be seen in Delhi for opting for less strict punitive measures when it comes to lynching (Figure 8.3).

Responses collected from various States and Union Territories were recorded and studied. When it comes to approximately 93% of the respondents choosing strict punishment for lynching, respondents from the state of Uttar Pradesh chose this response the most. That would mean that among all the respondents for strict punishments, a trend can be seen in UP for opting for strict punitive measures when it comes to solving lynching (Figure 8.4).

12 Hypothesis Testing

In the present research study, the hypothesis for punitive trends was tested. It was assessed whether there is a positive relation between the general perspective of the pro-deterrence position and the preferred criminalization trend for the criminal act of lynching among people in India. That would mean that the general trend for choosing strict punishment for reducing crime in India has a positive relation with the trend for choosing strict punitive measures against lynching as well. For the same purpose null hypothesis was formulated –
Ho: There is no relation between the trend for general punishment perspective and the specific punitive trend for lynching in India.

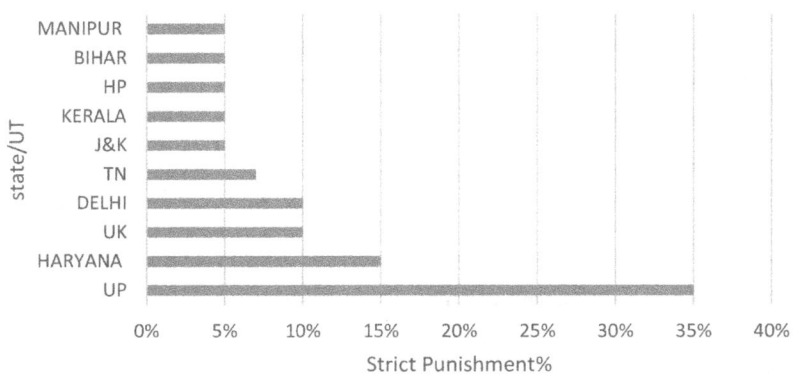

FIGURE 8.4   State/UT-wise trend for lynching

TABLE 8.5   Regression statistics

Regression statistics

Multiple R	0.143893
R Square	0.020705
Adjusted R Square	0.016086
Standard Error	0.396766
Observations	214

Following is the regression analysis for the same: In the aforementioned analysis, it can be seen that p-value is 0.03 which is less than 0.05. That means the null hypothesis is rejected, and it can be deduced that there is a weak positive relation between the general punishment perception among the people and specific punitive measures for lynching. In conclusion, with the increase in the trend towards general pro-deterrence perception for crimes in general, strict punitive beliefs against lynching would also rise.

TABLE 8.6 ANOVA

ANOVA					
Df	*SS*	*MS*	*F*	*Significance F*	
Regression	1	0.705626	0.705626	4.48234	0.035412
Residual	212	33.37381	0.157424		
Total	213	34.07944			

13 Legislative Analysis for Lynching

As our research approaches its conclusion, it's crucial to provide an updated analysis of the legislative landscape concerning lynching in India, including insights regarding Bharatiya Nyaya Sanhita (BNS). This section enables us to compare our research findings with the latest legal developments, particularly within the framework of BNS. Under Article 21 of the Indian Constitution, which guarantees the Right to Life (Constitution of India, n.d., Art. 21), legislative measures have been implemented to address the menace of lynching. While the Indian Penal Code (IPC) contains provisions to address acts of murder or culpable homicide under sections 300 and 302, the absence of a specific definition for lynching poses a challenge (India Today, 2018). However, recent legislative efforts, including the introduction of BNS, have aimed to address this issue comprehensively.

Bharatiya Nyaya Sanhita (BNS), also known as the Indian Penal Code, represents a comprehensive overhaul of India's legal framework, encompassing both substantive and procedural laws. BNS seeks to modernize and streamline India's legal system, addressing emerging challenges such as lynching through clear definitions and stringent penalties (Raut, Pal, & Tripathi, 2024).

In response to the alarming rise in lynching incidents, several states have enacted new laws to combat this heinous crime, aligning with the principles outlined in BNS. States like Manipur, West Bengal, Rajasthan, Jharkhand, and others have introduced specific anti-lynching legislation, proposing stricter penalties and expeditious legal procedures for lynching cases, pending Presidential assent (The Hindu, 2022). Additionally, Uttar Pradesh drafted a bill in 2019 aimed at curbing lynching, reflecting a growing recognition of the need for legislative action in line with BNS (The Economic Times, 2020 182).

Moreover, recent judicial directives have bolstered efforts to tackle lynching, with courts invoking the principles enshrined in BNS to deliver justice.

For instance, in landmark cases like Tehseen S Poonawalla v. Union of India in 2018, the judiciary has intervened to develop concrete punitive measures against lynching, drawing upon the guidelines laid out in BNS (Tehseen S Poonawalla v. Union of India, 2018).

Despite these advancements, challenges persist, particularly regarding the lack of formal data tracking lynching incidents. However, the proactive stance of the judiciary and legislative initiatives in alignment with BNS signify progress in addressing this pressing issue. Moving forward, it's imperative for legislative bodies to continue enacting comprehensive anti-lynching laws in line with BNS, defining and penalizing this crime effectively. Additionally, efforts to collect and analyze data on lynching incidents must be intensified to inform evidence-based policymaking and uphold the principles of justice and equality outlined in BNS.

14   Conclusion

Considering all the aforementioned information, the readers can easily conclude a few things. Firstly, the hypothesis set by the paper was met. Secondly, this study has successfully established a relationship between the punishment trends followed in India and the upcoming lynching developments. Thirdly, it also studied the perception of people regarding the criminal act of lynching comprehensively. This research was a mixture of empirical data analysis and a thereby link with the doctrinal study of lynching.

What can be finally deduced from this chapter is that coherent discourse, along with legal developments, are required to happen simultaneously. One without the other would lead to incomplete development. By furthering discussions regarding the same, our Indian society would come closer to defining lynching in the best manner that would suit the society the best.

Bibliography

Bajpai, G. S., Pal, G., Singh, T., & Tambe, A. (2023). *Hate Crime in India: Understanding Nuanced Discrimination Against North-Eastern Population.* Springer Cham.

Bharatiya Nayaya Sanhita. (2023).

Bhatia, A. (2018). *Lynching: A Study in Sociology.* Rawat Publications. Constitution of India, 1950.

Dixit, M. (2020). *The Politics of Mob Lynching in India.* Oxford University Press.

Hindustan Times. (2022, April 16). Palghar lynching case: Two years on. *Hindustan Times*. Retrieved from https://www.hindustantimes.com/cities/mumbai-news/palghar-lynching-case-two-years-on-101650048601368.html.

India Today. (2018, July 17). What is lynching and why killer mob goes unpunished. *India Today*. Retrieved from https://www.indiatoday.in/india/story/lynching-india-1287911-2018-07-17.

Indian Penal Code, 1860.

Jha, M. K. (Ed.). (2019). *Lynching, Cultural Violence and Justice: From Rajasthan to Dadri*. Sage Publications.

Live Law. (2021, September 7). Pehlu Khan Lynching Case: Rajasthan High Court Issues Bailable Warrants Against 6 Accused On Kin's Plea Against Their Acquittal. *Live Law*. Retrieved from https://www.livelaw.in/news-updates/pehlu-khan-lynching-rajasthan-high-courtbailable-warrants-accused-kin-acquittal-181068?infinitescroll=1.

Live Law. (2023, April 2). Kerala Court Convicts 14 In Madhu Lynching Case, Acquits Two. *Live Law*. Retrieved from https://www.livelaw.in/news-updates/kerala-court-madhu-lynching-veridct-225477.

Live Law. (2023, June 5). Tabrez Ansari Lynching Case: Jharkhand Court Convicts 10 Accused, Sentences Them To 10 Years Each. Live Law. Retrieved from https://www.livelaw.in/news-updates/tabrez-ansari-lynching-case-jharkhand-court-convicts-10-accused-sentenced-10-years-each-231989.

Live Law. (2023, May 25). Rakbar Khan Lynching Case 2018: Alwar Court Finds Four Guilty, Get 7-Year Jail Term Each; One Accused Acquitted. *Live Law*. Retrieved from https://www.livelaw.in/news-updates/rakbar-khan-lynching-case-2018-alwar-court-finds-four-guilty-acquits-one-229437.

Ministry of Home Affairs. (2019). *Action Taken Report on Mob Lynching*. Government of India.

National Crime Records Bureau. (2022). *Accidental Deaths & Suicides in India – 2021*. Ministry of Home Affairs, Government of India. Retrieved from https://ncrb.gov.in/en/accidental-deaths-suicides-india-2021.

NDTV. (2022, August 31). Maharashtra Man Beaten To Death By Mob Over Suspicion of Theft: Police. *NDTV*. Retrieved from https://www.ndtv.com/india-news/maharashtra-man-beaten-to-death-by-mob-over-suspicion-of-theft-police-3168754.

People's Union for Civil Liberties v. State of Maharashtra, (2014) 10 SCC 635. R v. Mastan, (2019) 3 SCC 107.

Raut, A. N., Pal, G., & Tripathi, A. (2024). *Decrypting the Sanhita: An Analysis of the Newly Introduced offences Under Bharatiya Nyaya Sanhita. (Latest 2024 Edition)*. Whitesmann Publishing Co. ISBN 9788119725955.

Scroll.in. (2023, August 21). Uttar Pradesh: 10 held after Muslim man thrashed, beard chopped by mob in Shamli. *Scroll.in*. Retrieved from https://scroll.in/latest/1011163/uttar-pradesh-10-held-after-muslim-man-thrashed-beard-chopped-by-mob-in-shamli.

Sen, S., & Varshney, A. (Eds.). (2021). *Mob Violence in India: Identity Politics, Citizens' Rights, and the State*. Cambridge University Press.

Singh, A., & Sharma, N. (2020). Understanding mob lynching in India: Prevalence, causes, and implications. *Journal of Social Issues, 76*(2), 243–259. https://doi.org/10.1111/josi.12368.

Tehseen S Poonawalla v. Union of India, (2018) 9 SCC 501.

The Economic Times. (2020 August 24). Uttar Pradesh government to examine anti-lynching proposal soon. Retrieved from https://economictimes.indiatimes.com/news/politics-and-nation/uttar-pradesh-government-to-examine-anti-lynching-proposal-soon/articleshow/77711987.cms?from=mdr.

The Hindu. (2022, February 15). The Anti-mob lynching bills passed by 4 Assemblies at various levels of non-implementation. *TheHindu*. Retrieved from https://www.thehindu.com/news/national/anti-mob-lynching-bills-passed-by-4-assemblies-at-various-levels-of-non-implementation/article65052872.ece.

The Hindu (2023, July 5), Tabrez Ansari lynching case: Jharkhand Court sentences 10 accused to 10 years of rigorous imprisonment *The Hindu*, retrieved from; https://www.thehindu.com/news/national/other-states/tabrez-ansari-lynching-case-jharkhand-court-sentences-10-accused-to-ten-years-of-rigorous-imprisonment/article67045516.ece.

The Indian Express. (2023, March 7). Nagaland mob lynching: No response from CM Rio even after 10 days, allege civil society groups. *The Indian Express*. Retrieved from https://indianexpress.com/article/north-east-india/nagaland/nagaland-mob-lynching-no-response-from-cm-rio-even-after-10-days-allege-civil-society-groups-7824023/.

The New Indian Express. (2022, March 16). Jharkhand government admits 46 mob-lynching cases reported since 2016. *The New Indian Express*. Retrieved from https://www.newindianexpress.com/nation/2022/mar/16/jharkhand-government-admits-46-mob-lynching-cases-reported-since-2016-2430657.html.

CHAPTER 9

Raising the Age of Trying People as Adults Back to 21

Antonio Reza

1   Introduction: Who Is an Adult?

In society, for the most part, we do not treat minors as adults because we recognize they are not fully functioning humans. Minors are cognitively and developmentally not the same as adults, and rightfully, are not held to the same standard as adults. It would be ridiculous to charge a 5-year-old with theft when they take a cookie from the cookie jar. Furthermore, we as a society would not brand that child with a criminal history or label them a thief for the rest of their lives. Which is precisely what bringing us to this point where we must ask the questions: What is an adult, and when do we hold people to that standard of being an adult in our criminal justice system?

What is an adult? The answer to this question will change depending on the context. This context could include: religion, jurisdiction, time in history, a topic at hand, profession, issue presented, an act that someone did, or an act that someone is allowed to do. Additionally, that context shifts multiple times within a person's life. For example, a Jewish boy becomes an adult multiple times during his life. He becomes a "man" when he turns 13 years old at his Bar Mitzvah (*Life Cycle: Coming of Age*, 2017). He then becomes a "man" and can be tried as an adult if he is 16 years old and accused of committing a crime (*O.G. v. Superior Ct. of Ventura Cty.*, 2021).[1] However, the case finding is new; before 2021 and without the help of Proposition 57 and SB 1391, he could have been tried as an adult when he was younger (*O.G. v. Superior Ct. of Ventura Cty.*, 2021). In American society, he also becomes a "man" when he turns 18 (*Legal Age*, n.d.). Nevertheless, again, in American society, he is not a "man" until he is 21 due to the legal drinking age (National Minimum Drinking Age Act, 1984: Sec. 158).[2] Finally, he becomes a "man" again medically when his brain fully develops at

---

1   California Supreme Court case finding 14 and 15-year-old children cannot be tried in adult court based on Prop. 57 and SB 1391.
2   The Act requires that States prohibit persons under 21 years of age from purchasing or publicly possessing alcohol.

around 25 (Campellone & Turley, n.d.). However, new medical research says the brain is fully developed at around 25, but that does not mean the brain is fully mature (Johnson, 2022). Full maturity would potentially come around 30 (Johnson, 2022). Clearly, there is no consensus around when this Jewish boy became a "man," and it is almost entirely based on the context at that moment in his life. This same line of thought of repeatedly joining adulthood for the Jewish boy would be the same for a Jewish girl, but the only difference would be that her 13th birthday would be a Bat Mitzvah (*Life Cycle: Coming of Age*, 2017).

This fluidity of becoming an "adult" change in different cultures and with other sexes. For example, in Latino cultures, a girl becomes a "woman" when she turns is 15, and the ceremony is called a Quinceanera (*About the Quinceanera Tradition*, 2021). Then, in America, a typical coming of age for "women" is when they turn 16 for their Sweet Sixteen (Picone, 2013). One interesting point to make is there is no such thing as a Quinceanero or a Sweet Sixteen for boys in Latino and American cultures. So, while girls become "women" at 15 and 16, boys do not become "men" until they are 18, and the only reason they became "men" is merely a legal and temporal technicality instead of a rite of passage. Then, in a more sinister line of thought, instead of a rite of passage to adulthood for boys, like a Sweet Sixteen or Quinceanera, once boys turn 16, they are now within the potential jurisdiction of the adult court, depending on the act they are charged with. Does that mean this is now a boy's coming-of-age moment? Did this boy come of age because the legal line of trying him as an adult has moved itself from 18 to 16 based on an act he is accused of? Again, this goes back to the original question: Who is an adult?

2   Why Do We Have Laws?

The simple answer is to avoid chaos. Thomas Hobbes would refer to this pre-law/pre-society time as the State of Nature, where we, as humans, would be in a state of perpetual and unavoidable war (Friend, n.d.). In order to avoid this dog-eat-dog world where only the strongest survive, we would create a civil society (Friend, n.d.). This civil society would originally stand on the Social Contract Theory, where people lived together under an agreement established by morals and rules of behaviour (McCombs School of Business, 2022). However, the social contract is still not good enough, nor is it what we use today.

The social contract would naturally go through its critical evolutionary phases to become what it is today. One of these evolutionary phases would be from having these morals and social rules passed around orally to being written. This codification of laws is done, in part, to avoid relativism while establishing consistency and certainty as to what conduct is permissible or not (Holt, 2020). Additionally, the codification of laws sets an objective standard to eschew subjectivism by removing the act from a single person's judgement and placing it to be judged in the hands of the collective and what the collective has regarded as permissible or not (Holt, 2020). While the judgement of that act is now in the hands of the collective, the law also binds the collective to that judgement (Judicial Learning Center, 2019). Therefore, enacting codified laws ensures consistency, objectivity, and safety amongst its members to protect against other citizens, organizations, or the government (Judicial Learning Center, 2019).

3 Why Do We Punish?

There is no point in having laws for society if nothing will happen to the people who transgress them. As a society, we want people to be held appropriately accountable for their actions and to get their just deserts when they have committed moral wrongdoing (Carlsmith et al., 2002). Theoretically, there are five rationales that punishment seeks to accomplish.

We punish people for the following purposes: (1) deterrence, (2) incapacitation, (3) rehabilitation, (4) restitution, and (5) retribution (Henderson, 2020). However, there are some exceptions to these punishments and why they are applied to a person when they have committed an illegal act. These reasons all roughly revolve around one's ability to truly appreciate their actions. This results in some being held to atone for their actions to the full extent of the law as adults, whereas others would be held to a different standard depending on the context.

3.1 *Three Main Legal Ways a Person Would Avoid Being Punished as an Adult*

There are three main instances in which a person would not be punished to the full extent of the law as an adult would if they committed the same crime. The first is when that person is legally insane, and that insanity is why that person committed the crime (*Insanity Defense*, n.d.). The second is when the person has diminished capacity (*Diminished Capacity*, n.d.) or is mentally incompetent (Lowe, 2017). The third is if the person was a minor when they committed the crime (Senate Bill No. 1391, 2018). The rationale supporting these three is that the person does not truly appreciate the ramifications of their crime.

These three carve-outs show up in other areas of the law. One example is contract law which is done roughly for the same reasons as criminal law (Stim,

2011). In contracts, a minor is not forced to uphold their end of a contract if they entered into it while they are under 18 (Stim, 2011). Even if a person is over 18 but does not have mental capacity, their contract could be voidable (*Mental Capacity to Contract: Everything You Need to Know*, n.d.). Lastly, if a person is mentally insane, the contract they entered into could be voidable (*Mental Incapacity & Contracts: Definition & Examples*, 2013). These are all supported by that individual lacking the mental capacity required to enter into a contract (*Mental Incapacity & Contracts: Definition & Examples*, 2013).

The only difference between contract law and criminal law in those three exception categories is that sometimes a minor can be tried as an adult in criminal law. In contrast, with contracts, the minor is not. In criminal law, society has made exceptions based solely on specific acts done by the minor to determine how we feel about that child and if we should hold them to the standard of an adult or not. Logically, this does not make sense because if that 16-year-old signed a contract, they could get out of it, but depending on what illegal act they did, they would not be able to get out of it, even if it was the same teenager. We have decided to be punitive and punish that child as an adult with a complete disregard for all of the science, evidence, and rationale we have for trying someone as an adult.

As a society, we have concluded that everyone cannot, and should not, be held to the same standard if they commit an illegal act. In essence, we have laws meeting people where they are because we acknowledge the purposes supporting why and how we punish people are not always applicable; especially when they fall into one of those three categories. This is because we have decided as a society that these people, when they commit their illegal acts, genuinely do not have an appreciation for their crimes. Therefore, how can we possibly effectively meet the purposes of punishment by employing: deterrence, incapacitation, rehabilitation, restitution, and retribution when their respective goals would not be met in their intended ways when dealing with those three demographics.

3.2 *The Problem Regarding the Bright-Line Rule for Trying People as Adult*

People who support trying kids as adults frequently say these two quotes: "Don't do the crime if you can't do the time." (Morgan & Grusin, 1975/1976) and "Adult time for adult crime." (Stimson, 2009) These quotes are problematic for a variety of reasons. When taking apart the quote: "Don't do the crime if you can't do the time." (*Baretta: Don't Do the Crime if You Can't Do the Time.*, n.d.) This quote is flawed because it assumes the act/crime someone does and the punishment allocated to that act/crime is are consistent with the truth (Perry,

2015). It assumes that the crime/act and the repercussions connected to it have always been that way, therefore, should stay that way. When in reality, crime and what is classified as deviant behaviour are more arbitrary and fluid. For example, marijuana was legal in California until 1913, and then it became illegal (Boslaugh, 2015). Nevertheless, it was still legal in many other states until the passage of the Marijuana Tax Act in 1937, making that plant illegal in the United States (Tikkanen, 2019). In 1969, marijuana was classified as a Schedule I drug under the Controlled Substances Act, categorising it with serious drugs such as heroin and LSD (Tikkanen, 2019). Then in 1996, California voters passed the Compassionate Use Act, which allowed for the use of medicinal marijuana (Department of Cannabis Control – State of California, n.d.). Then in November of 2016, the voters in California passed the Adult Use of Marijuana Act, also known as Proposition 64, which legalized the use of marijuana again for either medical or recreational purposes so long as the individual is over the age of 21 (*California Proposition 64, Marijuana Legalization*, 2016). However, federally, a person could still potentially receive a 3-year sentence in prison and a fine of $5,000 (*Federal Marijuana Charges*, 2019). With the quick history regarding our ever-shifting stance with a plant, there is no such thing as a capital T Truth with crime and punishment. Thus, the phrase: "Don't do the crime if you can't do the time." (Morgan & Grusin, 1975/1976) is flawed.

That same flawed reasoning of applying a capital T Truth to: "Don't do the crime if you can't do the time." (Morgan & Grusin, 1975/1976) applies to the phrase: "Adult time for adult crime." (Stimson, 2009) As established above, "adult time" (Stimson, 2009) is fluid because we, as a society continue to change what is considered deviant behaviour and how much punishment we allot to that act. Additionally, as stated above, society has a fluid stance on what an adult is. Therefore, how can one do adult time for an adult crime if crimes are defined and frequently redefined while simultaneously contending with the fact that the qualifications for what classifies a person as an adult is also fluctuating depending on the context?

All of this points to the problem with a bright-line rule of mandatorily trying people as adults when they turn 18 (Wishnia, 2021). This arbitrary bright-line rule is problematic and begins to show its ludicrousness instantly. For starters, there is nothing inherently special about turning 18. Nothing magical happens that would induce someone to instantly be cognitively and developmentally an adult when they turn 18. To further show the bright-line's absurdity, a person can turn 18 while still attending high school, which means they would have to raise their hand in a classroom to get permission to use the restroom, yet that same person is an "adult" in the eyes of the law. Additionally, the bright line holds no cultural relevance in America like a Bat Mitzvah, Quinceanera, or

Sweet Sixteen. Moreover, this age does not hold historical merit in the United States either because 18 was not always the age of trying people as an adult. The bright line holding fast at 18 has not always been the standard and needs to be readjusted back to where it was.

Lastly, biologically, people who are 18 should not be tried as adults. The human brain does not finish developing until 25 (Campellone & Turley, n.d.) and the last part of the brain to finish developing is the frontal cortex which is in charge of decision-making and impulse control (Campellone & Turley, n.d.). Additionally, the human brain is not done fully maturing until around the age of 30 (Johnson, 2022). This scientifically proves that trying people as adults when they are 18 is not reasonable or rational.

3.3   Biologically 18-Year-Olds Should Not Be Tried as Adults
As stated above, the human brain does not stop growing until someone is 25 years old (Campellone & Turley, n.d.).

The last part of the brain to develop is the frontal lobe (S. B. Johnson et al., 2009). The frontal lobe controls the planning, working memory, impulse control, and decision-making portion of the brain (S. B. Johnson et al., 2009). Additionally, it is also the last area of the brain that matures (S.B. Johnson et al., 2009). The development and maturity can potentially last up "until halfway through the third decade of life." (S. B. Johnson et al., 2009) A teenager's brain is biologically different from adults; specifically, the decision-making portion of the brain where that person can plan and weigh the outcomes of their actions down the road. Thus, without having this development yet, teenagers do not have a true appreciation of the ramifications of their actions.

Many crimes have a *mens rea* requirement or element incorporated into it. *Mens Rea* refers to criminal intent. The literal translation from Latin is "guilty mind." (*Mens Rea*, n.d.) Which begs the question: How can a teenager meet that element for crimes when that specific part of their brain is not fully functioning? Teenager does not truly appreciate their acts or the ripple effect they would have on their lives and everyone involved. Also, a teenager would be more impulsive and act rashly because that portion of their brain is not done growing or maturing. Therefore, biologically, trying people as adults at 18 is not medically sound and goes in the opposite direction of what logic would dictate.

3.4   History around the Trying People as Adults
The age at which we currently try, charge, and convict someone as an adult is when they are 18 years of age or older (*Age Matrix*, n.d.). This bright-line rule magically appears because we, as a society, say that that is the age to charge

people as an adult no matter what they do. However, this bright line of trying people as adults when they reach 18 has not always been the standard in the United States. The age of trying someone as an adult used to be 21 years old; it was later reduced from 21 to 18 in 1971 (SCOCAL, n.d.). It changed simultaneously with the passage of the 26th Amendment, which dropped the age to vote from 21 to 18 (*The 26th Amendment*, 2021).

Since the passage of Assembly Bill 2887 in 1971, much legislation has gone back and forth regarding minors entering the criminal legal system. For example, in 2000, Proposition 21 was passed, which required prosecutors to charge minors 14 years old or older directly in criminal court. (Welf. & Inst. Code, § 602, former subd. (b), repealed by Prop. 57, § 4.1.) (*Proposition 21*, n.d.) Proposition 21 gave prosecutors discretion to directly charge minors 14 or older in criminal court instead of the juvenile court for other specified serious offences. (Welf. & Inst. Code, § 707, former subd. (d), repealed by Prop. 57, § 4.2.) (*Proposition 21*, n.d.).

As a pushback to Proposition 21 in November 2016, Proposition 57 was enacted [*California Proposition 57: Parole for Non-Violent Criminals and Juvenile Court Trial Requirements*, 2016 (hereinafter "*California Proposition 57*, 2016")]. Proposition 57 amended the Welfare and Institutions Code to eliminate direct filing by prosecutors so that prosecutors would not send children directly to adult court (*California Proposition 57*, 2016). "The measure was designed to make judges, rather than prosecutors, decide whether to try juveniles as young as 14 years old in adult court." (*California Proposition 57*, 2016) However, minors can still be tried in criminal court after a juvenile court judge conducts a transfer hearing to consider the minor's maturity, degree of criminal sophistication, prior delinquent history, and whether the minor can be rehabilitated (*California Proposition 57*, 2016). "All remnants of Proposition 21 were deleted by the passage of Proposition 57. (*K.L., supra*, 36 Cal.App.5th at p. 534 fn. 3.)" (*O.G. v. Superior Ct. of Ventura Cty.*, 2021).

Then in 2019, Senate Bill 1391 amended Proposition 57 by eliminating the transfer of juveniles accused of committing crimes when they are 14 or 15 years old unless they are first apprehended after the end of juvenile court jurisdiction (*O.G. v. Superior Ct. of Ventura Cty.*, 2021). (See Welf. & Inst. Code, § 707, subd. (a)(1)– (2), as amended by Stats. 2018, ch. 1012, § 1.) Thus, making 16 the minimum age for transferring a minor to criminal court.

Since 1970, and the passage of Assembly Bill 2887, the United States "incarcerated population has increased by 500% – 2 million people in jail and prison today, far outpacing population growth and crime." (*Mass Incarceration*, 2022) One can deduce this dramatic increase is partly due to lowering the age of trying people as adults from 21 to 18 and, in turn, having the punishments for adults applied to a broader range of people. This egregious mistake needs remediation.

3.5 *The Sad History of Trying and Punishing Children as Adults*

3.5.1 The Youngest Child Sentenced to Death Was 10

The U.S. government executed James Arcene by hanging in Arkansas. He was Native American and the youngest person ever to be sentenced to death in the United States for his participation in murder and robbery when he was ten years old (Streib, 1987). He was hung when he was 23 years old, on June 18, 1885.

3.5.2 The Youngest Child Executed Was 14

The state of South Carolina sentenced and executed the child, George Stinney Jr., at 14 years old by means of the electric chair, making him the youngest person in modern history to be put to death (Bever, 2014). This African American child was arrested in March of 1944, had a 2-hour trial, the jury deliberated and convicted him in 10 minutes of murder on April 24, 1944, and he was executed on June 16, 1944 (Bever, 2014). He was found innocent and exonerated 70 years after his execution (Bever, 2014).

3.5.3 The Youngest Child to Receive LWOP Was 12: Overturned

In modern history, Florida sentenced the youngest person, Lionel Tate, to life in prison without the possibility of parole (cbs News, 2006). This African American boy was born in 1987 and was only 12 years old when he received his sentence (cbs News, 2006). However, that ruling was overturned in 2004 by an appeals court because it was not clear he understood the charges (cbs News, 2006). Sadly, this second chance was squandered; after his release, he recidivated and was sentenced to 30 years (cbs News, 2006).

3.5.4 Current Youngest Child to Receive LWOP Was 14: Standing

The state of Alabama currently holds the record for the youngest person sentenced in the modern history of the United States to life without the possibility of parole (Faulk, 2021). Miller was 14 years old at the time of his original conviction (Faulk, 2021). Recently, Miller was re-sentenced to life without parole in 2021 for his capital murder conviction in 2003 (Faulk, 2021).

Although Miller is still in prison for his crimes, his case has helped others around the nation. For example, in the state of Washington, Miller's case helped Barry Massey. "In 1987, Massey became the youngest person in the country to be given a life without the possibility of parole sentence." (Lynch, 2016) After 28 years in prison, Massey was released due to a landmark United States Supreme Court ruling (Lynch, 2016). That decision came from the 2012 ruling in *Miller v. Alabama*, where "the U.S. Supreme Court held that a mandatory life sentence without the possibility of parole was unconstitutional for juveniles" (Lynch, 2016). Since then, in 2014, "the Washington state legislature passed a bill that provided a process for individuals like Barry to potentially be released." (Lynch, 2016) "In February 2016, Massey was finally released from prison." (Lynch, 2016) It stands to reason although Massey and the state of Washington at one point had the nation's record for sentencing the youngest person to life without parole, it is now because of Miller and his case that the title has moved to Alabama (Lynch, 2016). It is ironic that Miller's case went up to the United States Supreme Court and won, causing over 2,000 inmates nationwide to get re-sentenced, but when Miller got re-sentenced in 2021, again, he got sentenced to life without parole (Lynch, 2016).

4   The Life-Long Punishment of Being Tried as an Adult

America has systematically set up barriers for people with records ("Getting Back to Work: Revamping the Economy by Removing Past Records," 2021). These barriers manifest themselves in many ways but the primary one would be "the box." ("Getting Back to Work: Revamping the Economy by Removing Past Records," 2021) The box appears on applications for housing, jobs, college, licensing, juries, and more. ("Getting Back to Work: Revamping the Economy by Removing Past Records," 2021) This box asks individuals about their criminal history. ("Getting Back to Work: Revamping the Economy by Removing Past Records," 2021) More often than not, when an applicant checks that box, they are excluded from that opportunity. ("Getting Back to Work: Revamping the Economy by Removing Past Records," 2021) This box directly contributes to recidivism due to the lack of opportunities it causes.

When people get convicted of crimes as children, it is much easier for them to seal or clean up their records, especially when they come of age. For example, some states will automatically expunge juvenile records once they turn 18 (Pirius, 2022). Though done for a variety of reasons, the main one is so that those mistakes do not follow them into adulthood and hinder them from being contributing members of society. It also bolsters the claim that these kids will be contributing members of society when they are older if given the chance to leave their record behind them because it is statistically proven that people age out of crime (*From Youth Justice Involvement to Young Adult Offending*, 2014). When legally classified as kids, they will still be held appropriately accountable for their actions in the immediate future while simultaneously helping them out in the far future because it will be easier to clean up their records.

Therefore, in the short term, society will get what it wants, and in the long term, society will win again because the person will almost inevitably age out of crime and no longer be a danger while simultaneously contributing in a positive and meaningful way to society.

By trying people as adults when they are still children at the age of 18, society is punishing them now, and punishing them perpetually when they come home. "At least 95% of all State prisoners will be released from prison at some point; nearly 80% will be released to parole supervision." (Huges & Wilson, n.d.) With all these people coming home, we do not want to hinder them from gaining gainful employment solely based on a criminal conviction. When they come home, society does not want them to recidivate because if they are not recidivating, they are not committing new crimes, and if fewer crimes are committed, there are fewer victims, which is what we all want. It is in the best interest of everyone to make it easier for these people to come home and rejoin society so they become contributing members instead of repeat offenders. One of the ways to do this is by making it easier for people to clean their records, and one of the ways to do that is to have more people be appropriately classified as minors. Thus, as stated above, outlining how much easier it is for minors to get their records cleaned compared to adults and combined with the fact people age out of crime, it is judicious and reasonable based on the United States legal history, to move this line back up from 18 to 21.

5 Conclusion: A Story from BIT141

Numbers are great for showing the magnitude of an issue. Science bolsters logical reasons supporting an issue. Facts are imperative in accompanying a position on an issue. History provides context to show us where we have been on an issue and hopefully guides us in avoiding repeating the mistakes. Nevertheless, nothing is more moving than anecdotal evidence to make real and tangible numbers, science, facts, and history on a particular issue. Therefore, I will end with the story of BIT141.

BIT141 was a young man who did not understand the lifelong impacts that having a criminal record would have. When BIT141 turned 19 years old, he thought he knew everything. After all, what teenager does not he had graduated high school in 2010, but between 2010 and 2011, he knew seven people who died. During the summer after graduation, he was kicked out of his house by his mother and was homeless. Eventually, with hard work, he was not homeless. Later, during a neighborhood party with some people, BIT141's friend pulled out a gun and said: "I'm tired of being hungry, and I'm tired of being homeless." When combined with the trauma of constant death and homelessness, those words provided the perfect storm for BIT141 to be a driver during a few armed robberies. Despite being a teenager, the actions of BIT141 resulted in him being charged with 4 counts of armed robbery and as if he was the perpetrator in the stores wielding the weapon.

Because BIT141 had crossed the bright line of 18, he was mechanically charged as an adult. This meant he went to adult jail and not the juvenile hall. To make matters worse, due to the multiple violent felony charges, he was in jail with every other adult male who was classified as a violent offender. Which included elder career criminals who had convictions, or current charges, of attempted murder, assault with a deadly weapon, and more.

Before BIT141 was 20, he was sent to an adult jail, tried as an adult, held in an adult faculty, housed with all the other serious violent adult felons, and convicted of the violent felony: armed robbery with the accompanying strike. It was not rehabilitative in any way, shape, or form for him, nor was it motivating for him to change his life and be a better person. It left him with resentment, further distrust in the system, and PTSD that lingers today. BIT141 was not a better person or ready to contribute to society after his experiences with the criminal justice system. However, with determination, intellect, hard work, support, and luck, he was successful despite the odds statistically stacked against him. Did BIT141 know what he was doing was wrong? Yes, the concept of right and wrong is instilled in everyone early. When people do something they should not be doing, they will naturally try to cover it up. This can appear as being criminally sophisticated and subsequently misclassified as an adult action because they took intelligent steps to get away with that act. However, they still do not truly appreciate the ramifications, severity, and gravity of their actions; this was particularly true for BIT141.

BIT141 did not have a proper understanding or appreciation of the impact that his actions would have. Nor did he clearly understand what the classification of a serious violent felon truly meant. For example, he did not know that he was facing over a decade in prison. He did not truly appreciate how long a decade is and how much life happens in that time. He did not know that being on 5-year felony probation meant that he would be under some sort of supervision by the criminal justice system his entire adult life and for 25% of his life as a whole up until he was 24 years old. He did not know that he would have a probation officer check in on him randomly to make sure he was not violating probation or be mandated to check into a probation office frequently to submit urine and do mouth swabs during drug tests. He did not know he would legally have a curfew requiring him to be indoors from 10pm until 6am until he was 24 because of his probation status. He did not know the police

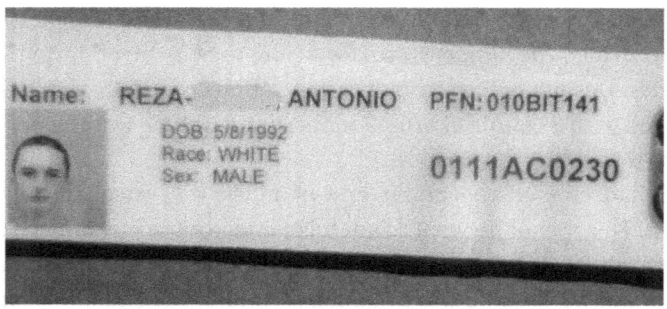

FIGURE 9.1 In this photograph of Reza's bracelet which consisted of his information and a mugshot
PHOTOGRAPHY TAKEN INSIDE A CORRECTIONAL FACILITY

would become familiar with him and use his probation status to pull him over and harass him legally. He did not know he would miss birthdays, barbeques, family events, and funerals due to being incarcerated or on probation.

He did not know the negative stigma that follows a person when they have a record, especially when the classification of felon accompanies it. He did not realize how many opportunities he would be excluded from based solely on the actions he took as a teenager. He did not realize the ripple effect it would have on his entire life or how impactful it would be. He had no idea how pervasive the box was. He had no idea the extra essays and paperwork he would always have to fill out to get into college and to have the same opportunities as his classmates have afforded to them. The list goes on as to what BIT141 missed out on and the impact it has had on his life. It far exceeded what he anticipated the potential punishment was going to be at that moment, and he never knew the punishment was perpetual post-incarceration. Nevertheless, the main thing he learned with age and maturity is that his actions impacted so many people around him and how genuinely sorry he is for the impact his actions had on the world. The story of BIT141 is my story. BIT141 was my assigned number. Below is a picture (Figure 9.1) of my bracelet that had my information on it and a mugshot taken inside a correctional facility. A picture paints a thousand words, and you can see I was a child despite being legally classified as an adult. So, was I an adult? Yes, legally, I was. Did I need to be held accountable for my actions? Yes, I broke the law. Did I need to experience everything that happened afterwards? I beg to differ. Therefore, with the culminating facts, history, and anecdotes, it stands to reason that the age of trying people as adults needs to be raised back to 21; where it once was.

Bibliography

About the Quinceanera Tradition. (2021). *Quinceanera-Boutique.com Inc.* Retrieved from https://www.quinceanera-boutique.com/quinceanera-tradition/.

Age Matrix. (2023, March). *Interstate Commission for Juveniles*. Retrieved from https://www.juvenilecompact.org/age-matrix.

Baumeyer, K. (2013, April 15). Mental Incapacity & Contracts: Definition & Examples. Retrieved from [Source URL].

Bever, L. (2014, December 18). It took 10 minutes to convict 14-year-old George Stinney Jr. It took 70 years after his execution to exonerate him. *Washington Post.* Retrieved from https://www.washingtonpost.com/news/morning-mix/wp/2014/12/18/the-rush-job-conviction-of-14-year-old-george-stinney-exonerated-70-years-after-execution/.

Boslaugh, S. E. (2015). *The SAGE Encyclopedia of Pharmacology and Society*. SAGE Publications.

California Proposition 57: Parole for Non-Violent Criminals and Juvenile Court Trial Requirements. (2016). *Ballotpedia*. Retrieved from https://ballotpedia.org/California_Proposition_57,_Parole_for_Non-Violent_Criminals_and_Juvenile_Court_Trial_Requirements_(2016).

California Proposition 64, Marijuana Legalization. (2016). *Ballotpedia*. Retrieved from https://ballotpedia.org/California_Proposition_64,_Marijuana_Legalization_(2016).

Campellone, J., & Turley, R. K. (n.d.). Understanding the Teen Brain. *Health Encyclopedia*. Retrieved from https://www.urmc.rochester.edu/encyclopedia/content.aspx?ContentTypeID=1&ContentID=3051.

Carlsmith, K. M., Darley, J. M., & Robinson, P. H. (2002). Why do we punish? Deterrence and just deserts as motives for punishment. *Journal of Personality and Social Psychology, 83*(2), 284–299. https://doi.org/10.1037/0022-3514.83.2.284.

CBS News. (2006, May 18). Lionel Tate gets 30 years in jail. *CBN News*. Retrieved from https://www.cbsnews.com/news/lionel-tate-gets-30-years-in-jail/.

Department of Cannabis Control – State of California. (n.d.). California's cannabis laws. *Department of Cannabis Control*. Retrieved from https://cannabis.ca.gov/cannabis-laws/laws-and-regulations/.

Diminished Capacity. *Legal Information Institute (Wex, Cornell Law School)*. Retrieved from https://www.law.cornell.edu/wex/diminished_capacity.

Faulk, K. (2021, February 18). A killer at 14, his case led to second chances for juvenile murderers. He may soon learn his fate. *Advance Local*. Retrieved from https://www.al.com/news/2021/02/a-killer-at-14-his-case-led-to-second-chances-for-juvenile-murderers-he-may-soon-learn-his-fate.html.

Federal Marijuana Charges. (2019, February 8). *Law Offices of David Sloane, The 420 Lawyer*. Retrieved from https://www.the420lawyer.com/marijuana-defense/marijuana-crimes/federal-marijuana-charges/.

Friend, C. Social Contract Theory. *Internet Encyclopedia of Philosophy*. Retrieved from https://iep.utm.edu/soc-cont/#SH2a.

From Youth Justice Involvement to Young Adult Offending. (2014, March 10). *National Institute of Justice*. Retrieved from https://nij.ojp.gov/topics/articles/youth-justice-involvement-young-adult-offending.

Getting Back to Work: Revamping the Economy by Removing Past Records. (2021, March). *Californians for Safety and Justice & UNITE-LA*. Retrieved from https://safeandjust.org/wp-content/uploads/GettingBacktoWork-3.2.2021.pdf.

Henderson, R. (2020). *Alaska Criminal Law*. Pressbooks by University of Minnesota Libraries Publishing. Retrieved from https://pressbooks.pub/alaskacriminallaw2022/chapter/1-5-the-purposes-of-punishment/.

Holt, D. (2020, October 30). PHI220 Ethics and Society. *Pressbooks/VIVA Open Publishing*. Retrieved from https://viva.pressbooks.pub/phi220ethics/chapter/what-is-subjectivism/.

Huges, T., & Wilson, D. J. *Revised Trends in the United States*. Bureau of Justice Statistics. Retrieved from https://bjs.ojp.gov/content/pub/pdf/reentry.pdf.

Insanity Defense. (n.d.). *Legal Information Institute (Wex, Cornell Law School)*. Retrieved from https://www.law.cornell.edu/wex/insanity_defense.

Johnson, S. (2022, January 31). Why is 18 the age of adulthood if the brain can take 30 years to mature? *Big Think*. Retrieved from https://bigthink.com/neuropsych/adult-brain/.

Johnson, S. B., Blum, R., & Giedd, J. N. (2009). Adolescent maturity and the brain: The promise and pitfalls of neuroscience research in adolescent health policy. *Journal of Adolescent Health, 45*(3), 216–221. https://doi.org/10.1016/j.jadohealth.2009.05.016.

Judicial Learning Center. (2019, August 7). Law and the Rule of Law. *Judicial Learning Center*. Retrieved from https://judiciallearningcenter.org/law-and-the-rule-of-law/.

Legal Age. *Legal Information Institute, Wex Cornell Law School*. Retrieved from https://www.law.cornell.edu/wex/legal_age.

Life Cycle: Coming of Age. (2017). *The Jewish Museum London*. Retrieved from https://jewishmuseum.org.uk/schools/asset/life-cycle-bar-bat-mitzvah/.

Lowe, M. (2017, March 29). Intellectually Disabled or Mentally Ill: Competency to Stand Trial and the Insanity Defense. *Dallas Justice Blog*. Retrieved from https://www.dallasjustice.com/intellectually-disabled-mentally-ill-competency-stand-trial-insanity-defense/.

Lynch, A. (2016, April 25). Barry Massey, youngest person sentenced to life, talks with LSJ students. *Law, Societies, and Justice*. Retrieved from https://lsj.washington.edu/news/2016/04/25/barry-massey-youngest-person-sentenced-life-talks-lsj-students.

Mass Incarceration. (2022, February 15). *American Civil Liberties Union*. Retrieved from https://www.aclu.org/issues/smart-justice/mass-incarceration.

McCombs School of Business. (2022, November 5). Social Contract Theory. *Ethics Unwrapped*. Retrieved from https://ethicsunwrapped.utexas.edu/glossary/social-contract-theory.

Mens Rea. *Legal Information Institute (Wex, Cornell Law School)*. Retrieved from https://www.law.cornell.edu/wex/mens_rea.

Mental Capacity to Contract: Everything You Need to Know. (n.d.). *UpCounsel*. Retrieved from https://www.upcounsel.com/mental-capacity-to-contract.

Morgan, A. & Grusin, D. (1975). Baretta's Theme (Keep Your Eye on the Sparrow). On *Baretta (TV Show)*. New York, NY: ABC Records. (1976).

National Minimum Drinking Age Act, 23 U.S.C. (1984). Retrieved from https://alcoholpolicy.niaaa.nih.gov/the-1984-national-minimum-drinking-age-act.

O.G. v. Superior Ct. of Ventura Cty., 11 Cal. 5th 82 (Cal. S.C. 2021).

Perry, J. (2015, December 27). Truth & Other Fictions. *Philosophy Talk*. Retrieved from https://www.philosophytalk.org/blog/truth-other-fictions.

Picone, K. (2013, August 17). The World's Coolest Coming of Age Traditions. *All That's Interesting, ATI*. Retrieved from https://allthatsinteresting.com/worlds-coolest-coming-of-age-traditions/3.

Pirius, R. (2022, September 7). Expunging or Sealing a Juvenile Court Record. *Criminal Defence Lawyer, NOLO*. Retrieved from https://www.criminaldefenselawyer.com/resources/expunging-or-sealing-a-juvenile-court-record.html.

Proposition 21. (n.d.). *The Legislative Analyst's Office, LAO*. Retrieved from https://lao.ca.gov/ballot/2000/21_03_2000.html.

SCOCAL. (n.d.). In re Thierry S., 19 Cal. 3d 727. *Stanford Law School*. Retrieved from https://scocal.stanford.edu/opinion/re-thierry-s-23096.

Senate Bill No. 1391. (CA. 2018). Retrieved from https://leginfo.legislature.ca.gov/faces/billTextClient.xhtml?bill_id=201720180SB1391.

Stim, R. (2011, October 10). Who lacks the capacity to contract? *NOLO*. Retrieved from https://www.nolo.com/legal-encyclopedia/lack-capacity-to-contract-32647.html.

Stimson, C. (2009). Adult Time for Adult Crimes. *The Prosecutor*. Retrieved from http://ndaa.org/wp-content/uploads/09_Oct_Dec_adult_time.pdf.

Streib, V. L. (1987). *Death Penalty for Juveniles*. Indiana University Press. Retrieved from https://books.google.com/books?id=3mdHAAAAMAAJ.

The 26th Amendment. (2021, June 17). *Richard Nixon Museum and Library, Nixon Library*. Retrieved from https://www.nixonlibrary.gov/news/26th-amendment.

Tikkanen, A. (2019, April 15). Why is marijuana illegal in the U.S.? *Encyclopedia Britannica*. Retrieved from https://www.britannica.com/story/why-is-marijuana-illegal-in-the-us.

Wishnia, J. (2021, October 26). Juvenile tried as an adult. *LegalMatch Law Library*. Retrieved from https://www.legalmatch.com/law-library/article/juvenile-tried-as-an-adult.html.

Index

Adolescents 2, 3, 7, 10, 11, 18, 19, 62
Adult 154, 183, 185, 186, 187, 191, 196, 197
Age 2, 3, 4, 5, 7, 8, 9, 9*f*1.2, 11, 16, 19, 20, 23, 24, 26, 30, 87, 88, 89, 117, 118, 120, 138, 148, 170, 171, 173, 173*t*8.2, 183, 183*n*2, 184, 187, 188, 189, 191, 192, 194, 195, 196, 197
Alcohol 55, 60, 61, 64
Animal 36, 43, 44
Article 14 91, 94
Article 21 41, 44, 47, 84, 86, 91, 94, 114, 179
Article 22 41
Atrocities 46, 52, 73, 83, 99

Bail 1, 2, 3, 12, 13, 14, 15, 16, 17, 19, 43, 46, 64, 102, 103, 103*n*3, 103*n*3, 103*n*5, 104, 108, 110, 111, 113, 113*n*10, 113*n*11, 115, 117, 122, 126*f*6.18, 130*f*6.22, 131, 131*n*15, 133, 133*f*6.23, 135, 136, 135*f*6.26, 137, 138, 139, 140, 144, 145, 149, 150
Brutality 46, 49

Colonial Conventions 77
Community Service 157, 164
Consent 2, 3, 4, 5, 6*f*1.1, 7, 8, 9, 10, 14, 17, 19, 20, 88, 89, 91, 155, 164
Constitution of India 32, 34, 40, 47, 52, 70, 73, 74, 75, 84, 89, 92, 95, 114, 179, 180
Constitutionalism 69, 84, 85, 94
Crime 2, 12*f*1.5, 14*f*1.7, 15*f*1.8, 16*f*1.9, 17, 17*f*1.10, 22, 24, 31, 32, 33, 48, 49, 51, 52, 58, 59, 61, 63, 74, 85, 86, 104, 105, 109, 123, 142, 155, 156, 157, 158, 159, 160, 162, 163, 164, 168, 174, 175, 176, 177, 179, 180, 183, 185, 186, 187, 189, 191, 192
Criminal Law 91
Criminal Procedural Code 31
Criminalization 2, 18, 19, 22, 54, 55, 67

Death Penalty Report 27, 32
Decolonization 69, 70, 71, 93
Detention 12, 13, 16, 26, 40, 41, 47, 111, 114, 115, 151, 152
Deterrence 44, 63, 65, 68, 169, 177, 178, 185, 186

Females 4, 7, 8, 118, 120, 122, 123, 130, 131, 139, 147

Inheritance 75, 100
Intervention 4, 104, 110, 117, 123*f*6.20, 130*f*6.22, 146, 150, 153, 157, 163

John Stuart Mill 58
Juvenile 131*n*17, 156, 157, 159, 160, 166, 189, 195, 197, 198

Law Commission of India 71, 72, 87, 89
Legal aid 106, 108, 124, 131, 151
Legal culture 159, 161, 163, 164, 166
LWOP 190
Lynching 168, 170, 171, 174*t*8.3, 175*t*8.4, 179, 180, 181

Minors 10, 20, 156, 157, 158, 159, 164, 183, 189, 192
Morals 58, 87, 184

Narcotics and Psychotropic Substances Act (NDPS) 42
National Legal Services Authority (NALSA) 37, 53, 95, 108, 152

Overcriminalization 3, 5, 13, 17, 45, 55, 57, 58, 59, 60, 65, 66, 67, 68, 168

Panel Advocate 103, 117, 123, 124, 140, 141, 149
Phone calls 136, 137
POCSO Act 1, 2, 3, 7, 10, 11, 12, 13, 14*f*1.7, 15, 17, 19, 20
Police 10, 12, 13, 17, 18, 25, 26, 27, 33, 36, 37, 38, 39, 40, 41, 42, 46, 47, 48, 49, 50, 50*n*1, 51, 52, 53, 72, 73, 76, 78, 79, 82, 83, 93, 94, 97, 103, 108, 109, 137, 138, 139, 144, 145*t*6.5, 146, 150, 194
Post-colonial 95, 108
Prison xvi, 22, 24, 28, 33, 102, 104, 105, 111, 112*t*6.3, 112*t*6.3, 113, 113*t*6.4, 118, 139, 141, 142, 150, 151, 152, 153, 154
Prisoners 102, 115, 138, 146, 147, 151, 153

Probation   122, 122*n*14, 154, 155, 156, 159, 160, 161, 163, 164, 166, 193
Punishment   3, 19, 25, 36, 41, 42, 43, 44, 45, 49, 54, 59, 63, 65, 68, 91, 123, 159, 168, 173, 174, 174*t*8.3, 174*t*8.3, 175, 175*t*8.4, 175*t*8.4, 176, 176*f*8.1, 177, 177*f*8.3, 178, 180, 185, 186, 187, 194, 195
Punitive   22, 61, 156, 168, 169, 170, 171, 174, 175, 176*f*8.2, 177, 178, 180, 186

Rape   1, 2, 3, 4, 5, 7, 12, 14, 17, 19, 20, 28, 48, 50, 52, 58, 91, 93, 94
Rehabilitation   33, 42, 106, 109, 110, 122*n*14, 139, 141, 142, 143, 144, 145*t*6.5, 150, 154, 162, 164, 185, 186
Rights   10, 31, 33, 37, 38, 41, 42, 47, 48, 50, 51, 52, 57, 60, 70, 73, 83, 84, 86, 87, 88, 90, 92, 94, 95, 97, 99, 100, 106, 108, 109, 110, 115, 122, 133, 146, 151, 155

Same-sex relationships   87
Sedition   88, 89, 90
Serious   2, 12, 41, 43, 44, 56, 61, 122, 123, 156, 156*n*2, 157, 158, 171, 187, 189, 193
Sexuality   1, 8, 18

Shell Law   75, 79
Sociological   32
Sodomy   85, 86
Statutes   5, 38, 39, 40, 59, 70, 72, 79, 97
Stereotypes   88
Stigmatization   10, 28, 99

The 26th Amendment, 2021   189
The Bihar Prohibition and Excise Rules   45
Transgender persons (protection of rights) Act   35, 46, 50, 51

Undertrials   12, 22, 103, 104, 105, 106, 107*f*6.2, 109, 111, 113, 113*n*11, 114, 115, 117, 118, 122, 123, 124, 125, 130, 131, 133, 135, 136, 137, 138, 142, 143, 148, 149, 150, 151, 153

Victim   7, 14*f*1.7, 15, 16, 19, 25, 31, 32, 33, 40, 42, 49, 93, 94, 109, 156, 157, 158, 165

Women   4, 7, 9*f*1.2, 10*f*1.3, 20, 24, 26, 28, 30, 32, 33, 34, 37, 39, 42, 51, 53, 60, 62, 63, 68, 94, 109, 112*t*6.3, 138, 139, 141, 147*n*23, 148, 148*n*24, 184

www.ingramcontent.com/pod-product-compliance
Lightning Source LLC
Chambersburg PA
CBHW070619030426
42337CB00020B/3858